File for Divorce in Georgia

File for Divorce in Georgia

Seventh Edition

Judge Charles T. Robertson II

and

Edward A. Haman
Attorney at Law

SPHINX® PUBLISHING
AN IMPRINT OF SOURCEBOOKS, INC.®
NAPERVILLE, ILLINOIS
www.SphinxLegal.com

Seventh Edition, 2007

Published by: **Sphinx® Publishing, An Imprint of Sourcebooks, Inc.®**

<u>Naperville Office</u>
P.O. Box 4410
Naperville, Illinois 60567-4410
630-961-3900
Fax: 630-961-2168
www.sourcebooks.com
www.SphinxLegal.com

This publication is designed to provide accurate and authoritative information in regard to the subject matter covered. It is sold with the understanding that the publisher is not engaged in rendering legal, accounting, or other professional service. If legal advice or other expert assistance is required, the services of a competent professional person should be sought.
From a Declaration of Principles Jointly Adopted by a Committee of the American Bar Association and a Committee of Publishers and Associations

This product is not a substitute for legal advice.

Disclaimer required by Texas statutes.

Library of Congress Cataloging-in-Publication Data
Robertson, Charles T.
  File for divorce in Georgia / by Charles T. Robertson II and Edward A. Haman. — 7th ed.
       p. cm.
    Includes index.

1. Divorce—Law and legislation—Georgia—Popular works. 2. Divorce suits—Georgia—Popular works. I. Haman, Edward A. II. Title.

KFG100.Z9R63 2007
346.75801'66—dc22
                                                    2007031055

Printed and bound in the United States of America.
LSI — 10 9 8 7 6 5 4 3 2

Contents

Using Self-Help Law Books

Before using a self-help law book, you should realize the advantages and disadvantages of doing your own legal work and understand the challenges and diligence that this requires.

The Growing Trend

Rest assured that you will not be the first or only person handling your own legal matter. For example, in some states, more than 75% of the people in divorces and other cases represent themselves. Because of the high cost of legal services, this is a major trend, and many courts are struggling to make it easier for people to represent themselves. However, some courts are not happy with people who do not use attorneys and refuse to help them in any way. For some, the attitude is, "Go to the law library and figure it out for yourself."

We write and publish self-help law books to give people an alternative to the often complicated and confusing legal books found in most law libraries. We have made the explanations of the law as simple and easy to understand as possible. Of course, unlike an attorney advising an individual client, we cannot cover every conceivable possibility.

Cost/Value Analysis

Whenever you shop for a product or service, you are faced with various levels of quality and price. In deciding what product or service to buy, you make a cost/value analysis on the basis of your willingness to pay and the quality you desire.

When buying a car, you decide whether you want transportation, comfort, status, or sex appeal. Accordingly, you decide among choices such as a Neon, Lincoln, Rolls Royce, or Porsche. Before making a decision, you usually weigh the merits of each option against the cost.

When you get a headache, you can take a pain reliever (such as aspirin) or visit a medical specialist for a neurological examination. Given this choice, most people, of course, take a pain reliever, since it costs only pennies; whereas a medical examination costs hundreds of dollars and takes a lot of time. This is usually a logical choice because it is rare to need anything more than a pain reliever for a headache. But in some cases, a headache may indicate a brain tumor, and failing to see a specialist right away can result in complications. Should everyone with a headache go to a specialist? Of course not, but people treating their own illnesses must realize that they are betting, on the basis of their cost/value analysis of the situation, that they are taking the most logical option.

The same cost/value analysis must be made when deciding to do one's own legal work. Many legal situations are very straightforward, requiring a simple form and no complicated analysis. Anyone with a little intelligence and a book of instructions can handle the matter without outside help.

But there is always the chance that complications are involved that only an attorney would notice. To simplify the law into a book like this, several legal cases often must be condensed into a single sentence or paragraph. Otherwise, the book would be several hundred pages long and too complicated for most people. However, this simplification necessarily leaves out many details and nuances that would apply to special or unusual situations. Also, there are many ways to interpret most legal questions. Your case may come before a judge who disagrees with the analysis of our authors.

Therefore, in deciding to use a self-help law book and to do your own legal work, you must realize that you are making a cost/value analysis. You have decided that the money you will save in doing it yourself outweighs the chance that your case will not turn out to your satisfaction. Most people handling their own simple legal matters never have a problem, but occasionally people find that it ended up costing them more to have an attorney straighten out the situation than it would have if they had hired an attorney in the beginning. Keep this in mind while handling your case, and be sure to consult an attorney if you feel you might need further guidance.

Local Rules   The next thing to remember is that a book which covers the law for the entire nation, or even for an entire state, cannot possibly include every procedural difference of every jurisdiction. Whenever possible, we provide the exact form needed; however, in some areas, each county, or even each judge, may require unique forms and procedures. In our state books, our forms usually cover the majority of counties in the state or provide examples of the type of form that will be required. In our national books, our forms are sometimes even more general in nature but are designed to give a good idea of the type of form that will be needed in most locations. Nonetheless, keep in mind that your state, county, or judge may have a requirement, or use a form, that is not included in this book.

You should not necessarily expect to be able to get all of the information and resources you need solely from within the pages of this book. This book will serve as your guide, giving you specific information whenever possible and helping you to find out what else you will need to know. This is just like if you decided to build your own backyard deck. You might purchase a book on how to build decks. However, such a book would not include the building codes and permit requirements of every city, town, county, and township in the nation; nor would it include the lumber, nails, saws, hammers, and other materials and tools you would need to actually build the deck. You would use the book as your guide, and then do some work and research involving such matters as whether you need a permit of some kind, what type and grade of wood is available in your area, whether to use hand tools or power tools, and how to use those tools.

Before using the forms in a book like this, you should check with your court clerk to see if there are any local rules of which you should be aware or local forms you will need to use. Often, such forms will require the same information as the forms in the book but are merely laid out differently or use slightly different language. They will sometimes require additional information.

Changes in the Law

Besides being subject to local rules and practices, the law is subject to change at any time. The courts and the legislatures of all fifty states are constantly revising the laws. It is possible that while you are reading this book, some aspect of the law is being changed.

In most cases, the change will be of minimal significance. A form will be redesigned, additional information will be required, or a waiting period will be extended. As a result, you might need to revise a form, file an extra form, or wait out a longer time period. These types of changes will not usually affect the outcome of your case. On the other hand, sometimes a major part of the law is changed, the entire law in a particular area is rewritten, or a case that was the basis of a central legal point is overruled. In such instances, your entire ability to pursue your case may be impaired.

Introduction

Going through a divorce is probably one of the most common, and most traumatic, encounters people have with the legal system. Paying a divorce lawyer can be expensive, and it comes at a time when you are least likely to have extra funds. In a contested divorce case, it is not uncommon for the parties to run up legal bills of over $10,000 each.

Horror stories abound of lawyers charging substantial fees with little progress to show for it. This book is designed to enable you to obtain a divorce without hiring a lawyer, and it also serves as a practical workbook for paralegals and legal secretaries. Even if you do hire a lawyer, this book will help you to work with him or her more effectively, which can also reduce your legal costs.

This is not a law school course, but a practical guide to get you through the system as easily as possible. Legal jargon has nearly been eliminated. For ease of understanding, this book uses the term *spouse* to refer to your husband or wife (whichever applies), and the terms *child* and *children* are used interchangeably.

Please keep in mind that different judges and courts in different counties may have their own particular (if not peculiar) procedures and ways of doing things. The Superior Court clerk's office can often tell you if they have any special forms or requirements. Court clerks cannot give legal advice, but they can tell you what their court or judges require. It is a good idea to go by the Superior Court clerk's office in person and ask for any particular forms that they require to be included in your divorce paperwork.

The first two chapters of this book give you an overview of the law and the legal system. Chapters 3 and 4 help you decide if you want an attorney and if you want a divorce. The remaining chapters show you what forms you need, how to fill out the forms, and what procedures to follow.

You will also find three appendices in the back of the book. Appendix A is a list of the Superior Court clerks' offices and is arranged alphabetically by county. Appendix B contains selected portions of the Georgia law dealing with property division, alimony, and child support. Although these provisions are discussed in the book, it is sometimes helpful to read the law exactly as the legislature wrote it. Please remember that the law is always changing. Interpretations of these statutes are the responsibility of the courts, and it sometimes happens that, in the interest of fairness, courts subtly (or dramatically) change interpretations of sections of law to conform to social agendas.

Appendix C contains the forms you will complete. You will not need to use all of the forms. This book will assist you in determining which forms you need, depending upon your situation.

Read this entire book before you prepare or file any papers. This will give you the information you need to decide which forms you need and how to fill them out.

Marriage Ins and Outs

Several years (or maybe only months or weeks) ago, you made a decision to get married, and now you are contemplating a divorce. This chapter will discuss, in a very general way, what you got yourself into and how you can get yourself out.

CEREMONIAL MARRIAGE

Marriage is frequently referred to as a *contract*. It is a legal contract, and for many, it is also a religious contract. This book will deal only with the legal aspects.

Prior to most marriages, a license is required. Georgia laws governing the rules of marriage licenses have changed a lot in the last few years. You may have heard about blood tests being needed, but as of July 1, 2003, there is no longer any requirement in Georgia to take a blood test to marry. Georgia does not issue licenses to same-sex couples, but will allow anyone over the age of 16 to marry after completing an application. The filing fee for a marriage license can be waived upon completion of a Premarital Education Program. The details get a little complicated, but you can get that information from your local probate court (which is the court that handles marriage licenses) or read through the rules on the Web at **www.gaprobate.org/licenses.php**.

Anyone under age 18 who wishes to marry will require parental consent, except in some extreme circumstances. This rule previously allowed any pregnant woman to marry without parental consent. However, a famous case involving a pregnant 38-year-old woman and her 15-year-old "boyfriend" caused that law to be reexamined. Their affair became public when the woman and the teen were married in November 2005 by a retired judge who performed the ceremony in his driveway. State law allowed people younger than 16 to marry if the bride was pregnant. The law was changed last year, and now 16- and 17-year-olds can wed only with the approval of both parents or guardians and a probate judge. (Hall County authorities arrested the woman the day after the wedding and charged her with sexually molesting a minor, and she ultimately spent time in jail.)

Once the procedures have been followed, a ceremony is performed. The wedding ceremony involves the bride and groom reciting certain vows, which are actually mutual promises about how they will treat each other. Legal papers are also signed, such as a marriage license and a marriage certificate.

These formalities combine to create certain rights and obligations for the husband and wife. Although the focus at the ceremony is on the emotional and romantic aspects of the relationship, the legal reality is that financial and property rights are being created. These financial and property rights and obligations cannot be broken without a legal proceeding.

Marriage will give each of the parties certain rights in property, and it creates certain obligations with respect to the support of any children they have together (or adopt). Unfortunately, most people do not fully realize that these rights and obligations are being created until it comes time for a divorce.

COMMON-LAW MARRIAGE

Sometimes there is a question about whether parties are married and if an informal arrangement conveys the same rights and responsibilities as a ceremonial marriage. The answer in Georgia, at one time, was *maybe*; but since January 1, 1997, the answer is *absolutely not* because of changes in the law. There is a rumor that you can be married at common law simply by living with someone; dating someone exclusively for some period of time; having sex with someone; or, by signing the same name on a motel registry. In fact, some of these elements could be important factors to consider in states that recognize *common-law marriages*, but none automatically mean that you are married.

Technically, to qualify as a marriage relationship, only three elements are required.

1. The parties are able to contract.

2. The parties actually do contract.

3. There is consummation according to law.

These requirements apply equally to common law as well as ceremonial marriages. In a ceremonial marriage, the consummation does not have to be sexual intercourse, but can be the marriage license or participation in the marriage ceremony. A common-law marriage usually requires that the parties have sexual relations.

In the absence of a formal ceremony, if there is a controversy about whether a marriage exists, Georgia courts used to look to such circumstantial evidence as continuous living together (the longer they have lived together, the stronger the case for marriage), general reputation, and statements from the parties themselves. If a child is born, the legal relationship may be affirmed in the eyes of the law with a much lower standard of proof. If no child is born, the burden of proving a marriage without a legal ceremony is much harder.

While Georgia still recognizes the common-law marriages of other states, Georgia has narrowed the requirements for a true common-law marriage, and in the opinion of one commentator, you just about have to go through a ceremony with an unauthorized official to qualify. In any event, an invalid marriage, whether ceremonial or common law, requires no court action for a divorce. However, if there is a possibility of a valid marriage, you may want to speak with an attorney and plan to go through a divorce, so that there are no problems with any future marriage.

DIVORCE

A *divorce* is the most common method of terminating or breaking the marriage contract. This procedure is sometimes referred to as a *dissolution of marriage* or even a *divorce a vinculo matrimonii*. In this book, the terms *divorce* and *dissolution of marriage* are used interchangeably and have the same meaning. In a divorce, the court declares the marriage contract broken, divides the parties' property and debts, decides if either party should receive alimony, and determines the custody, support, and visitation for any children the parties may have.

Traditionally, a divorce could only be granted under very specific circumstances, such as *adultery* or *mental cruelty*. These were called *fault grounds*, and divorce did not happen easily. Fault had to be proven at trial, and a simple wish to be single by one party was generally insufficient.

No-Fault Divorce

Today, a mobile society has demanded easier divorces, and Georgia has adopted what is commonly referred to as *no-fault* divorce. A divorce must be granted simply because one or both of the parties want one. The wording used to describe the situation is that "the marriage is irretrievably broken." There simply is no situation in Georgia that prevents any party in a marriage from divorcing if he or she chooses, and the spouse is powerless to prevent the occurrence, although he or she could make it unpleasant, expensive, and time-consuming.

Fault Grounds for Divorce

There are still twelve fault grounds for divorce in Georgia. There may be a reason in your particular circumstance to use a fault ground. Most people do not, and if you think you should, consult an attorney. The twelve grounds stand as follows.

1. *Improper intermarriage.* Hereditary diseases are much more likely to appear in marriages between people who are closely related by bloodline. Most societies have forbidden these relationships, and in Georgia, if the parties seeking to marry are too closely related, they are prohibited from marrying. For the purposes of this book, this applies to such situations as fathers and daughters, uncles and nieces, etc.

2. *Mental incapacity at the time of the marriage.* Unfortunately, your belief that your spouse has recently lost his or her mind does not qualify for this category of divorce.

3. *Impotency at the time of the marriage.*

4. *Pregnancy of the wife by someone other than the husband* at the time of the marriage and unknown to the husband.

5. *Force, menace, duress, or fraud in obtaining the marriage.*

6. *Adultery of either party after the marriage.* This is especially noteworthy because this ground may prevent the adulterous party from receiving alimony.

7. *Wilful desertion* continuing for a period of one year.

8. *Conviction for an offense of moral turpitude,* which results in a prison conviction of two or more years.

9. *Habitual intoxication.*

10. *Cruel treatment,* usually the willful infliction of physical or mental pain upon the complaining party.

11. *Incurable mental illness.* This category requires some professional certification and refers to situations where a spouse is institutionalized or has been diagnosed as having an incurable mental condition.

12. *Habitual drug addiction.* While occasional drug use will not go over well with the court, this category does not usually apply to circumstances of infrequent social use of illicit substances.

Occasionally, there are very good reasons to allege one or more of these grounds, if true, for strategic purposes. On the other hand, although these grounds may be present in many divorces, most divorces by agreement simply refer to the marriage as being irretrievably broken, a *no-fault divorce.* Making a claim for a fault-based divorce may require other court procedures and involve fairly complicated evidence issues. If you are seeking a divorce on any of these grounds, you should consult a lawyer.

ANNULMENT

The basic difference between a divorce and an *annulment* is that a divorce says, "this marriage is broken," and an annulment says, "there never was a marriage." An annulment is more difficult and often more complicated to prove, so it is not used very often. Annulments are only possible in a few circumstances, usually where one party deceived the other or minors were involved. If you decide you want an annulment, you should consult an attorney. If you are seeking an annulment for religious reasons and need to go through a church procedure (rather than, or in addition to, a legal procedure), you should consult your priest or minister.

A divorce is generally easier to obtain than an annulment. This is because all you need to prove to get a divorce is that your marriage is broken. You prove this simply by saying it. The *Petition for Divorce* that you will file states, "The marriage between the parties is irretrievably broken." That is all you need. However, in order to get an annulment, you will need to prove more. This proof will involve introducing various documents into evidence and having other people testify at the court hearing.

Grounds for Annulment

Annulments are usually only appropriate under one of the following circumstances:

- ✪ *If one of the parties was too young to get married.* In Georgia, both parties must be at least 16 years old to get married but must have parental consent if under 18. There are a few exceptions, such as if the woman is pregnant or the parties are already biological parents.

- ✪ *If one of the parties is guilty of fraud.* For example, where one party got married only in order to have the right to inherit from the other with no intention of ever living together as husband and wife.

- ✪ *If one party was under duress when he or she got married.* Duress means that the person was being threatened or was under some kind of pressure so that he or she did not get married voluntarily. Usually, in Georgia duress refers to substantial threat, such as being at the point of a gun. Duress cannot be used as a substitute for a drunken bad decision or a sudden change of mind. This ground is to be used in the event of the famous *shotgun wedding*.

✪ *If one party did not have the mental capacity to get married.* This means the person was suffering from mental illness or mental disability (such as being severely retarded) to such an extent that the person did not understand that he or she was getting married or possibly did not even understand the concept of marriage.

✪ *If one party was already married to another person.* This might occur if one party married while mistakenly believing his or her divorce from his or her previous spouse was final. In this era of mobile lifestyles, this happens much more often than you think. If your spouse was previously married, a quick check to be sure the divorce is final is not a difficult process to undertake, but you may want to ask an attorney how to go about it.

✪ *If the marriage is incestuous.* Georgia law prohibits marriage between certain family members, such as brother and sister, aunt and nephew, or uncle and niece.

If your spouse wants to stop an annulment, there are several arguments he or she could make to further complicate the case. This area of the law is not as well defined as divorce. There are Georgia Code Sections outlining the proper procedures to follow, but annulments are much less common than divorces. The annulment procedure can be complicated. If you believe that it would be the most beneficial process, you should consult a lawyer.

LEGAL SEPARATION

Georgia law permits a legal separation and refers to the process as *separate maintenance*. This procedure is used to divide property and provide child support when the husband and wife live separately but remain married. This is usually used to break the financial rights and obligations of a couple whose religion does not permit divorce, in situations arising from either mutual agreement to separate or one party's voluntary departure, or to maintain insurance coverage for a separated spouse. It is an old procedure that is gradually fading out. It is possible to obtain support without getting a divorce, but that procedure is beyond the scope of this book.

Changes in Georgia law on the subject have made the area of separation agreements even more treacherous ground, as a separation agreement could provide the settlement terms for an eventual divorce. Also, since a divorce is usually inevitable in separate maintenance situations, the process is at least twice as expensive as a divorce alone. If you believe this process is somehow the most appropriate for your circumstances, seek legal counsel.

DO YOU REALLY WANT A DIVORCE?

Getting a divorce is one of the most emotionally stressful events in a person's life. Only the death of one's child or spouse creates more stress than a divorce. It will also have an impact on several aspects of your life and can change your entire lifestyle.

So, before beginning the divorce process, you need to take some time to think about how it will affect your life. This section will help you examine these things and offers alternatives if you want to try to save your relationship. Even if you feel absolutely sure that you want a divorce, you should still read this material so you are prepared for what may follow.

Legal Consequences

Dealing with lawyers, clerks, and judges is exhausting, but this is the easiest part of divorce. The stress of going through a court system procedure and having to deal with your spouse as you go through it is tough. It can be confrontational and emotionally explosive. However, when compared to the other aspects of divorce, the pain of having to deal with the system is not as piercing as the pain of losing a partner and friend.

The journey through the legal system generally has three direct consequences.

1. The divorce of two people. Basically, this gives each the legal right to marry someone else.

2.   The division of their property (and responsibility for debts).

3.   The care and custody of their children.

Although it is theoretically possible for the legal divorce to be concluded within a few months, the legalities usually continue for years. This is mostly caused by the emotional aspects leading to battles over the children. For example, a couple divorcing with small children will have to anticipate dealing with each other for nearly two decades. These relationships as ex-spouses routinely extend far longer than the marriage itself.

Social and Emotional Effects

Divorce will have a tremendous impact on your social and emotional lives, and the effects will continue long after you are legally divorced.

Lack of companionship. Even if your relationship is quite stormy, you are probably still accustomed to just having your spouse around. You may be able to temporarily put aside your problems and at least somewhat support each other in times of mutual adversity (such as in dealing with a death in the family, the illness of your child, or storm damage to your home). You may also feel a little more secure at night by not being alone in the house. Even if your marriage is one of the most miserable, you may still notice at least a little emptiness, lone-liness, or solitude after the divorce. It may not be that you miss your spouse in particular, but just miss another person being around.

Grief. Divorce may be viewed as the death of a marriage or maybe the funeral ceremony. Like the death of anyone or anything you have been close to, you will feel a sense of loss. This aspect can take you through all of the normal feelings associated with grief, such as guilt, anger, denial, and acceptance. You will get angry and frustrated over the years you have wasted. You will blame yourself, your spouse, your parents, and your lawyer for the problems resulting from this unpleasantness. You will feel guilty because you failed to make the marriage work. You will find yourself saying, *I cannot believe this is happening to me.* For months or even years, you will spend a lot of time thinking about your marriage. It can be extremely difficult to put it all behind you and to get on with your life.

Dating. After your divorce, your social life will change. If you want to avoid solitary evenings in front of the TV, you will find yourself trying to get back into the singles' scene. This will probably involve a change in friends, as well as a change in lifestyle.

First, you may find that your current married friends no longer find you, as a single person, fitting in with their circle. Gradually, or even quickly, you may find yourself dropped from their guest list. Now you have to start making an effort to meet single people at work, going out on the town, and even dating! This experience can be very frightening, tiring, and frustrating after years of being away from this lifestyle. It can also be very difficult if you have custody of the kids. Also, the dating scene is (or at least should be) entirely changed with the ever-present threat of AIDS, sexually transmitted diseases, and other communicable diseases.

Financial Certainties

The financial changes brought about by divorce can be a very long and drastic adjustment. Divorce has a significant financial impact in almost every case. Many married couples are just able to make ends meet. After getting divorced, there are suddenly two rent payments, two electric bills, and so on. If there are children involved, for the spouse without custody, there is also child support to be paid.

Mathematically, the costs rise without any increase in income. Also, once you have divided your property, each of you will need to replace the items the other person got to keep. If she got the bedroom furniture and the pots and pans, he will need to buy his own. If he got the TV and the sofa, she will need to buy her own TV and sofa.

Children and Divorce

The effect of a divorce upon your children and your relationship with them can often be the most painful and long-lasting aspect of divorce. Your family life will be permanently changed, as there will no longer be a family. Even if you remarry, stepparents rarely bring back that same family feeling. Your relationship with your children may become strained as they work through their feelings of blame, guilt, disappointment, and anger. Your children may even need professional counseling. Also, as long as there is child support and visitation involved, you will be forced to have at least some contact with your ex-spouse.

ALTERNATIVES TO DIVORCE

By the time you have purchased this book and read this far, you have probably already decided that you want a divorce. However, if what you have just read and thought about has changed your mind or made you want to make a last effort to save your marriage, there are a few things you can try. These are only very basic suggestions. Details can be offered by professional marriage counselors.

Talk to Your Spouse

Choose the right time (not when your spouse is trying to unwind after a day at work or is trying to quiet a screaming baby) and talk about your problems. It is highly recommended that this discussion take place in a public place, such as a restaurant, so that there is some social pressure to keep things sensible. It is pretty easy for emotions to get out of hand at times. Wherever it occurs, try to establish a few ground rules for the discussion, such as:

- ✪ talk about how you feel, instead of making accusations that may start an argument;

- ✪ each person listens while the other speaks (no interrupting); and,

- ✪ each person must say something positive about the other and their relationship.

As you talk, you may want to discuss such things as where you would like your relationship to go, how it has changed since you got married, and what can be done to bring you closer together.

Change Your Thinking

Many people get divorced because they will not change something about their outlook or their lifestyle. Then, once they get divorced, they find they have made that same change they resisted for so long.

Example 1:

Cheryl and Henry were unhappy in their marriage. They did not seem to share the same lifestyle. Henry felt overburdened with responsibility and bored. He wanted Cheryl to be more independent and outgoing, to meet new people, to handle the household budget, and to go out with him more often. Cheryl was more shy and reserved, was not confident in her ability to find a job, and preferred to stay at home. Cheryl wanted Henry to give up some of his frequent days golfing out with the guys, to help with the cooking and laundry, to stop leaving messes for her to clean up, and to stop bothering her about going out all the time. However, neither would try change, and eventually all of the little things built up into a divorce.

After the divorce, Cheryl was forced to get a job to support herself. Now she has made friends at work, goes out with them two or three nights a week, is successful and happy at her job, and is quite competent at managing her own budget. Henry now has his own apartment and has to cook his own meals (something he finds he enjoys) and do his own laundry. He has also found it necessary to clean up his own messes and keep the place neat, especially if he is going to entertain guests.

Both Cheryl and Henry have changed in exactly the way the other had wanted. It is just too bad they did not make these changes before they got divorced! If you think some change may help, give it a try. You can always go back to a divorce if things do not work out.

Example 2:

James and Kelly were both very angry and distant and their divorce case was very unpleasant. During the separation James enrolled in an Internet dating service. Kelly was shown the ad by a mutual friend. At first, she was outraged at what she saw as the fictional self-portrayal of her long-time partner. However, her mood changed pretty dramatically when she read what kind of woman he was interested in meeting. It described almost to a letter the kind of person that Kelly thought she was. That ad was the beginning of a struggle between the two of them to rebuild the relationship. It may not be a bad idea, before you file for divorce, to write your own Internet ad for what you are looking for, and see if perhaps some of the elements are closer than you think.

Counseling Counseling is not the same as giving advice. A counselor should not be telling you what to do. A counselor's job is to assist you in figuring out what you really want to do by asking questions that will get you thinking.

Low-cost or free counseling is available through nonprofit community groups such as your local mental health association, YMCA, YWCA, Jewish Community Centers (JCC), or family support groups. Religious organizations, such as Catholic charities, offer sliding scale fees to make counseling affordable to all.

When consulting a religious group for counseling, check to see what kind of approach is taken. You do not necessarily have to be a member of the faith of the group offering the counseling, but check the rules of the group when you call for an appointment.

Local colleges and universities may have counseling available through family institutes, psychology departments, and social work departments. Ask your local librarian at your public library for help in finding community resources.

Actually, just talking things out with your spouse is a form of self-counseling. The only problem is that it is difficult to remain objective and nonjudgmental. You both need to be able to calmly analyze what the problems are and discuss possible solutions.

Very few couples seem to be able to do this successfully, which is why there are professional marriage counselors. As with doctors and lawyers, good marriage counselors are usually best discovered by word of mouth. You may have friends who can direct you to someone who helped them. You can also check with your family doctor or your clergyperson for a referral, or even the Yellow Pages under "Marriage and Family Counselors" or some similar category. You can see a counselor either alone or with your spouse. It may be a good idea to see a counselor even if you are going through with the divorce. It may make the process go smoother, or at least provide some closure to the ending relationship.

Another form of counseling is talking to a close friend. Just remember the difference between counseling and giving advice. Do not let your friend tell you what you should do.

Trial Separation

Before going through the time, expense, and trouble of getting a divorce, you and your spouse may want to try just getting away from each other for awhile. This can be as simple as taking separate vacations, or as complex as actually separating into separate households for an indefinite period of time, a legal process called *separate maintenance*. This may give each of you a chance to think about how you would like living alone, how important or trivial your problems are, and how you really feel about each other. However, be careful about how you structure this arrangement. There are a number of details to be worked out that parallel a divorce agreement, such as support, custody, and debt payments.

The Legal System

This chapter gives you a general introduction to the legal system. These are things you need to know in order to obtain a divorce (or help your lawyer get the job done) and to get through any encounter with the legal system with minimal stress. These are some of the realities of our system. If you do not learn to accept these realities, you will experience much stress and frustration.

THEORY VS. REALITY

The United States legal system is a system of rules, and there are basically three types of rules.

- ✪ *Rules of Law*—such as a law telling a judge how to go about dividing your property.

- ✪ *Rules of Procedure*—such as requiring court papers to be in a certain form, or filed within a certain time.

- ✪ *Rules of Evidence*—such as the certain way in which facts need to be proven.

According to theory, these rules allow each side to present evidence most favorable to that side, and an independent person or persons (the judge or jury) will be able to figure out the truth. Then certain legal principles will be applied to that truth, which will give a fair resolution of the dispute between the parties. These legal principles are supposed to be relatively unchanging, so that anyone can know what will happen in any given situation and can plan accordingly. This provides order and predictability to society. Any change in the legal principles is supposed to occur slowly, so that the expected behavior in our society is not confused from day to day.

The System is Not Perfect

Contrary to how it may seem, legal rules are not made just to complicate the system and confuse everyone. The rules attempt to make the system as fair and just as possible. They have been developed over several hundred years, and in most cases, they do make sense. Unfortunately, our efforts to find fairness and justice have resulted in a complex set of rules. The underlying problem with our system is that it attempts to provide a framework against which all human problems can be addressed with fairness to all sides. In practice, there are simply too many possibilities in human relationships, and the results can sometimes be unsatisfactory. However, keep in mind that on the whole, the system works pretty well.

Judges Do Not Always Follow the Rules

It is a shocking discovery, even for many young lawyers, that judges do not always follow the rules. Many judges may make decisions simply on what they think seems fair under the circumstances. Unfortunately, what seems fair to a particular judge may depend upon his or her personal ideas and philosophy.

For example, there is nothing in the divorce laws that gives one parent priority in child custody; however, it is generally conceded that a majority of judges believe that a child is better off with his or her mother, especially if the child is very young. All other things being equal, these judges will find a way to justify awarding custody to the mother. These decisions may be based on procedures or policies of which you are unaware, and the result can make you wonder about their rationality.

The System is Often Slow

Even lawyers get frustrated with how long it can take to get a case completed (especially if they do not get paid until it is done). Whatever your situation, things will take longer than you expect. Patience is required to get through the system with a minimum of stress. Do not let your impatience or frustration show. No matter what happens, keep calm and be courteous.

No Two Cases are Alike

Just because your friend's case went a certain way does not mean yours will have the same result. The judge can make a difference, but more often it is the circumstances that make a difference. Even if your coworker makes the same income as you and has the same number of children, you cannot assume you will be ordered to pay the same amount of child support. There are usually other circumstances your coworker chooses not to relate or may not understand.

Half of the People Lose

Remember, there are two sides to every legal issue, and there is usually only one winner. Do not expect to have every detail go your way. If you leave anything to the judge to decide, you can expect to have some things go your spouse's way. It has been said that a perfect compromise leaves both sides a little disappointed. Under the circumstances, prepare to be a little disappointed in any compromise you work out with your spouse.

Justice is Not Guaranteed

In America, the system gives everyone an opportunity for justice. However, everyone does not realistically have equal financial access to the system. It has proven painfully true to some that you are only guaranteed as much justice as you can afford. This is another reason why trying to work out your individual circumstances is often preferable to leaving your fate in the uncertain hands of the system.

THE PLAYERS

The law and the legal system are often compared to games, and just like games, it is important to know the players.

The Judge

In Georgia, the Superior Court judge is the single most powerful individual in the county. He or she has the power to change the title of property, assign custody, and in criminal cases, sentence someone to death. Further, in domestic cases, it often requires the majority of justices on the Supreme Court of Georgia to overturn his or her decisions. It makes sense that you should invest your time in convincing him or her of the reasonableness of your position. The judge has the power to decide whether you can get divorced, how your property will be divided, which of you will get custody of the children, and how much the other will pay for child support. In short, the judge is the last person you want to make angry with you.

In general, judges have large caseloads and like it best when your case can be concluded quickly and without hassle. This means that the more you and your spouse agree upon, and the more complete your paperwork, the better the judge will like it. Most likely, your only direct contact with the judge will be at the final hearing, which may last as little as five minutes. (See Chapters 6 and 10 for more about how to deal with the judge.)

The Judge's Secretary

The judge's secretary sets the hearings for the judge and can frequently answer many of your questions about the procedure, and what the judge would like or requires. You do not want to make an enemy of the secretary. This means that you do not call often and do not ask too many questions. A few questions are okay, and you may want to start off saying that you just want to make sure you have everything in order for the judge. Be friendly and courteous, even if the secretary happens to be brusque. He or she has a large caseload, just as the judge does, and may be suffering from stress—or he or she may just be an unpleasant person. However, you will get further by being nice than by arguing with or complaining to him or her.

The Court Clerk

While the secretary usually only works for one judge, the court clerk handles the files for all of the judges. The clerk's office is the central place where all of the court files are kept. The clerk files your court papers and keeps the official records of your divorce. Most people who work in the clerk's office are friendly and helpful. While they cannot give you legal advice (such as telling you what to say in your court papers), they can help explain the system and the procedures (such as telling you what type of papers must be filed).

Many Georgia courts have mediation processes that are mandatory in domestic actions. Some courts require that the parents in a divorce case attend seminars about the effects of the divorce on the children. You should specifically ask the clerk if such requirements are in place in your county. Often these requirements are spelled out on the court clerk's website.

The clerk has the power to accept or reject your papers, so you do not want to anger the clerk either. If the clerk tells you to change something in your papers, just change it; never argue or complain.

NOTE: *Judges, secretaries, and law clerks are generally very patient and conscientious; however, if you anger the judge, his or her secretary, or the clerk, any one of them can delay your divorce or cause you a number of problems. Be polite, courteous, and friendly to all of these people.*

Lawyers   Lawyers can serve as guides through the legal system. They guide their own client, while trying to confuse, manipulate, or outmaneuver their opponent. In dealing with your spouse's lawyer (if he or she has one), try to be polite. You will not get anywhere being antagonistic or argumentative. The lawyer is just doing his or her job to get the best situation for his or her client.

A lawyer can sometimes get you through the legal system faster, while helping you avoid the dangers along the way. Just as a wilderness guide can take you faster along the trail, a lawyer's help can be invaluable. However, if the trail is well marked and there are not many serious dangers along the way, you may decide not to hire a guide. So it is with lawyers and divorce. Chapter 4 provides more information about whether you need a lawyer.

Paralegals   In Georgia, the term *paralegal* is often used interchangeably with *legal assistant*, *lawyer's assistant*, and sometimes, *secretary*. Some paralegals have American Bar Association credentials, law school educations, certified paralegal certification, and twenty years of experience in the field. Others merely call themselves paralegals despite both a lack of experience or even a high school diploma. Usually, a paralegal in the courthouse or in the employ of an attorney can be expected to be relatively well informed and less expensive than the corresponding attorney, but be careful. The title can easily be abused by individuals with little concern for their responsibilities or their impact on client's lives.

This Book   This book will serve as your map of the trail through the legal system. In most cases, the dangers along the way are relatively small. If you start getting lost or the situation seems to be getting worse, then you can always hire a lawyer to jump to your aid.

DIVORCE LAW AND PROCEDURE

This section gives you a general overview of the law and procedures involved in getting a divorce. To most people, the law appears very complicated and confusing. Fortunately, many areas of the law can be broken down into simple and logical steps. Divorce is one of those areas.

The Law   The law relating to divorce, as well as to other areas of social interaction, comes from the *Official Code of Georgia Annotated* (OCGA), published by the Michie Company under contract with the State of Georgia. These are the laws passed by the Georgia Legislature and are often collectively called *statutes*.

This book is designed so that you will not need to look up the law. However, a portion of this law, relating to property division, alimony, and child support, can be found in Appendix B.

Residency Requirement. One basic law you need to be aware of is that in almost every case, either you or your spouse must live in Georgia for at least six months immediately before filing a petition with the court.

The other source of law is the past decisions of the Georgia courts. The reason past decisions are important is that the courts deeply value consistency. If some aspect of your case has already been decided by the courts in a certain way, your judge will want to follow that decision. This *case law* is much more difficult to locate and follow than statutes.

For most situations, the law is clearly spelled out in the statutes, and the past court decisions are not all that important. However, if you wish to learn more about how to find these court decisions, see the last section of this chapter, entitled "Legal Research."

The Procedure   The law can be very simple in most divorce cases. How to apply that law to your situation and the procedures to follow can sometimes seem more confusing. However, whether your divorce is contested or uncontested, you will need to show the judge the following five things. In no particular order, the points that must be made are:

- ✪ who you are, and that you are in the right court;

- ✪ when you married, and when you separated;

- ✪ why you are entitled to a divorce;

- ✪ what should be done with your assets and liabilities; and,

- ✪ how custody of your children should be apportioned, and how they should be supported.

It is a requirement in Georgia that the parties be *legally separated* for thirty days prior to the entry of any final decree of divorce. This usually refers to sexual intimacy, but may also reflect a date long after any sexual relations when one spouse has left the marital residence or begun residing in another area of the house.

In Georgia, attorneys commonly refer to divorces as being *contested* or *uncontested*. In general, an uncontested divorce refers to a situation in which the parties have worked out all of their differences and are prepared to have their agreed upon terms put into a judge's order. In a contested divorce, some of the issues are not agreed upon by the parties, and the parties are basically presenting their sides of the case to the judge for a decision. His or her final decision, in either case, is called a **FINAL JUDGMENT AND DECREE**. (see form 18, p.255, or form 17, p.253.)

Uncontested Divorce

The basic uncontested divorce process may be viewed as a five-step process.

1. The parties work out the terms of their divorce, such as child custody and support, alimony, and division of property and debts. While these agreements are generally upheld by the courts, there are some basic guidelines that have to be followed.

2. One party files court papers that have been agreed to by the other party, asking the judge to grant a divorce. These papers are called the **PETITION FOR DIVORCE**, the **AGREEMENT**, and may include an **AFFIDAVIT REGARDING CUSTODY**, as well as additional forms. New Georgia rules require additional forms for child support. Because they are pretty complicated, you need to follow the directions in Chapter 7 closely and add these, whether your divorce is contested or uncontested.

3. The court must be sure that the other party has proper legal notice of the divorce process and that he or she will be legally bound by the court's decision.

4. A hearing date must be set.

5. On the date of the hearing, whoever was the filing party appears in front of the judge. The evidence is presented, the **AGREEMENT** is reviewed for formality, and a judgment is issued granting the divorce.

Later chapters tell you how to carry out these steps, but you should find the following preliminary information helpful.

Work out the settlement terms. This may be simple or impossible, or anywhere in between. You can expect that the complexities of your circumstances will be much greater for a longer relationship. Chapter 5 includes a discussion on how to get an idea of what you have and to what you may be entitled. It discusses property, alimony, child support, and custody, and can give you a good idea of your exposure.

Petition for Divorce. A Petition for Divorce is nothing more than a written request for the judge to grant you a divorce and divide your property. A **PETITION FOR UNCONTESTED DIVORCE** is provided in Appendix C. (see form 12, p.233.) Instructions are provided in later chapters. Once the form is completed, it is filed with the court clerk. You may also hear this petition referred to by the older term—*complaint*.

Notifying your spouse. After you have prepared the **PETITION FOR UNCONTESTED DIVORCE**, you need to officially notify your spouse. Even though your spouse may already know that you are filing for divorce, you still need to have him or her officially notified. This is done by having a copy of your **PETITION** delivered to your spouse. This must be done in a certain way, which is explained in detail on page 77. It can also be done by agreement, and the **ACKNOWLEDGMENT OF SERVICE AND CONSENT TO JURISDICTION** is the more convenient approach if the divorce is by agreement. (see form 24, p.269.)

Obtaining a hearing date. Once all of your paperwork is in order and has been filed, you need to set a date for a hearing. The hearing date in Georgia must be more than forty-five days after the **PETITION**

FOR **UNCONTESTED DIVORCE** is filed, except in certain circumstances by agreement. A hearing is simply a meeting with the judge so that he or she can give you a divorce. This is usually done by contacting the Superior Court Clerk and asking for a hearing date. Sometimes you will be referred directly to the judge's secretary. This can often be done over the telephone.

Attend the hearing. Finally, you go to the hearing. The judge will review the papers you have submitted and any additional information you have and will make a decision about whether to grant the divorce, how your property should be divided, who should have custody of your children, and how the children are to be supported. If it applies to your situation, he or she may also decide whether alimony will be paid. If you and your spouse agree on these matters, the judge will likely approve your agreement.

Contested Divorce

Very simply, any case that is not uncontested is contested. If you and your spouse need assistance with any aspect of the divorce, there is a controversy. The problem with contested divorces is that often the issues of agreement are so involved that if the parties are not in total agreement, they are effectively in total disagreement. However, if there are only minor disagreements, you may still be able to effectively resolve your situation without an attorney. If you really have a contested divorce, it may do you well to seriously consider professional assistance, as the intricacies of evidence and procedure are difficult. It is not illegal to try it yourself, just dangerous and possibly irreversible.

The steps in a contested divorce have similarities to an uncontested divorce, except that a judge does the *working it out* part, based upon the evidence presented. These steps are as follows.

- ✪ One party files papers asking the judge to grant a divorce. These papers are called the **PETITION FOR CONTESTED DIVORCE** and may include an **AFFIDAVIT REGARDING CUSTODY**, as well as additional forms. New Georgia rules require additional forms for child support. Because they are pretty complicated, you need to follow the directions in Chapter 7 closely and add these, whether your divorce is contested or uncontested.

- ✪ The court must be sure that the other party has proper legal notice of the divorce process, and that he or she will be legally bound by the court's decision.

✪   A temporary hearing date must be set.

✪   On the date of the temporary hearing, both parties appear in front of the judge, the evidence is presented, and the judge makes the decisions regarding the position of the parties in an abbreviated hearing. A **TEMPORARY ORDER** is issued that applies to such items as who will live where until the divorce is final, who keeps the children, and what support is to be paid.

✪   If the parties can live with the **TEMPORARY ORDER**, they can make it the final order of the court. If either party does not like the order, they can request a judge or jury trial called a *final hearing*.

Again, each step is covered in detail in later chapters, but some preliminary information is helpful.

Petition for Divorce. Just like an uncontested divorce, the Petition for Divorce is nothing more than a written request for the judge to grant you a divorce and divide your property. A **PETITION FOR CONTESTED DIVORCE** is provided in Appendix C, and full instructions for preparing it are provided in Chapter 8. Once the **PETITION FOR CONTESTED DIVORCE** is completed, it is taken to the court clerk to be filed.

Notifying your spouse. After you have prepared the **PETITION**, you need to officially notify your spouse. Even though your spouse may already know that you are filing for divorce, you still need to have him or her officially notified. This is done by having a copy of your **PETITION FOR CONTESTED DIVORCE** delivered to your spouse (this is called service of process). In a contested divorce, it is much more likely that you will have service of process than in an uncontested divorce. This must be done in a certain way, which is explained in detail on page 77. It can also be done by agreement. The **ACKNOWLEDGMENT OF SERVICE AND CONSENT TO JURISDICTION** remains the more convenient approach even if the divorce is not by agreement. (see form 24, p.269.)

Obtaining a temporary hearing date. Once all of your paperwork is in order and is filed, you need to set a date for a hearing. The temporary hearing date in Georgia must be more than ten days from the day the **PETITION FOR CONTESTED DIVORCE** is served on your spouse, except in certain circumstances. A temporary hearing is usually requested by including a **RULE NISI** (form 6, p.219.) with your divorce petition when you file your papers with the Superior Court Clerk. A **RULE NISI** is simply a form that gets served with your **PETITION FOR CONTESTED DIVORCE** stating what day the temporary hearing is held. This is rarely accomplished over the phone.

The temporary hearing. Finally, you go to the temporary hearing. The judge will review the papers you have submitted and any additional evidence both parties present, and make a decision regarding temporary issues, such as temporary child support and custody. If it applies to your situation, he or she may also decide whether temporary alimony will be paid. You are only allowed one witness at the temporary hearing. Affidavits, if they can be introduced into evidence at all, must be provided to the opposing party at least twenty-four hours before the hearing. Since a temporary hearing may be held in a couple of weeks, and a contested jury trial in a major metropolitan county can take eighteen months to even begin, the temporary hearing can be incredibly important. Also, your conduct during the time you are waiting for a final hearing could be used against you. Evaluate your personal circumstances carefully before trying this yourself.

The final hearing. If either party is unhappy with the judge's **TEMPORARY ORDER**, the party may request a final hearing. This generally is requested within six months of the date of the temporary hearing or the date of the judge's order, whichever is later.

The final hearing will be in front of a judge only, unless one party requests a jury. Juries only determine property issues and do not decide custody claims. Most juries are six-person juries. Either the judge or the jury will reach a decision, commonly called a verdict. This verdict is incorporated into a **FINAL JUDGMENT AND DECREE**, which formally destroys the union of the parties.

Military Personnel

There are special rules for military personnel. A military divorce can be filed in Georgia by either party in a court in the country contiguous to the military base. One of the parties has to be stationed at that base to acquire residency. It works a lot better in an uncontested divorce, but this jurisdictional exception can be used in a contested contest at times as well. You will probably want to talk with a military officer in the legal department of the base if this applies to you. While some people think that it is unbecoming conduct to file for divorce against someone serving in the military, you have to make that decision for yourself. Georgia also has laws that protect active duty military personnel from contested civil and criminal claims.

If you are a military spouse, and have an uncontested divorce, read the section on "Military Divorces" in Chapter 12 and file in the county next to the military base.

LEGAL RESEARCH

This book is not a course in legal research, and for most simple cases, you do not need to do legal research. However, if your case becomes complicated or you simply have an interest in checking the divorce law in Georgia, this section gives you some basic guidance.

Official Code of Georgia Annotated

The main source of information on Georgia divorce law is the Official Code of Georgia Annotated (OCGA). These are numerous volumes that contain the laws passed by the Georgia Legislature. Each section is followed by summaries (called *annotations*) that discuss that section. For example, if you are looking for information about temporary alimony, you would find Section 19-6-3. This would give you the exact language of the statute, which would be followed by summaries of court opinions explaining the temporary alimony statute.

These volumes are supplemented as needed. It is important to note that in the backs of some of the books will be paper inserts that comprise the latest legislative activity on a particular area. It is essential to look both in the main text of the book and in the back section to make sure there have not been any changes since the last publication of that volume. A set can usually be found at the public library, although check to be sure they have the most recent set. You will primarily be concerned with Chapter 19 of the Georgia Code, although you can look for other subjects in the index volume.

In addition to the laws passed by the legislature, law is also made by the decisions of the judges in various cases each year. To find this *case law* you will need to go to a law library. Each county has a law library connected with the court, so you can ask the court clerk where the library is located. Be aware that some law libraries do not encourage casual research by untrained individuals, so govern your actions accordingly.

Law schools have libraries that may be open to the public. Do not be afraid to ask the librarian for assistance. They cannot give you legal advice, but they can tell you where the books are located and might even be kind enough to give you a short course on legal research. In addition to OCGA, there are several types of books used to find the case law.

Georgia Digest

The *Georgia Digest* is a set of volumes that gives short summaries of cases and the place where you can find the court's full written opinion. The information in the *Georgia Digest* is arranged alphabetically by subject. Look first in the index (a four volume set divided alphabetically) and find the heading for "Divorce." Then look for the specific subject area you want to investigate.

South Eastern Reporter

The *South Eastern Reporter* is a large set of books where the appeals courts publish their written opinions on the cases they hear. There are two series of the *South Eastern Reporter*. The older cases are found in the *South Eastern Reporter* (S.E.) and the newer cases are found in the *South Eastern Reporter 2d. Series* ("S.E.2d"). For example, if the digest tells you that the case of *Smith v. Smith* is located at "349 S.E.2d 721 (1991)," you can find the case by going to Volume 349 of the *South Eastern Reporter 2d Series* and turning to page 721. In its opinion (which was printed in 1991), the court discusses what the case was about, what questions of law were presented for consideration, and what the court decided and why.

Uniform Superior Court Rules

The *Uniform Superior Court Rules* are the rules that are applied in the various courts in Georgia, and they also contain approved forms. These rules mainly deal with forms and procedures. You would be primarily concerned with the "Rules of Civil Procedure."

Alternative Dispute Resolution

Traditionally, disputes in Georgia have been resolved by individuals and attorneys presenting contested issues to judges for resolution. However, there is a growing trend in Georgia courts favoring alternative means of resolving disputes. In the case of a divorce, disputes are common, and unresolved disputes are fatal to any expectation of a simple, uncontested divorce. If you have reached a point in your divorce process where you and your spouse are unable to reach an agreement, some form of resolution will be required. It is important to understand both the underlying causes of the disputes and some alternatives that may be presented or available to you.

GETTING YOUR SPOUSE TO AGREE

If you are reading this section, you understand there is a possibility that you and your spouse will not agree on one or more issues, and that you may reach an impasse. Before you can determine an appropriate way to deal with the impasse, it is very important to try and understand why it may exist. Generally, there are four primary reasons for an inability to reach an agreement:

1. unrealistic expectations from one or both parties;

2. secondary personal issues involved in the negotiation process;

3. fear of reaching a resolution or conclusion; and/or,

4. impossibility.

One or more of these issues may apply to you or your spouse, and an understanding of some of the underlying themes may assist you in deciding a course of action. Keep in mind that this section assumes that your spouse is not habitually under the influence of drugs or alcohol, suffering from a clinical mental illness, or physically violent. If any of these cases exists, please do not attempt to resolve the issues on your own. These types of cases are difficult even for trained professionals.

– Caution –

If you are a battered spouse, all sources agree that violence itself cannot be the subject of mediation, and that mediation is not a substitute for counseling, education, and legal sanctions. As a general rule, no criminal cases involving domestic violence should ever be mediated. The violent act or acts must be dealt with through the actual court procedure in order to emphasize the seriousness of the act and the fact that domestic violence, when proved, is indeed against the law.

Unrealistic Expectations

The only way to deal with the problem of unrealistic expectations is education. You must understand that it is your responsibility to yourself and your children to understand the true community standards of support, alimony, custody, and division of property. You can get this information in casual conversation with lawyers, mediators, judges, or financial planners. You often cannot get accurate information from friends or family who believe they have gone through, or worse yet know someone who has gone through, the same situation.

If you do speak with an attorney, make it very clear that you do not plan to retain him or her for an adversarial process (this keeps the attorney in the mode of a neutral rather than an advocate) and ask for his or her view of the legal landscape. While this should not be the only basis for your expectations, it is a good place to start. If you know that your expectations are realistic, and your spouse's are dramatically different, you might ask (in a nonconfrontational manner) the basis for his or her calculation and then make available corrective information. If your husband believes that he will only have to pay 15% of net income for child support in Georgia for two children or your wife believes that a jury will award her unlimited lifetime alimony, then try to determine how he or she came to that conclusion and see if there is an available education process, as common ground is vitally important before you can progress to the next stage.

Secondary Personal Issues

Often emotion—jealously, rage, pain, depression—gets in the way of rational thought and behavior. When secondary personal issues are driving the situation, lawyers often become very wealthy. These cases are the most difficult to work around from a dispute-resolution perspective.

Infidelity is a common theme, and often the victimized spouse has no real interest in the practical disposition of assets and liabilities but wants to be sure that there are no resources for the other party to use to enjoy his or her new life. This is the equivalent of *scorched earth battlefield tactics*, in which one party will destroy every asset just to be sure the other party cannot use it. An equally common theme is the *guilty spouse phenomenon*, in which one party gives away everything as penance for a misdeed.

It is probably a mistake to expect to ever reach an understanding if harsh emotions prevent discussions of issues, but understand that both of these are foolish positions. In the long run, the guilty spouse will just be back in court for the children or resources after the initial shock wears off, or the scorched earth spouse will find that destroying everything leaves nothing for him or her either.

In these cases, mediation is premature. Counseling is necessary for one or both of you to be able to communicate before you can reach a point of seeking a genuine consensus. If you are the injured party, try to talk to a professional. He or she will probably try to help you reach a point in which you can understand that your spouse is still the person you once loved, and that the spouse will bear the consequences of the bad decisions for a lifetime, regardless of who gets the dishwasher.

Fear of Reaching a Conclusion

Often conflict is the thread that keeps parties tied together—sometimes for life. They substitute bickering for affection and anger for passion, and silence becomes the agreed upon form of pleasant communication. You may have seen this in your friends through a couple that has been divorced for years and continues to battle over visitation, flaunts the new house or car, or takes a vicious delight in showing off the new boyfriend or girlfriend.

Many times one spouse will take a position with respect to one issue (an heirloom from the other's family, pictures, or an interest in a family timeshare) that has very little financial value but for which the other side has a passionate interest. Many times, the spouse knows there can be no resolution, but keeps this argument alive for the sake of contact with the spouse. (Many times this can be seen with one spouse leaving stuff at the house after the divorce, sometimes for years!)

The solution to this is to recognize the issue and come to grips with it, because it can only exist in a two-way street. If you do not care what your spouse thinks or does, then it is very difficult for the spouse to continue any form of relationship. Many people do not understand that the opposite of love is not hate, but rather indifference. Once you reach a point of indifference, you will naturally sever any ties to the relationship and allow nature to take its course.

Impossibility

Some situations are simply impossible, and every outcome is bad. Sometimes religious beliefs, joined family business interests, or situations in which two people physically do not have the resources to be able to divide everything and maintain separate lives prevent people from reaching an agreement. The only solution to impossible situations is to grit your teeth and take the best of whatever bad options you have, but be open to all options, including putting the divorce on hold while interpersonal issues are resolved.

ALTERNATIVE DISPUTE RESOLUTION OPTIONS

If you have reached a point of disagreement and believe that some form of dispute resolution would be appropriate, there are several things to consider. Terms may be presented to you including *independent mediation, court-ordered mediation, arbitration, guardian ad litem,* or *collaborative mediation.* Each of these terms is something different, and your community may even have other options. To determine the options available in your community, ask your Superior Court Clerk's office for a list of approved mediators and what may be available.

Independent Mediation

Independent mediation involves talking to your spouse and going directly to a professional mediator. There are several advantages to independent mediation, including:

- ✪ the process is private and confidential;

- ✪ the issues can be addressed fairly quickly; and,

- ✪ many side issues of family and friend involvement are minimized.

This is probably one of the more expensive mediation options because you will be paying the prevailing rate for the mediator, and the mediator will be taking the case from start to finish. However, often the most expensive mediated case is less than an average litigated case.

Most professionals will suggest that each party at least speak with an attorney before the mediation, so that they have some idea of the process and goals. Mediators will often provide ground rules prior to the mediation, and require the parties to exchange complete financial information.

Court-Ordered Mediation

In many courts, the judge will order the parties to participate in mediation prior to the judge hearing the case. If this is the case in your jurisdiction, the court also has probably capped the costs and required participating mediators to serve at an artificially reduced rate in exchange for being on the *approved list.* The Ninth Judicial Circuit, for example, requires mediators to charge no more than $75 per hour ($37.50 per party). Other jurisdictions provide the mediator for free.

If your court requires mediation, then participate willingly and with a spirit of good faith and cooperation. You will find that this is a pretty cost-effective option for the cost of mediators, but you have probably spent a lot of money on attorneys to get here.

In mediation, the idea is that the parties are brought to a consensus by a trained professional who works with both parties to find a solution that is tailored to fit their personal expectations. Generally, it is thought that both parties should be a little disappointed in mediation.

Arbitration

Arbitration is a less formal form of litigation, and the parties have input but no part in the decision process. In arbitration, each party presents his or her case and the arbitrator makes a decision.

Guardian Ad Litem

Many courts use a version of dispute resolution in custody cases called a *guardian ad litem*. A guardian ad litem is appointed by the court to represent the interests of a child or an incapacitated adult. The guardian investigates the family situation and makes a report to the court with a recommendation regarding custody. In some courts the guardian is paid by the court, and in others, the parties are charged for the guardian. The vast majority of guardians are caring, capable professionals who are worth far more than they are paid. Generally the parties agree on a guardian, and if one is necessary in your case, pay close attention to the selection of the guardian. Check résumés and get a contract cost of the guardian before agreeing to one. Understand that he or she becomes the most important witness for custody and distribution of assets in the case.

Collaborative Mediation

In *collaborative mediation*, the parties use attorneys or representatives who agree not to act like advocates and instead serve as counselors or collaborators. Each party is required to fully disclose all assets and liabilities. Custody is determined by a professional psychologist who facilitates a parenting schedule, and the representatives of each party are required to be pleasant and respectful in an effort to work together to find a solution. This is often easier said than done, but may work in your case. Look on the Internet for devotees of this practice and see if it fits with your own personal cost-benefit analysis. Collaborative mediation works very well in cases where there are enough assets to pay the costs of the professionals involved.

Church Programs

Many churches, especially the larger ones, have faith-based programs that try first to repair the damage. If that is not possible, they often provide direction for the divorce with a biblical perspective. Some religions have divorce intervention programs. One example is a program offered by the Church of Scientology. You do not necessarily have to be a member of a church to participate in one of their programs.

Larger churches are often open during the week. Go in and talk to a pastor or one of the assistants and see what is available. You will find that there are some tremendous options available.

CONCLUSION

In closing, litigation can be very negative and professionals have come up with many alternatives that are designed to improve the process. Some of these may be appropriate for you, but first determine the reason for the impasse and often the appropriate solution will be fairly easily determined.

Lawyers

Georgia courts do not usually require an attorney to represent you. A party in Georgia has a constitutional right to represent him- or herself. Whether you need an attorney will depend upon many factors, such as how comfortable you feel handling the matter yourself; whether your situation is more complicated than usual; how much opposition you get from your spouse; and, whether your spouse has an attorney. It may also be advisable to hire an attorney if you encounter a judge with a hostile attitude, or if your spouse gets a lawyer who wants to fight. There are no court-appointed lawyers in divorce cases, so if you want an attorney, you will have to hire one. It is also against the law in Georgia for an attorney to handle a divorce case on a *contingency fee* basis, so be prepared to discuss money fairly early in the conversation.

A very general rule is that you should consider hiring an attorney whenever you reach a point in which you no longer feel comfortable representing yourself. This point will vary greatly with each person, so there is no easy way to be more definite. The cases in which attorneys are rarely required are marriages of very short duration that resulted in neither children nor substantial possessions and were not complicated by many assets or liabilities. In cases in which your spouse refuses to come to some agreement, retirement benefits or tax complications exist, or custody is challenged, attorneys are inevitable.

Rather than asking if you *need* a lawyer, a more appropriate question is, *Do you want a lawyer?* The next section discusses some of the pros and cons of hiring a lawyer, and some of the things you may want to consider in making this decision.

WANTING A LAWYER

One of the first questions you will want to consider, and most likely the reason you are reading this book, is, *How much will an attorney cost?* Attorneys come in all ages, shapes, sizes, sexes, races, ethnicities, and price ranges. For a very rough estimate, you can expect an attorney to charge anywhere from $80 to $1,500 total for an uncontested divorce and from $1,500 and up (for each of you) for a contested divorce. Lawyers usually charge an hourly rate for contested divorces, ranging from about $75 to $300 per hour. Most new (and often less expensive) attorneys are quite capable of handling a simple divorce, but if your situation became more complicated, you would probably want a more experienced lawyer.

Advantages to Having a Lawyer

The following are some of the advantages to hiring a lawyer.

○ *Judges and other attorneys may take you more seriously.* Most judges prefer both parties to have attorneys. They feel this helps the case move in a more orderly fashion because both sides will know the procedures and relevant issues. Persons representing themselves very often waste a lot of time on matters that have absolutely no bearing on the outcome of the case.

○ *A lawyer will serve as a buffer between you and your spouse.* This can lead to a quicker passage through the system by reducing the chance for emotions to take control and confuse the issues.

○ *Attorneys often prefer to deal with other attorneys.* However, if you become familiar with this book and conduct yourself in a calm and proper manner, you should have no trouble. (Proper courtroom manners are discussed in Chapter 6.)

○ *You can let your lawyer worry about all of the details.* By having an attorney, you only need to become generally familiar with the contents of this book, as it will be your attorney's job to file the proper papers in the correct form, and to deal with the court clerks, the judge, the process server, your spouse, and your spouse's attorney.

✪ *Lawyers provide professional assistance with problems.* In the event your case is complicated, or suddenly becomes complicated, it is an advantage to have an attorney who is familiar with your case. It can also be comforting to have a lawyer to turn to for advice and to get your questions answered.

Advantages to Representing Yourself

There are also significant advantages to representing yourself.

✪ *You save the cost of a lawyer.* In a time of strained finances, this can be very helpful.

✪ *Sometimes judges feel more sympathetic toward a person not represented by an attorney.* Sometimes this results in the unrepresented person being allowed a certain amount of leeway with the procedure rules.

✪ *The procedure may be faster.* Two of the most frequent complaints about lawyers are the delay in completing the case and a failure to return phone calls. Most lawyers have a heavy caseload, which sometimes results in cases being neglected for various periods of time. If you are following the progress of your own case, you will be able to push it along the system diligently.

✪ *Selecting an attorney is not easy.* As the next section shows, it is hard to know whether you will be happy with the attorney you select.

Advantages to the Middle Ground

You may want to look for an attorney who will be willing to accept an hourly fee to answer your questions and give you help as you need it. This way you will save some legal costs but still get some professional assistance. For malpractice purposes, many attorneys may be reluctant to accept this arrangement unless it is outlined in detail (and at your expense) in an agreement between the two of you.

There are also nonlegal avenues of assistance available, such as FindLaw (**www.findlaw.com**) and LegalZoom (**www.legalzoom.com**), which are designed to help with filling out forms. Often they provide simple forms for you. There are several simple divorce computer programs available, but remember that most are not specifically designed for Georgia, and are certainly not designed for all 150 or more Georgia counties. If you use one of these, or any other product, to handle your divorce, be sure to carefully read and understand what you are signing. Further, some paralegal companies have been formed that offer assistance in these matters. However, know that because of state rules, paralegals acting independently of lawyers are on very shaky legal ground. While a paralegal may provide you with a certain level of legal information to assist in filing your forms, he or she cannot provide any legal advice, nor appear in court on your behalf. To do so would be engaging in the unauthorized practice of law. It is against the law in Georgia to engage in, or assist anyone else in engaging in, the unauthorized practice of law.

It is also theoretically possible for both you and your spouse to hire one attorney. However, *be careful*. This arrangement is not favored in Georgia, and the attorney will only be able to represent one of you (or neither of you) and will require you to sign lots of releases explaining that you understand that one attorney cannot represent two people in a divorce. However, if the case is uncontested, and you simply want the attorney to draft the documents, it is possible to use only one attorney.

SELECTING A LAWYER

Selecting a lawyer is a two-step process. First you need to decide with which attorney to make an appointment. Then you need to decide if you want to hire that attorney. The next section helps you with the second step.

Finding Lawyers

The following suggestions may help you locate a few lawyers for further consideration.

- ✪ *Ask a friend.* A common, and frequently the best, way to find a lawyer is to ask someone you know to recommend one to you. This is especially helpful if the lawyer represented your friend in a divorce or other family law matter.

- ✪ *Lawyer referral service.* You can find a referral service by looking in the Yellow Pages phone directory under "Attorney Referral Services" or "Attorneys." This is a service, usually operated by a bar association, that is designed to match a client with an attorney handling cases in the area of law the client needs. The referral service does not guarantee the quality of work nor the level of experience or ability of the attorney. Finding a lawyer this way will at least connect you with one who is interested in divorce and family law matters and probably has some experience in this area.

- ✪ *Yellow Pages.* Check under the heading for "Attorneys" in the Yellow Pages. Many of the lawyers and law firms will place ads indicating their areas of practice and educational backgrounds. Look for firms or lawyers that indicate they practice in areas such as "divorce," "family law," or "domestic relations."

- ✪ *Ask another lawyer.* If you have used the services of an attorney in the past for some other matter (for example, a real estate closing, a traffic ticket, or a will), you may want to call and ask if he or she could refer you to an attorney whose ability in the area of family law is respected.

- ✪ *Signs in the neighborhood.* Look for signs in your neighborhood, shopping district, or on your way to and from work. Attorneys who practice in your area of town are probably very familiar with the economics of the community and are often familiar with general practice issues like simple divorces.

- ✪ *Bar association.* Look in the phone book for your local county or state bar association. Call them and ask for a referral to a member of a domestic relations or family law practice section committee. This is routinely provided as a low-cost or free service by bar associations.

- ✪ *Internet.* Check the Internet. Many domestic attorneys have Web pages, many firms are listed, and most major online services have extensive domestic relations sections.

EVALUATING A LAWYER

From your search you should select three to five lawyers worthy of further consideration. Your first step will be to call each attorney's office, explain that you are interested in seeking a divorce, and ask the following questions.

- Does the attorney (or firm) handle this type of matter?

- How much can you expect it to cost? (Do not expect to get much of a definite answer, but you should be able to obtain an hourly rate, a range of total costs for a simple case, and information about what variables might increase the costs. However, you may need to discuss this with the attorney, rather than the person answering the phone at the attorney's office.)

- How soon can you get an appointment?

If you like the answers you get, ask if you can speak to the attorney. Some offices will permit this, but others will require you to make an appointment. Make the appointment if that is what is required. Once you get in contact with the attorney (either on the phone or at the appointment), ask the following questions.

- How much will it cost?

- How will the fee be paid? (Many attorneys will accept credit cards or promissory notes secured by property in which you have personal equity. It never hurts to ask.)

- Can you see a copy of his or her standard fee agreement or letter?

- How long has the attorney been in practice?

- How long has the attorney been in practice in Georgia?

- What percentage of the attorney's cases involve divorce cases or other family law matters? (Do not expect an exact answer, but you should get a rough estimate that is at least 20%.)

✪ How long will it take? (Do not expect an exact answer, but the attorney should be able to give you an average range and discuss things that may make a difference.)

If you get acceptable answers to these questions, it is time to ask yourself the following questions about the lawyer.

✪ Do you feel comfortable talking to the lawyer?

✪ Is the lawyer friendly to you?

✪ Does the lawyer seem confident in him- or herself?

✪ Does the lawyer seem to be straightforward and able to explain things so you understand?

Some part of your evaluation may include the attorney's office. You should probably expect to see some evidence of computerization to help keep costs down, but you will have your own opinions as to whether you prefer your professionals to be more or less technologically inclined. Also, the attorney's office and car may provide some clue to his or her success, but beware of relying on just the image.

Your attorney should not act like he or she is too important for you, nor should you be looking for a best friend. Domestic matters are times of tremendous emotional upheaval, and you are entitled to someone who will be absolutely straightforward, even if there is unpleasant information to convey.

Check the state bar website (**www.gabar.org**) or call the state bar association to see if there are any unresolved complaints against the attorney. Domestic relations cases are fairly high on the list of state bar complaints, so do not be surprised if your attorney has been involved in an investigation. However, an inordinate number of unhappy clients is probably a bad omen.

Finally, how accessible is he or she? Is the attorney's residence number in the phone book, or does he or she give clients his or her home phone number for emergencies? Does the attorney carry and answer a cell phone or have a service for after-hours crises? Do not expect much sympathy from an attorney you try to call in the wee hours of the morning to referee a domestic argument, but it may be comforting to know that he or she can be reached in an emergency.

If you get satisfactory answers, you probably have a lawyer with whom you will be able to work. Most clients are happy with an attorney who makes them feel comfortable.

WORKING WITH A LAWYER

You will work best with your attorney if you keep an open, honest, and friendly attitude. You should also consider the following suggestions.

Starting Early   Do your research before a crisis starts while you have an opportunity to make decisions based on considered judgment rather than emergencies. Attorneys are trained to work in emergency situations, but the environment is expensive and the results more uncertain.

Leave your embarrassment at home. You will probably be discussing personal details with your attorney that you may never have even mentioned to your best friend. Your sexual and social practices are going to be a topic of conversation. If this type of frank discussion is unpleasant for you, you should prepare for it.

Communicating with Your Attorney   If you want to know something or if you do not understand something, ask your attorney. If you do not understand the answer, tell your attorney and ask him or her to explain it again. There are many points of law that many lawyers do not fully understand without study, so you should not be embarrassed to ask questions. Many people who say they have had a bad experience with a lawyer either did not ask enough questions, or had a lawyer who would not take the time to explain things to them. If your lawyer is not taking the time to explain what he or she is doing, it may be time to look for a new lawyer.

Give your lawyer complete information. Anything you tell your attorney is confidential. An attorney can lose his or her license to practice if he or she reveals information without your permission. So do not hold back, even if the issues are extremely personal. Tell your lawyer everything, even if it does not seem important to you. There are many things that seem unimportant to a non-attorney but can change the outcome of a case. Also, do not hold something back because you are afraid it will hurt your case. It will definitely hurt your case if your lawyer does not find out about it until he or she hears it in court from your spouse's attorney. If your attorney knows in advance, he or she can plan to eliminate or reduce damage to your case.

Accept reality. Listen to what your lawyer tells you about the law and the system. It will do you no good to argue because the law or the system does not work the way you think it should. For example, if your lawyer tells you that the judge cannot hear your case for two weeks, do not try demanding that an emergency hearing be set tomorrow. By refusing to accept reality, you are only setting yourself up for disappointment. Remember, it is not your attorney's fault that the system is not perfect or that the law does not say what you would like it to say.

Be patient. Be patient with the system (which is often slow), as well as with your attorney. Do not expect your lawyer to return your phone call within an hour. He or she may not be able to return it the same day either. Most lawyers are very busy and overworked. It is rare that a busy attorney can maintain a full caseload and still make each client feel as if he or she is the only client.

Talk to the secretary. Your lawyer's secretary can be a valuable source of information, so be friendly and get to know him or her. Often the secretary will be able to answer your questions, and you will not get a bill for the time you talk to him or her.

Let your attorney deal with your spouse. It is your lawyer's job to communicate with your spouse or with your spouse's lawyer. Let your attorney do this job. Many lawyers have had clients lose or damage their cases when the client decides to say or do something on their own. However, if lawyers are involved and the parties wish to settle the case themselves, but the lawyers seem to be part of the problem rather than part of the solution, remember that attorneys are ultimately employees who can be hired and fired.

Doing Your Part

There are certain things you can do to move your case along and build a good relationship with your attorney. The first is to be on time to appointments with your lawyer and especially to court hearings.

Keep your case moving. Many lawyers operate on the old principle of the squeaky wheel gets the oil. Work on a case sometimes gets put off until a deadline is near, an emergency develops, or the client calls. The reason for this is that many lawyers take more cases than can be effectively handled in order to earn the income they desire. Your task is to become a squeaky wheel that does not squeak too much. Whenever you talk to your lawyer, ask the following questions.

○   What is the next step?

○   When do you expect it to be done?

○   When should I talk to you next?

If you do not hear from the lawyer when you expect, call him or her the following day. Do not remind him or her that he or she did not call—just ask how things are going.

How to save money. Of course you do not want to spend unnecessary money for an attorney. Here are a few things you can do to avoid excess legal fees.

○   Do not make unnecessary phone calls to your lawyer.

○   Give information to the secretary whenever possible.

○   Direct questions to the secretary. He or she will refer to the attorney if he or she cannot answer it.

○   Plan your phone calls so you can get to the point and take less of your attorney's time.

○   If you leave a message on an answering machine or voice mail, leave the number where you can be reached. Often attorneys will return calls from court, pay phones, or car phones, and they do not have access to your personal phone numbers. Make it easy for them.

○   Do some of the legwork yourself. Pick up and deliver papers yourself, for example. Ask your attorney what you can do to assist with your case.

✪   Be prepared for appointments. Have all related papers with you, plan your visit to get to the point, and make an outline of what you want to discuss and what questions you want to ask.

✪   *Be smart!* Think about the consequences of what you want to gain from a settlement. It is crazy to pay a lawyer $100 to fight for a lawn mower that you can buy used for $50. On the other hand, a difference of $20 per week in child support for a two-year-old child amounts to $16,640 during the time the child is dependent on child support. It is probably worthwhile to spend a few dollars making sure this number is as low or as high as possible.

Pay your attorney bill when it is due. No client gets prompt attention like a client who pays his or her bill on time. However, you are entitled to an itemized bill, showing what the attorney did and how much time it took. Many attorneys will have you sign an agreement that states how you will be charged, what is included in the hourly fee, and what is extra.

Review your bill carefully. There are numerous stories of people paying an attorney $500 or $1,000 in advance, only to have the attorney make a few phone calls to the spouse's lawyer, then ask for more money. If your attorney asks for $500 or $1,000 in advance, you should be sure that you and the lawyer agree on what is to be done for this fee. For $1,000 you should at least expect to have a petition prepared, filed with the court, and served on your spouse (although the filing and service fees will probably be extra).

If you truly have an uncontested divorce for a short-term marriage that involves neither custody, nor real estate, nor retirement benefits, for $1,000 you should at least expect the lawyer to prepare an uncontested divorce agreement. Your spouse can come by the attorney's office to sign the documents or you could take them to your spouse and save the delivery charges. However, there are a lot of variables, and filing fees and copy charges are almost always additional charges.

FIRING YOUR LAWYER

If you find that you can no longer work with your lawyer, or do not trust your lawyer, it is time to either go to it alone or get a new attorney. You will need to send your lawyer a letter stating that you no longer desire his or her services, and are discharging him or her from your case. Also state that you will be coming by the office the following week to pick up your file. (Of course, you will need to settle any remaining fees charged.)

The attorney does not have to give you his or her own notes or other work that is in progress, but he or she must give you the essential contents of your file (such as copies of papers already filed or prepared and billed for, and any documents you provided). If the attorney refuses to give you this information, contact the state bar association regarding a grievance procedure. Quite frankly, most attorneys would much rather work out their problems with you than defend themselves from a complaint to the bar association.

Under the State Bar of Georgia Fee Arbitration program, if you have a dispute with your lawyer regarding fees, you might consider *fee arbitration*. The process is very straightforward. The phone number for the bar association is 404-527-8700. A lawyer cannot force a client to participate if a client declines; however, if a client wants to arbitrate and the lawyer refuses, the process may continue without the lawyer's participation as a party at the hearing. If the client prevails in such a hearing, the award becomes evidence in any future litigation over the fee, and the client may be furnished with free counsel if such future litigation is needed.

Evaluating Your Situation

chapter 5

Before you file any papers with the court, you need to evaluate your situation. The following points should be considered before you begin the divorce process.

RELATIONS WITH YOUR SPOUSE

First, you need to evaluate your situation with respect to your spouse. Have you both already agreed to get a divorce? If not, what kind of reaction do you expect from him or her? The expected reaction can determine how you will proceed. If he or she reacts in a rational manner, you can probably use the uncontested procedure. However, if you expect an extremely emotional and possibly violent reaction, you will need to take steps to protect yourself, your children, and your property. You should start out expecting to use the contested procedure.

Unless you and your spouse have already decided together to get a divorce, you do not want your spouse to know that you are thinking about filing for divorce. This is a defense tactic, although it may not seem that way at first. If your spouse thinks you are planning a divorce, he or she may do things to prevent you from getting a fair result. These things include withdrawing money from bank accounts and hiding information about income and assets. So do not let on until you have collected all the information you need and are about to file with the court, or until you are prepared to protect yourself from violence, if necessary.

– Caution –

Tactics such as withdrawing money from bank accounts and hiding assets are dangerous. If you try any of these things you risk looking like the bad guy before the judge. This can result in anything from having disputed matters resolved in your spouse's favor to being ordered to produce the assets (or be jailed for contempt of court).

Georgia also requires that the assets of the parties in a divorce be held in trust until the ownership is resolved. It is a dangerous situation to take items that belong to both of you and try to dispose of them yourself.

Theoretically, judges prefer you to keep evidence of the assets (such as photographs, sales receipts, or bank statements) to present to the court if your spouse hides them. Then your spouse will be the bad guy and risk being jailed. However, once your spouse has taken assets and hidden them or sold them and spent the money, even a contempt order may not get the money or assets back.

If you determine that you need to get the assets in order to keep your spouse from hiding or disposing of them, be sure you keep them in a safe place and disclose them on your **Domestic Relations Financial Affidavit**. (see form 13, p.235.) Do not dispose of them. If your spouse claims you took them, you can explain to the judge why you were afraid that your spouse would dispose of them, and that you merely got them out of his or her reach.

FINANCIAL INFORMATION

It is extremely important that you collect all of the financial information you can get. This information should include originals or copies of the following:

- ✪ your most recent income tax return (and your spouse's if you filed separately);

○ the most recent W-2 tax forms for yourself and your spouse;

○ any other income reporting papers (such as interest, stock dividends, etc.);

○ your spouse's most recent pay stub, showing year-to-date earnings (otherwise, try to get copies of all pay stubs since the beginning of the year);

○ deeds to all real estate;

○ titles to cars, boats, and other vehicles;

○ your and your spouse's will;

○ life insurance policies;

○ stocks, bonds, or other investment papers;

○ pension or retirement fund papers and statements;

○ health insurance card and papers;

○ bank account or credit union statements;

○ your spouse's Social Security number and driver's license number;

○ names, addresses, and phone numbers of your spouse's employer, close friends, and family members;

○ credit card statements, mortgage documents, and other credit and debt papers;

○ a list of vehicles, furniture, appliances, tools, etc., owned by you and your spouse (See the next section on "Property and Debts" for forms and a detailed discussion of what to include.);

○ copies of bills or receipts for recurring, regular expenses, such as electric, gas, or other utilities, car insurance, etc.;

✪ copies of bills, receipts, insurance forms, or medical records for any unusual medical expenses (including for recurring or continuous medical conditions) for yourself, your spouse, or your children;

✪ any other papers showing what you and your spouse earn, own, or owe; and,

✪ any information about personal injury or workers' compensation cases your spouse may be involved with, as well as any inheritance, trust, or estate issues with which he or she may be involved.

Make copies of as many of these papers as possible and keep them in a safe and private place where your spouse will not find them. Try to make copies of new papers as they come in, especially as you get close to filing court papers and as you get close to a court hearing.

PROPERTY AND DEBTS

This section is designed to help you get a general idea of where things stand regarding the division of your property and debts and to prepare you for completing the court papers you need to file. The following sections deal with the questions of alimony, child support, custody, and visitation. If you are still not sure whether you want a divorce, these sections may help you decide.

Property   Trying to determine how to divide assets and debts can be difficult. Under Georgia's *equitable distribution* law, assets and debts are separated into two categories—*marital* (meaning it is both yours and your spouse's) and *nonmarital* (meaning it is yours or your spouse's alone). In making this distinction the following rules apply.

✪ If the asset or debt was acquired after the date you were married, it is presumed to be a marital asset of debt. It is up to you or your spouse to prove otherwise.

✪ In order to be a nonmarital asset or debt, it must have been acquired before the date of your marriage. Also, it is nonmarital if you acquired it through a gift or inheritance (as long as it was not a gift from your spouse). This includes income from nonmarital property.

Example 1:

You receive rent from an investment property you had before you got married. If you exchange one of these assets or debts after your marriage, it may still be nonmarital.

Example 2:

You had a $6,000 car before you got married. After the marriage, you traded it for a different $6,000 car. The new car is probably also nonmarital.

Finally, you and your spouse may sign a written agreement that certain assets and debts are to be considered nonmarital. These agreements, if executed prior to the marriage, may or may not be enforceable. Unfortunately, Georgia law does not favor contracts in contemplation of marriage (sometimes called *prenuptial agreements*), and they can be looked at very closely. Most court arguments over property involve controversies over what is marital property and what is not. If this becomes a contested issue in your case, and valuable property is at stake, you may want to consult a lawyer.

✪ Marital assets and debts are those that were acquired during your marriage, even if they were acquired by you or your spouse individually. This also includes the increase in value of a nonmarital asset during the marriage or due to the use of marital funds to pay for or improve the property.

Example:

You owned your home before getting married and decide to rent it after moving in with your spouse. To rent it, you and your spouse have a new roof put on it. If you then decided to sell it, the increase in value of the property due to the roof would be marital property.

Usually, all rights accrued during the marriage in pension, retirement, profit-sharing, insurance, and similar plans are marital assets. It is also possible for one spouse to make a gift of nonmarital property to the other spouse, thereby making it marital property.

✪ Real estate that is in both names is considered marital property, and it is up to the spouse claiming otherwise to prove it.

✪ Finally, the value of an asset, as well as the question of whether an asset or debt is marital or nonmarital, is determined as of the date of the settlement agreement, or the date the petition was filed, whichever is first. However, Georgia law says that, even if you separate, marital assets can still accumulate. (This is another reason to watch out for separate maintenance.)

Property Inventory

The following information will assist you in completing the **PROPERTY INVENTORY**. (see form 1, p.181.) This form is a list of all of your property and key information about that property. You will notice that this form is divided into nine columns, designated as follows.

◈ Column (1): You will check the box in this column if the piece of property is nonmarital property. This is property that either you or your spouse acquired before you were married, or was given to you or your spouse separately, or was inherited by you or your spouse separately.

◈ Column (2): Describe the property in this column. A discussion regarding what information should go in this column will follow.

◈ Column (3): This column is used to write in the serial number, account number, or other number that will help clearly identify that piece of property.

◈ Column (4): This is for the current market value of the property.

◈ Column (5): This will show how much money is owed on the property, if any.

⬥ Column (6): Subtract the balance owed from the value. This will show how much the property is worth to you (your *equity*).

⬥ Column (7): This column will show the current legal owner of the property. (H) designates the husband, (W) the wife, and (J) is for jointly owned property (in both of your names).

⬥ Column (8): This column will be checked for those pieces of property you expect the husband will keep.

⬥ Column (9): This column is for the property you expect the wife will keep.

Use columns (1) through (7) to list your property, including the following.

Cash. List the name of the bank, credit union, etc., and the account number for each account. This includes savings and checking accounts and certificates of deposit (CDs). The balance of each account should be listed in the columns entitled VALUE and EQUITY. (Leave the BALANCE OWED column blank.) Make copies of the most recent bank statements for each account.

Stocks and bonds. All stocks, bonds, or other paper investments should be listed. Write down the number of shares and the name of the company or organization that issued them. Also copy any notation such as *common* or *preferred* stock or shares. This information can be obtained from the stock certificate itself or from a statement from the stockbroker. Make a copy of the certificate or the statement.

Real estate. List each piece of property you and your spouse own. The description might include a street address for the property, a subdivision name and lot number, or anything that lets you know the piece of property to which you are referring. There probably will not be an ID number, although you might use the county's tax number. Real estate (or any other property) may be in both of your names (joint), in your spouse's name alone, or in your name alone. The only way to know for sure is to look at the deed to the property. (If you cannot find a copy of the deed, try to find mortgage papers or payment coupons, homeowners insurance papers, or a property tax assessment notice.) The owners of property are usually referred to on the deed as the *grantees*. Real estate is also called *real property*.

In assigning a value to the property, consider the market value, which is how much you could probably sell the property for. This might be what similar houses in your neighborhood have sold for recently. You might also consider how much you paid for the property or how much the property is insured for. Do not use the tax assessment value, as this is usually considerably lower than the market value.

Vehicles. This category includes cars, trucks, motor homes, recreational vehicles, motorcycles, boats, trailers, airplanes, and any other means of transportation for which the state requires a title and registration. Your description should include the following information (which can usually be found on the title or on the vehicle itself).

- ✪ Year it was made.

- ✪ Make: The name of the manufacturer, such as "Ford," "Honda," "Chris Craft," etc.

- ✪ Model: You know it is a Ford, but is it a Mustang, an F-150, or an Explorer? The model may be a name, a number, a series of letters, or a combination of these.

- ✪ Serial Number/Vehicle Identification Number (VIN): This is most likely found on the vehicle, as well as on the title or registration. This information is required to keep you from owing the state of Georgia a transfer tax of 10% of the value of the vehicle as a result of changing the name on the title.

Make a copy of the title or registration. Regarding a value, you can go to the public library and ask to look at the *blue book* for cars, trucks, or whatever it is you are looking for. A blue book (which may actually be yellow, black, or any other color) gives the average values for used vehicles. Your librarian can help you find what you need. Another source is to look in the classified advertising section of a newspaper to see what similar vehicles are selling for. You might also try calling a dealership to see if it can give you a rough idea of the value. Be sure you take into consideration the condition of the vehicle. You can also go to the Internet to determine the market value of your car, boat, trailer, or other vehicle. Edmunds.com (**www.edmunds.com**) and the National Automobile Dealers Association (**www.nada.com**) have good online products to estimate the value of used vehicles. Be sure to deduct the amount of any outstanding loan from any value you determine.

Furniture. List all furniture as specifically as possible. You should include the type of piece (such as sofa, coffee table, etc.), the color, and if you know it, the manufacturer, line name, or style. Furniture usually will not have a serial number, although if you find one be sure to write it on the list. Just estimate a value, unless you know what it is worth.

Appliances, electronic equipment, yard machines, etc. This category includes such things as refrigerators, lawn mowers, and power tools. Again, estimate a value, unless you are familiar enough with them to simply know what they are worth. There are too many different makes, models, accessories, and age factors to be able to figure out a value otherwise. These items will probably have a make, model, and serial number on them. You may have to look on the back, bottom, or other hidden place for the serial number, but try to find it.

Jewelry and other valuables. You do not need to list inexpensive costume jewelry. You can plan on keeping your own personal watches, rings, etc. However, if you own an expensive piece, then you should include it in your list along with an estimated value. Be sure to include silverware, original art, gold, coin collections, etc. Again, be as detailed and specific as possible.

Life insurance with cash surrender value. This is any life insurance policy that you may cash in or borrow against, and therefore, has value. If you cannot find a cash surrender value in the papers you have, you can call the insurance company and ask.

This information is important because a spouse usually removes his or her partner as the beneficiary during the divorce. The spouse will probably name a new beneficiary, but what if he or she does not? Upon the death of the insured, there may be a dispute between the ex-spouse and the family of the deceased.

There are many cases in which a husband names "my wife" as beneficiary of the life insurance policy (or pension, 401(k), or other assets). In the event of a divorce and remarriage of the husband to another, who should receive the money? Did the husband intend for the ex-wife or the current wife to have the money? Many court cases have addressed this type of problem that could be avoided if proper attention was paid during the divorce to the financial details.

Other big ticket items. This is simply a general reference to anything of significant value that does not fit in one of the categories already discussed. Examples might be a portable spa, an above-ground swimming pool, golf clubs, guns, pool tables, camping or fishing equipment, farm animals, or machinery.

Pensions and military benefits. The division of pensions, and of military and retirement benefits, can be a complicated matter. Whenever these types of benefits are involved, you will need to consult an attorney or a CPA to determine the value of the benefits and how they should be divided. (Be sure to read the section in Chapter 12 on pension plans.)

What not to list. You will not need to list your clothing and other personal items. Pots, pans, dishes, and cooking utensils ordinarily do not need to be listed, unless they have some unusually high value.

Once you have completed your list, go back through it and try to determine who should end up with each item. The ideal situation is for both you and your spouse to go through the list together and divide the items fairly. However, if this is not possible, you will need to offer a reasonable settlement to the judge. Consider each item and make a check mark in either column (8) or (9) to designate whether that item should go to the husband or wife. You may make the following assumptions:

- ✪   your nonmarital property will go to you;

- ✪   your spouse's nonmarital property will go to your spouse;

- ✪   you should get the items that only you use;

- ✪ your spouse should get the items only used by your spouse; and,

- ✪ the remaining items should be divided, evening out the total value of all the marital property, and taking into consideration who would really want particular items. The general rule is that each party is entitled to a property division of half of the assets and half of the liabilities of the marriage.

To somewhat equally divide your marital property, you first need to know the total value of your property. First of all, do not count the value of the nonmarital items. Add the remaining amounts in the EQUITY column of form 1, which will give you an approximate value of all marital property.

In an uncontested case, often the parties simply go room by room, taking turns picking items that they particularly wish to keep. This arrangement works best when the parties can keep in mind that they were at one time friends, and that the current circumstances should be kept as pleasant as possible.

If it comes time for the hearing and you and your spouse are still arguing over some or all of the items on your list, you will be glad that you made copies of the documents relating to the property on your list. Arguments over the value of property may need to be resolved by hiring appraisers to set a value; however, you will have to pay the appraiser a fee. (See Chapter 8 for information on dividing property in contested cases.)

This is a good time to take pictures of the home and its contents. Give the photographs or videos to a trusted friend to hold, or rent a safe-deposit box. It is not a good idea to keep important divorce papers and records in the trunk of your car. Concentrate on furniture and expensive items such as china, crystal, and silver. Be certain to document items of sentimental value to you, even if they are not expensive, such as high school memorabilia, baby books and family pictures, and videos.

It is best to do this when your spouse is not home, especially if you have not told your spouse of your intentions to file for divorce. These records could be very useful in a fight over personal and real property.

Debts   This section relates to the **DEBT INVENTORY** (form 2, p.183), which lists your debts. Although there are cases in which, for example, the wife gets a car but the husband makes the payments, generally whoever gets the property also gets the debt owed on that property. This seems to be a fair arrangement in most cases.

In the case of credit cards, it is important to know who is authorized to sign on the account. Removing your name from an account does not necessarily relinquish your liability. Check with your credit card issuer for more details on how to limit the authorized users on cancelled accounts.

You should also cancel home equity loans and lines of credit if you can. If it is a joint account, notify the lender that you are going through a divorce. Insist that the lender notify you if your spouse tries to withdraw funds.

On form 2 you will list each debt owed by you or your spouse. As with nonmarital property, there is also nonmarital debt. This is any debt incurred before you were married, and that is yours alone. Form 2 contains a column for "N-M" debts, which should be checked for each nonmarital debt. You will be responsible for your nonmarital debts, and your spouse will be responsible for his or hers.

To complete the **DEBT INVENTORY**, list each debt as follows.

    ✦   Column (1): Check if this is a nonmarital debt.

    ✦   Column (2): Write in the name and address of the creditor (the bank, company, or person to which the debt is owed).

    ✦   Column (3): Write in the account, loan, or mortgage number.

    ✦   Column (4): Write in any notes to help identify what the loan was for (such as "Christmas gifts," "Vacation," etc.).

    ✦   Column (5): Write in the amount of the monthly payment.

    ✦   Column (6): Write in the balance still owed on the loan.

◈   Column (7): Write in the date (approximately) when the loan was made.

◈   Column (8): Note whether the account is in the husband's name (H), the wife's name (W), or jointly in both names (J).

◈   Columns (9) & (10): These columns note who will be responsible for the debt after the divorce. As with your property, each of you will keep your nonmarital debts, and the remainder should be divided, taking into consideration what the loan was for and equally dividing the debt. (See Chapter 8 for information on dividing debts in contested cases.)

CHILD CUSTODY AND VISITATION

As with everything else in divorce, things are ideal when both parties can agree on the question of custody of the children. Generally the judge will accept any agreement you reach, provided it does not appear that your agreement will cause harm to your children.

With respect to child custody, Georgia law makes three significant statements. First, the court is to inquire as to the *best interests of the child,* and that the preferred method of custody is to maximize the child's contact with both parents. Second, the statutes state very clearly that the party not in default is entitled to custody. How each judge resolves this conflict is the subject of much discussion among attorneys and parents, but a judge's decision, if carefully made, is rarely overturned. Third, if the child is over the age of 14, he or she may choose with which parent to live.

Although there is no law supporting it, you may expect that most judges are from the old school of thought on the subject of custody and believe that, all things being equal, a young child is better off with the mother. The judge may go to great lengths to justify an award of custody to the mother. It happens day after day throughout the state, and it is a reality with which you may have to deal. If you are the husband and believe your particular circumstances are such that you would be a better parent, you must determine how much you can afford to prove it.

Joint Custody   *Joint custody* is a great idea in its concept, but it is usually not a very practical one. Originally, this type of custody contemplated parents separated by great distances who each kept the child for an extended period of time. The term has evolved to mean a significant shared custody arrangement with quality time divided, more or less, along equal bounds. When it works, it works wonderfully. When it does not work, there are some predictable problems.

Very few parents can put aside their anger toward each other to agree on what is best for their child. Joint custody often makes this worse and leads to more fighting. Even if joint custody is ordered, a child can only have one primary residence. So the judge may still decide with which parent the child will mainly live, as well as how decisions regarding such things as education and medical care will be made.

If you and your spouse cannot agree on how these matters will be handled, you will be leaving this important decision up to the judge. The judge cannot possibly know your child as well as you and your spouse, so it makes sense for you to work this out yourselves. Otherwise you are leaving the decision to a stranger.

If the judge must decide the issue, there is only one question to be answered—*What is in the best interest of the child?* The judge could consider such things as:

- which parent is most likely to allow the other to visit the child;

- the love, affection, and other emotional ties existing between the child and each parent;

- the ability and willingness of each parent to provide the child with food, clothing, medical care, and other material needs;

- the length of time the child has lived with either parent in a stable environment;

- the permanence, as a family unit, of the proposed custodial home (this relates to where one of the parties will be getting remarried immediately after the divorce, or more often, to petitions to change custody at a later date);

❂   the moral fitness of each parent;

❂   the mental and physical health of each parent;

❂   the home, school, and community record of the child;

❂   the preference of the child, providing the child is of sufficient
intelligence and understanding; and,

❂   any other fact the judge decides is relevant.

One Superior Court judge has admitted that he uses the *diaper rule*
in the case of arguments involving small children. For the decision as
to the custodial parent, that judge wants to know who has changed
the bulk of the diapers, prepared the bulk of the meals, taken the
child to the doctor, and read the child to sleep at night. While all
judges certainly are not following this formula, you might keep it in
mind.

It is impossible to predict the outcome of a custody battle, and anyone
who tells you otherwise is nuts. There are too many factors and individual circumstances to make such a guess. The only exception is
where one parent is clearly unfit and the other can prove it, but unfitness can be awfully subjective.

Drug abuse is probably the most common charge against a spouse,
but unless there has been an arrest and conviction, it is difficult to
prove. In general, do not charge your spouse with being unfit unless
you can prove it.

Child abuse is also a common charge, but this explosive issue should
not be raised lightly. Judges are not impressed with unfounded allegations, and they can do more harm than good.

Under some recent Georgia court decisions, homosexuality, by itself,
cannot be a factor in a custody decision.

If your children are older (not infants), it may be a good idea to seriously consider their preference for with whom they would like to live.

Your respect for their wishes may benefit you in the long run. Just be sure that you keep in close contact with them and visit them often.

Georgia also allows children over the age of 14 to elect their custodial parent. The child can change his or her mind at trial, and the judge does not have to agree with the child. However, most of the time, the minor's election carries a tremendous amount of weight.

If divorce is inevitable, take your spouse and meet with a counselor for nothing but visitation issues. Let the counselor work out what is really best for the children (and not for the parents). One judge is known for ordering quarreling parents to leave the children in the house and for the parents to each rotate every two weeks so that the children are not inconvenienced. Parents are generally appalled by this idea, but the light goes on when they think about what a bad experience this would be for adults, and it sticks with them when they think about shifting around the children.

CHILD SUPPORT

As of January 1, 2007, Georgia changed its entire child support code. The new rules are all found in the OCGA 19-6-15 and a copy is in Appendix B. Before going any further, it is recommended that you take a really deep breath. This is NOT impossible, but it is unnecessarily complicated. While most practitioners will privately tell you that this is job security for attorneys, it must be stressed that it is possible to do this yourself.

How Child Support is Determined

Across the nation, there are several different ways to calculate how to apportion the costs of children after the biological parents separate. Until 2007, Georgia child support was based on a percentage formula (in the industry, this is called a *Wisconsin plan*, for various unimportant reasons). Using this type of calculation, the person who had custody of children received support based on the percentage of the other party's income. For example, one child would be awarded 17–22% of the payor's gross income, two children would be awarded 20–25%, and so on. Many people who think about this area of society believe that percentage formulas are especially rough on the poor. As of January 1, 2007, Georgia joined a number of other states and adopted an *income shares model*, which is supposed to be more fair.

Income shares is a fancy economist term for *shared expenses based on income*. Under income shares, you take all the money that both parents make, then a rocket scientist somewhere decides how much parents with that much money should be paying for the kids they have. The problem with income shares is that you have to calculate income, and then have a formula for apportioning payments. Attached in form 3 is the complete Georgia workbook—44 pages. Only about six pages will be important for most of us, and we are going to concentrate on those.

There are several ways to do this. One way is to go to **www.georgia childsupport.com** and fill out the forms online. Another is to fill them out by hand. Online is easier, since the calculations are done for you, but this section walks through the process of doing it manually.

Child Support Worksheet

First, understand that you will have to complete a **Child Support Guidelines Worksheet** (form 3, p.185). It looks pretty overwhelming, but it can be made much more simple by taking it step by step. First, fill in the **Child Support Guidelines Worksheet** with the names of the plaintiff and defendant, and the names and birthdates of the children of the marriage. Notice there is a box next to the children's names. If the children are subject to support, check the box. If the children are from another relationship, do not check the box. Then check the box for either an initial filing or a first-time action—usually a divorce. Otherwise, you would check "Modification" if this is an action to change an order previously entered. Once you are done with that, put that paper aside for a while.

Next, determine the gross monthly income of both the mother and father. (Be careful not to use annual income—use monthly income.) When you have that number, find Schedule A and enter those numbers at the top of the form. Reading the form, you will see that there are some other categories of income to figure out. If those apply, add them to the appropriate parent, until you reach a total at the bottom of the page. (Important! Remember that for most of the numbers you are going to have to come up with, you are going to complete "schedules" that will fill in the blanks on the forms that the court requires.)

Next, add each parent's adjusted income together to arrive at the combined adjusted income amount, and then go to the tables and find the dollar figure that corresponds with the combined adjusted income amount and the number of children for whom support is being determined. For example, assume that the parents make a total of $2,000 per month and they are figuring support for two kids. The correct schedule would show that the appropriate amount of support is $624.

Now comes a pretty tricky bit of math that will be helpful in the future—you are going to figure out the percentage that each parent should provide of the child support. To get that percentage, take the total income of the first parent and DIVIDE it by the total for both parents, and you will have a percentage number. Then take the income of the second parent and DIVIDE it by the total for both parents, and you will have another percentage number. (If you have done this right, the two numbers will add together and be awfully close to 100.) For example, if each parent makes $1,000 per month, and both parents together make $2,000 a month, you would divide $1,000 by $2,000 and get 50% for each parent. When required, from this point forward, *prorate* the expenses between the parties using those same pro rata percentages.

Now take the support number and multiply it by the parent percentage, and you will have a base number that Georgia expects to be paid by each parent. Multiply each parent's pro rata percentage by the Basic Child Support Obligation amount to determine each parent's child support responsibility. (see form 3, p.188.) You are now in the home stretch.

Deviations from Child Support Amount

If there are health insurance premiums and/or work-related child care costs, enter these costs in Schedule D. These costs are added together and prorated between the parties. If either parent is already paying these costs, credit the parent who is paying or will pay the expense. The prorated Basic Child Support Obligation, after the adjustments for health insurance and work-related child care costs, results in the *Presumptive Amount of Child Support*, which is just a fancy name for child support amount.

It is possible to get deviations from this number, but obviously it is easiest to stop here. If there are no deviations, the noncustodial parent owes the custodial parent the Presumptive Amount of Child Support, which is the total of his or her pro rata share of the Basic Child Support Obligation and the mandatory additional expenses of health insurance and work-related child care costs.

If there are deviations, the Presumptive Amount of Child Support may be deviated upward or downward, if applicable, and the calculations are entered on Schedule E. Any deviated amount from the Presumptive Amount of Child Support must be supported by the court's written findings or a jury's special interrogatory findings. The findings of fact must state the reasons for the deviation; the amount of child support that would have been required if the Presumptive Amount of Child Support had not been rebutted; and, both of the following: (1) the application of the Presumptive Amount of Child Support would be unjust or inappropriate considering the relative ability of each parent to pay, and (2) how the best interest of the child for whom support is being determined will be served by deviating from the Presumptive Amount of Child Support. Loosely translated, this means that deviating from the base child support amount is time-consuming and expensive.

On a case-by-case basis, if the parties prove extraordinary educational expenses, extraordinary medical expenses, and/or special expenses incurred for child rearing, these expenses are to be prorated between the parties. If special expenses exist, the amount of special expenses must exceed 7% of the Basic Child Support Obligation threshold. Additional special expenses over the threshold can be considered, if appropriate.

If a noncustodial parent's gross income is at or below $1850 per month, consider whether a low-income deviation would be appropriate. To calculate whether the noncustodial parent's Presumptive Amount of Child Support may be adjusted by ensuring that the noncustodial parent has a self-support reserve ($900 per month), do the following.

✪   Subtract $900 from the noncustodial parent's adjusted income.

✪   If the resulting amount is less than the noncustodial parent's pro rata responsibility of the Presumptive Amount of Child Support, then the Presumptive Amount may be deviated.

✪   However, the calculation will not be complete until the court or jury considers the financial impact that a reduction in the amount of child support paid to the custodial parent would have on the custodial parent's household. No award may

impair the ability of the custodial parent to maintain minimally adequate housing, food, clothing, and other basic necessities for the child.

Other specific deviations include upward deviations for high income
as well as deviations for parenting time; travel expenses for
visitation; dental, vision, or life insurance; child and dependent tax
care credit; permanency of foster care plan; and, payment of alimony
or a mortgage or shelter provided to the custodial parent.

After adjusting the Presumptive Amount of Child Support for any
potential deviations, the resulting dollar amount equals the Final
Child Support Order amount. This amount will be entered on the
Child Support Worksheet and more deviations can be made for the
percentage of the allocation of uninsured health care expenses
between the parents, either pro rata or as otherwise specified by the
court. These expenses are not a part of the support awarded or part
of the calculation, but indicated here for future reference when the
uninsured health care expenses come due.

The gross income of either parent may be reduced based upon one or
more of the following reasons, and calculated on Schedule B if, for
example, a parent is self-employed. (If that is the case, adjust the
monthly gross income by reducing the gross income by 6.2% for FICA
(up to the annual maximum amount allowed) and 1.45% for Medicare.)

If there are preexisting child support orders, reduce the monthly
gross income by the amount of monthly current support the parent
has been paying consistently for a specific period (twelve months if
the order has been in effect for at least one year). If less than full
payments have been made, use the average of the amount of current
support actually paid.

If either parent is supporting his or her other children living in the
home, who are not the subject of the case before the court or any other
child support order, then the court may in its discretion find that:

❂   the failure to consider the parent's other child in the home
     would cause a substantial hardship to the parent and

✪   such adjustment is in the best interest of the child in the current case.

You may then calculate a *Theoretical Support Order*. Using the Basic Child Support Obligation Table, locate the Basic Child Support Obligation by determining the dollar figure corresponding to that parent's gross income and the number of qualified other children. Multiply that dollar figure by 75% and reduce the parent's gross income by that number.

ALIMONY

Types of Alimony

Georgia law provides that alimony may be granted to either the husband or the wife. (See Appendix B for the statute explaining the factors involved in deciding the issue of alimony.) In reality, there are few cases where a wife will be ordered to pay alimony to her husband.

There are two types of alimony.

1.   *Temporary alimony*, which is for a limited period of time and is to enable one of the spouses to get the education or training necessary to find a job. This is usually awarded when one of the parties has not been working during the marriage.

2.   *Permanent alimony* continues for a long period of time, possibly until the death or remarriage of the party receiving the alimony. This is typically awarded when one of the parties is unable to work due to age, physical or mental illness, or for reasons of fairness.

The only common area in which alimony is excluded is where the spouse seeking alimony is guilty of adultery, not condoned by the other innocent party, and the adultery is the cause of the divorce. However, the factors considered in determining the type and amount of alimony also give clues as to when alimony might be awarded.

The law requires the judge to consider the following factors:

✪   the standard of living established during the marriage;

- ✪ the length of time the parties were married;

- ✪ the age and the physical and emotional condition of each party;

- ✪ the financial resources of each party;

- ✪ the time necessary for either party to obtain education and training in order to obtain appropriate employment;

- ✪ the contribution of each party to the marriage (such as services rendered in homemaking, child care, and the education and career building of the other party);

- ✪ the condition of the parties, including their separate estate, earning capacity, and fixed liabilities;

- ✪ any other relevant economic factor; and,

- ✪ any other factor the judge finds necessary to reach a fair result.

As an alternative to alimony, you may want to negotiate to receive a greater percentage of the property instead. This may be less of a hassle in the long run, but it may change the tax consequences of your divorce. (See Chapter 12 regarding taxes.) Be prepared, though, to justify any distribution that changes your personal tax situation. The IRS can be rather particular about schemes designed to evade taxes.

TWO AVAILABLE DIVORCE PROCEDURES
Technically, there are two divorce procedures. These are:

1. uncontested divorce procedure and

2. contested divorce procedure.

The uncontested and contested divorce procedures use some of the same forms, but the contested will require additional steps.

Chapter 7 describes the uncontested procedure, and Chapter 8 describes the contested divorce. You should read this entire book before you begin filling out any court forms.

Uncontested Divorce Procedure

– Caution –

Before you can use any procedure, you or your spouse must have lived in Georgia for at least six months before filing your petition (unless you or your spouse are in the military).

The uncontested procedure is designed for those who are in agreement (or can reach an agreement) about how to divide the property, custody, the amounts of support, and visitation. This is also referred to as a *consent divorce*. The uncontested procedure may also be used when your spouse does not respond to your petition. If your spouse cannot be located, you can use the same forms, but although you can get a divorce and custody, it is sometimes difficult to get any alimony or property your spouse currently has, or to make your disappeared spouse responsible for any debts.

Contested Divorce Procedure

The contested procedure will be necessary when you and your spouse are arguing over any single issue, or combination of issues, and cannot resolve it. This may be the result of disagreement over custody of the children, the payment of child support or alimony, the division of your property, or any combination of these items. The section of this book dealing with the contested procedure builds on the uncontested procedure section. First you will need to read Chapter 6 to get a basic understanding of the forms and procedures. Then read Chapter 8 for additional instructions on handling the contested situation. Be sure to read through both chapters before you start filling out any forms. Keep in mind that a contested divorce may increase the likelihood that you will find the services of a lawyer to be valuable, either to consult or to totally handle your case.

General Procedures and Forms

Most of the forms in this book follow forms approved by statute and tested by practice. The forms in this book are legally correct; however, one occasionally encounters a troublesome clerk or judge who is very particular about how he or she wants the forms.

When you go to file your forms, do not be surprised if you get hassled by the clerk. Some courts object to a fill-in-the-blank format, which will require you to retype the entire form with the appropriate information included. Although there is no good reason for this requirement, retyping the forms to satisfy the clerk will be easier, cheaper, and less time-consuming than hiring a lawyer to sue the clerk (and possibly the judge) to try to force acceptance of the preprinted forms.

If you encounter any problem with the forms in this book being accepted by the clerk or the judge, you can try one or more of the following suggestions.

- ✪ Ask the clerk or judge what is wrong with your form, then try to change it to suit the clerk or judge.

- ✪ Ask the clerk or judge if any bar association forms are available. If they are, find out where you can get them, get them, and use them. The instructions in this book will still help you to fill them out.

- ✪ Consult a lawyer.

To use the forms in Appendix C, you will need to photocopy the forms in this book because the forms you file with the clerk should only have writing on one side. This will also allow you to have the blank forms in case you make a mistake.

The instructions in this book will tell you to type in certain information. Typed information is required under the Uniform Rules of the Superior Court. While some clerks will allow handwritten forms, it is best not to take the chance. In an emergency, just be sure your handwriting can be easily read or the clerk may not accept your papers for filing regardless of his or her sympathy for your situation.

Each form is referred to by both the title of the form and a form number. Be sure to check the form number because some of the forms have similar titles. The form number is found in the top outside corner of the first page of each form. Also, a list of the forms, by both number and name, is found at the beginning of Appendix C.

Case Heading

You will notice that most of the forms in Appendix C of this book have the same heading. Generally, the forms without this heading are not filed with the court but are for your use only. However, the top portion of each of these court forms will all be completed in the same manner. The heading at the very top of the form tells which court your case is filed in. You will need to type in the name of the appropriate county where the court is located.

Next, you need to type your full name and your spouse's on the lines at the left side of the form, above the words "Plaintiff" and "Defendant," respectively. Do not use nicknames or shortened versions of names. You should use the names as they appear on your marriage license, if possible. You will not be able to type in a "Case Number" until after you file your PETITION FOR DIVORCE with the clerk. The clerk will assign a case number and will write it on your petition and any other papers you file with it. You must type in the case number on all papers you file later.

The top part of the form is called the *style* of the case, and when completed, the top portion of your forms should look something like the following example.

IN THE SUPERIOR COURT OF THE COUNTY OF

_____

STATE OF GEORGIA

_____	)	
Plaintiff	)	
	)	Civil Action File Number
v.	)	
	)	
_____	)	_____
Defendant	)	

FILING WITH THE COURT CLERK

Georgia has over 150 counties. Each county has a superior court, and each superior court has a clerk. As a general rule, if you and your spouse live in the same county, file with your county clerk. In most cases, if you and your spouse have separated, you must file your contested or uncontested divorce *in the county where your spouse lives*, if different from your own. If your spouse has only recently separated and is temporarily residing in another county while you have been in the same county for some time, you may want to file in your county and have the sheriff of the spouse's county serve your spouse. If this sounds somewhat complicated, it is. Hundreds of cases every year involve the question of which Georgia county is the proper county in which to bring suit. If your circumstances are complex, this is the type of question an attorney should be able to address for a modest fee.

Once you have decided which forms you need and have prepared them all, it is time to file your case with the court clerk. First, make at least three copies of each form (the original for the clerk, one copy for yourself, one for your spouse, and one extra just in case the clerk asks for two copies or you decide to hire an attorney later).

Filing is actually about as simple as making a bank deposit, although the following information will help things go smoothly. Call the court clerk's office. You can find the phone number under the county government section of your phone directory. There is also a list of clerk's offices by county in Appendix A. Ask the clerk the following questions (along with any other questions that come to mind, such as where the clerk's office is located and what the hours are).

- ✪ How much is the filing fee for a divorce?

- ✪ Can I pay by cash, check, or credit card?

- ✪ Does the court have any special forms that need to be filed with the petition? (If there are special forms that do not appear in this book, you will need to go down to the clerk's office and pick them up. There may be a fee, so ask.)

- ✪ How many copies of the petition and other forms do you need to file with the clerk?

Next, take your petition and any other forms you need to the clerk's office. The clerk handles many different types of cases, so be sure to look for signs telling you which office or window to go to. You should be looking for signs that say such things as "Civil Division," "Superior Court Filing," etc. If it is too confusing, ask someone where to go to file a petition for divorce.

Once you have found the right place, simply hand the papers to the clerk and say, "I'd like to file this." The clerk will examine the papers, then do one of two things—either accept it for filing (and either collect the filing fee or direct you to where to pay it) or tell you that something is not correct. If you are told something is incorrect, ask the clerk to explain what is wrong and how to correct the problem.

Although clerks are not permitted to give legal advice, the types of problems they spot are usually very minor things that they can tell you how to correct. Often it is possible to figure out how to correct it from the way they explain what is wrong. Some clerks, due to busy schedules or the fact that most clerks are not attorneys, try to avoid giving any specific advice. If the clerk will not take your papers and will not tell you what the problem is, you might ask for the legal aid office, or perhaps ask an attorney to simply review your papers for a modest fee.

NOTIFYING YOUR SPOUSE

You do not need to worry about this section if you and your spouse are in total agreement about every aspect of the divorce. You both simply sign and file an **AGREEMENT**. (see form 14, p.239.) However, in all other cases, you are required to notify your spouse that you have filed for divorce. This gives your spouse a chance to respond to your **PETITION FOR DIVORCE**. (If you are unable to find your spouse, you will also need to read Chapter 11.)

Acknowledgment of Service and Consent to Jurisdiction

If you and your spouse have agreed to all terms, it is customary to simply sign an **ACKNOWLEDGMENT OF SERVICE AND CONSENT TO JURISDICTION**. (see form 24, p.269.) It includes a paragraph in which the other party consents to the jurisdiction of the court, and is filed along with the **PETITION FOR DIVORCE**. This form is very simple. Put the name of the county in the first blank at the top of the form. Then write your name as "Plaintiff" and your spouse's name as "Defendant," both in the heading and twice in the body of the form. The clerk will give you the civil action file number when you sign this form. Have your spouse sign before a notary public on the line above the word "Defendant." If your spouse will not sign this form, see the section on the next page entitled "Sheriff's Entry of Service."

Along with the previous forms, at least one copy of the **SUMMONS** will be required. (see form 4, p.215.) The information on the **SUMMONS** is identical to the information for either the **ACKNOWLEDGMENT OF SERVICE AND CONSENT TO JURISDICTION** (form 24) or the **SHERIFF'S ENTRY OF SERVICE** (form 5, p.217).

Summons

To complete the **SUMMONS** you need to do the following.

◈ Complete the top portion according to the instructions at the beginning of this chapter, except type in your name and address on the lines above the word "PLAINTIFF" and your spouse's name and address on the lines above the word "DEFENDANT."

◈ Type your name and address again in the space after the first paragraph. After your name, type in the words "Pro Se." This form is designed for an attorney's name to go in this space, and "Pro Se" means that you do not have an attorney.

⟐   Go to the clerk's office and have the clerk sign and date the **Summons** when you file your pleadings. The bottom portion of this form is for the sheriff deputy to complete when he or she serves your spouse.

Sheriff's Entry of Service

If your spouse will not sign an **Acknowledgment of Service and Consent to Jurisdiction** (form 24), or for some reason simply cannot, then use the **Sheriff's Entry of Service**. (see form 5, p.217.) A sheriff's deputy will personally deliver the papers to your spouse. Of course, you must give the sheriff accurate information about where your spouse can be found. If there are several addresses where your spouse might be found (such as home, a relative's, or work), enclose a letter to the sheriff with all of the addresses and any other information that may help the sheriff find your spouse (such as the hours your spouse works).

The **Sheriff's Entry of Service** is the form the deputy will fill out and file with the clerk to verify that the papers were delivered (including the date and time they were delivered). The **Sheriff's Entry of Service** form in Appendix C is an example of a commonly used form, but first call the court clerk in your county and ask if your county uses a particular form.

If you need to provide the sheriff with this form, use the **Sheriff's Entry of Service** and complete it as follows.

⟐   Type in the county and case number at the very top of the form.

⟐   In the upper right part of the form, type in your name on the line above the word "Plaintiff" and your spouse's name on the line above the word "Defendant." Place an "x" in the box after the word "Defendant." Type in your spouse's address on the line above the word "Address." Ignore the lines for a garnishee.

⟐   Type in your name and address on the lines below the words "Attorney or Plaintiff's Name & Address." Again, add the words "Pro Se" after your name.

⟐   Give this form to the sheriff, who will complete the rest of the form, and file it with the court clerk after your spouse has been served.

You may be able to pay the service fee (about $30) and leave the form with the court clerk when you file your **Petition for Divorce**. The sheriff may also send you a copy, but you may need to check your file at the clerk's office to see if your spouse has been served. Since you are filing this action in the county of your spouse's residence, the clerk will probably accept the service fee when you file your **Petition for Divorce**. If not, call the county sheriff's office in the county where your spouse lives and ask how much it will cost to have him or her served with divorce papers.

Other Notices   If a hearing on your case should be necessary, the notice of the hearing date and time is called a **Rule Nisi**. (see form 6, p.219.) Complete the **Rule Nisi** as follows.

⬧ Fill in the top portion of the form according to the instructions at the beginning of this chapter.

⬧ In the main paragraph, cross out either the word "Plaintiff" or the word "Defendant," whichever is appropriate. If you are the plaintiff, you would cross out the word "Defendant" in the first line; the word "Plaintiff" in the fourth line; and, the word "Defendant" in the fifth line.

⬧ Fill in the date and time of the hearing if you know it. Otherwise the clerk or judge's secretary can provide you with this information when you arrange a date and time.

⬧ Type your name on the line above the words "Pro Se" and your address and telephone number where indicated.

Take the **Rule Nisi** form to the clerk, who will assign a hearing date and time. If you have an **Acknowledgment of Service and Consent to Jurisdiction**, or if the sheriff has already served the papers and your spouse has filed an **Answer**, just mail a copy of the **Rule Nisi** to your spouse along with a completed **Certificate of Service**. (see form 7, p.221.) If you have not filed an **Acknowledgment of Service and Consent to Jurisdiction** and your spouse has not answered your **Petition for Divorce**, the **Rule Nisi** will have to be served by the sheriff in the same manner as described in the section on "Sheriff's Entry of Service."

Once your spouse has been served with the **PETITION FOR DIVORCE**, you may simply mail him or her copies of any papers you file later. All you need to do is sign a statement (called a *certificate of service*) that you mailed copies to your spouse. Some of the forms in this book will have a certificate of service for you to complete. If any form you file does not contain one, you will need to complete a **CERTIFICATE OF SERVICE**. (see form 7, p.221.) To complete form 7, type in the name of the document being sent to your spouse on the line in the main paragraph; the date you mail it on the date line; and, your name and address at the bottom. Cross out either the word "Plaintiff" or "Defendant," whichever does not apply to you. Attach this form to whatever document you are sending your spouse. File one copy with the court and keep a copy for yourself.

SETTING A COURT HEARING

You will need to set a hearing date for the temporary or final hearing or for any preliminary matters that require a hearing (these are discussed later). The court clerk may be able to give you a date, but you will probably have to get a date from the judge's secretary. (If you do not know which judge, call the court clerk, give the clerk your case number, and ask for the name and phone number of the judge assigned to your case.) You can then either call or go see that judge's secretary and tell him or her you would like to set a final hearing date for a divorce (or for whatever preliminary motion needs a hearing). Usually the judge's phone number can be found in the government section of your phone book.

The secretary may ask you how long the hearing will take. If you and your spouse have agreed on everything (an uncontested divorce), tell the secretary it is an uncontested divorce and ask for ten minutes (unless the secretary advises you differently). If you have a contested divorce, it could take anywhere from thirty minutes to several days, depending upon such things as what matters you disagree about and how many witnesses will testify.

One general rule is that the more time you need for a hearing, the longer it will take to get the hearing. Also, it is better to overestimate the time required, rather than not schedule enough time and have to continue the hearing for several weeks. Judges do not like to go over the time scheduled.

The secretary will then give you a date and time for the hearing, but you will also need to know where the hearing will be held. Ask the secretary for the location. You will need the street address of the courthouse, as well as the room number, floor, or other location within the building.

COURTROOM MANNERS

There are certain rules of procedure that are used in a court. These are really the rules of good conduct, or good manners, and are designed to keep things orderly. Many of the rules are written down, although some are unwritten customs that have just developed over many years. They are not difficult, and most of them do make sense. Following these suggestions will make the judge respect you for your maturity and professional manner. It will also increase the likelihood that you will get the things you request.

- ✪ *Show respect for the judge.* Showing respect basically means not doing anything to make the judge angry with you, such as arguing with him or her. Be polite, and call the judge "Your Honor" when you speak to him or her, such as "Yes, Your Honor" or "Your Honor, I brought proof of my income." Although many lawyers address judges as "Judge," this is not proper.

    Many of the following rules also relate to showing respect for the court. This also means wearing appropriate clothing, such as a coat and tie for men and a dress or suit for women.

    Rise when the judge enters and leaves the room, and if you are not in the witness box, rise when you speak with the judge. Ask permission to approach the judge with evidence or documents. This is because in many courts the bailiff or deputy in the courtroom will consider such an approach a potential threat and respond accordingly. With the heightened sense of security in most public offices, it is very easy to unintentionally make court personnel very nervous.

- ✪ *Whenever the judge talks, you listen.* Even if the judge interrupts you, stop talking immediately and listen.

○ ***Only one person can talk at a time.*** Each person is allotted his or her time to talk in court. The judge can only listen to one person at a time, so do not interrupt your spouse when it is his or her turn. As difficult as it may be, stop talking if your spouse interrupts you. (Let the judge tell your spouse to keep quiet and let you have your say.)

○ ***Talk to the judge, not to your spouse.*** Many people get in front of a judge and begin arguing with each other. They actually turn away from the judge, face each other, and begin arguing as if they are in the room alone. This generally has several negative results. The judge cannot understand what either one is saying since they both start talking at once, they both look like fools for losing control, and the judge gets angry with both of them. So whenever you speak in a courtroom, look only at the judge. Try to pretend that your spouse is not there. Remember, you are there to convince the judge that you should have certain things. You do not need to convince your spouse.

○ ***Talk only when it is your turn.*** The usual procedure is for you to present your case first. When you are done saying all you came to say, your spouse will have a chance to say whatever he or she came to say. Let your spouse have his or her say. When he or she is finished, you will get another chance to respond to what has been said.

○ ***Stick to the subject.*** Many people cannot resist the temptation to get off the track and start telling the judge all the problems with their marriage over the past twenty years. This just wastes time and aggravates the judge. Stick to the subject and answer the judge's questions simply.

○ ***Keep calm.*** Judges like things to go smoothly in their courtrooms. They do not like shouting, name calling, crying, or other displays of emotion. Generally, judges do not like family law cases because they get too emotionally charged. Give your judge a pleasant surprise by keeping calm and focusing on the issues.

✪ ***Show respect for your spouse.*** Even if you do not respect your spouse, act like you do. All you have to do is refer to your spouse as "Mr. Smith" or "Ms. Smith" (using his or her correct name, of course).

DOMESTIC STANDING ORDERS

Almost every court in Georgia requires upon the filing of a **PETITION FOR DIVORCE** that the parties behave civilly to each other and to any children. A **DOMESTIC STANDING ORDER** will be given to you by the court in which you file your divorce and will be the guideline the court follows in expecting the parties to act kindly to one another. (see form 33, p.___.)

Uncontested Divorce

This chapter provides an explanation of the uncontested divorce procedure. Chapter 8 discusses the contested divorce procedure. Remember that this chapter assumes you have prepared the papers discussed in Chapter 6 regarding notifying your spouse. What you are now preparing are the documents stating what you want to do.

For purposes of this book, a *contested* case is one in which you and your spouse will be doing your arguing in court, and leaving the decision up to the judge. An *uncontested* case is one in which you will do your arguing and deciding before court, and the judge will only be approving your decision.

Example:

Most lawyers have had the following experience—a new client comes in, saying she wants to file for divorce. She has discussed it with her husband, and it will be a simple, uncontested divorce. Once the papers are filed, the husband and wife begin arguing over a few items of property. The lawyer then spends a lot of time negotiating with the husband. After much arguing, an agreement is finally reached. The case will proceed in the court as uncontested, but only after a lot of contesting out of court.

You probably will not know whether you are going to have a contested case until you try the uncontested route and fail. Therefore, the following sections are presented mostly to assist you in attempting the uncontested case. (Chapter 8 specifically discusses the contested case.)

There are actually two ways that a case can be considered uncontested. The first is when you have your spouse served and he or she does not respond. The other is when you and your spouse reach an agreement on every issue in the divorce. To be in this situation you and your spouse must be in agreement on the following points:

- ✪ how your property is to be divided;

- ✪ how your debts are to be divided;

- ✪ which of you will have custody of the children;

- ✪ how much child support is to be paid by the person not having custody; and,

- ✪ whether any alimony is to be paid, and if so, how much and for how long a period of time.

Forms   To begin an uncontested case, the following forms should be filed with the court clerk in all cases. (See Chapter 6 for filing instructions.)

- ✪ **DOMESTIC RELATIONS CASE FILING INFORMATION FORM** (form 9);

- ✪ **DISCLOSURE STATEMENT** (form 8);

- ✪ **PETITION FOR DIVORCE** (form 12);

- ✪ **REPORT OF DIVORCE, ANNULMENT, OR DISSOLUTION OF MARRIAGE** (form 25); and,

- ✪ **SHERIFF'S ENTRY OF SERVICE** (form 5) or **ACKNOWLEDGMENT OF SERVICE AND CONSENT TO JURISDICTION** (form 24).

Other forms you determine to be necessary may also be filed, either with your **PETITION FOR DIVORCE** or at any time before the final hearing, depending upon your situation.

The following forms will be prepared in advance, but will not be filed until the final hearing:

✪   **FINAL JUDGMENT AND DECREE** (form 17);

✪   **DOMESTIC RELATIONS CASE FINAL DISPOSITION INFORMATION FORM** (form 10); and,

✪   **AGREEMENT** (form 14).

Once all of the necessary forms have been filed, you will need to call the judge's secretary to arrange for a hearing date for the final judgment. (See Chapter 6 regarding setting a hearing.) You should tell the secretary that you need to schedule a "final hearing for an uncontested divorce." Such a hearing should not usually take more than ten minutes. (See Chapter 10 for information on how to handle the final hearing.) The following sections give instructions for when you need each form and how to complete it.

DISCLOSURE STATEMENT

To complete the **DISCLOSURE STATEMENT** (form 8, p.223), simply type your name as "Plaintiff," and your spouse's as "Defendant" in the upper left-hand corner. If you have an **AGREEMENT** (form 14, p.239) already prepared, check line #2, "Divorce with Agreement Attached." If you have not yet prepared your **AGREEMENT**, check line #1, "Divorce without Agreement Attached."

DOMESTIC RELATIONS CASE FILING INFORMATION

The **DOMESTIC RELATIONS CASE FILING INFORMATION FORM** must be completed in all cases. (see form 9, p.225.) Fill in the county, your name, and address as the "Plaintiff," and your spouse's name and address as the "Defendant." In the part of the form designated "Check Case Type," you will check the box for "Divorce." The clerk will fill out the other blanks.

Your **PETITION FOR DIVORCE** is now ready for filing. If your spouse needs to be served by the sheriff, be sure to prepare the **SUMMONS** (form 4, p.215) to go along with your **PETITION**.

PETITION FOR DIVORCE

The **PETITION FOR DIVORCE** (form 12) must be completed in all cases. This is the paper you file with the court to begin your case and to ask the judge to give you a divorce. The **PETITION FOR DIVORCE** must be accompanied by your **DOMESTIC RELATIONS FINANCIAL AFFIDAVIT**, which gives the judge part of the financial information he or she will need. (see form 13, p.235.) The **PETITION FOR DIVORCE** may also be accompanied by other affidavits, depending on your situation. Together, these papers give the judge an idea of what your situation is and of what you want him or her to do.

Complete your **PETITION FOR DIVORCE** as follows.

◈ Complete the top portion of the form according to the instructions in Chapter 6 on page 74.

◈ In paragraph 1, type your name after the word "Plaintiff".

◈ In paragraph 2, type your spouse's name after the word "Defendant" and the city and county name where your spouse lives.

◈ In paragraph 3, type the date of your marriage and the date of your separation.

◈ In paragraph 4, check the first box if you have no children. If you do have children, check the second box, and identify the children by name, age, and date of birth. If you have children, you will also need to include an **AFFIDAVIT REGARDING CUSTODY** (see form 15, p.249.)

⬥   While you do not have to fill out anything for Paragraph 5, you should attach your prepared **AGREEMENT** (form 13) to divide your assets.

⬥   At the bottom of the last page, type in your name, address, and telephone number next to "Plaintiff." Do not sign the form yet.

⬥   Take this form to a notary and sign it before the notary on the line marked "Plaintiff."

AGREEMENT

The **AGREEMENT** is used if you and your spouse can agree on the division of your property. (see form 14, p.239.) This form includes provisions for agreements on child support and custody, alimony, and attorney's fees. Whether you and your spouse agreed on everything from the start or whether you have gone through extensive negotiations to reach an agreement, you need to put your agreement in writing. This is done through a settlement agreement. Even if you do not agree on everything, you should put what you do agree on into a written agreement.

Complete your **AGREEMENT** as follows.

⬥   Complete the top portion according to the instructions in Chapter 6 on page 74.

⬥   Type in the date you were married and date you were separated on the lines in the first two paragraphs beginning with the word "WHEREAS."

⬥   In each section there are choices for you to make regarding your personal circumstances. Choose the provision that applies to your situation. Read through each one and look for places where you need to check a box or type in information to fit your situation.

⬥   In the section on CHILD CUSTODY & VISITATION, check the first box if there are no minor children. Check the second box if one of you will have custody, and check the box for which of you (Plaintiff or Defendant) will have custody. Check the third box if you and your spouse will have joint custody, and check the box for which of you will provide the children's primary residence. Any special arrangements you wish to include can be typed in by the last box in this section.

– Caution –

Georgia judges have a bias against any situation in which there is shared custody and no child support is paid. Many courts will simply not approve such an arrangement, even if the parents agree, without lawyers presenting it. The standard configuration is for one spouse to have primary custody and responsibility for the children, and the other to pay a percentage of income for support. If you think your circumstances vary dramatically from this standard, you may want to consult an attorney.

◈   If there are no minor children, check the first box in the section on CHILD SUPPORT. If there are children, check the second box and type in the amount and payment period, such as "$583.20" per "month." This amount must fall within the guidelines found in the **Child Support Guidelines Worksheet** (form 3, Schedule A, p.201).

◈   In the section on ALIMONY, check the first box if you and your spouse agree that neither of you will pay alimony. If alimony is to be paid, check the second box and complete that paragraph by also checking a box for who is to pay alimony and filling in an amount, the payment period, and when alimony will end.

◈   For the section on DIVISION OF PROPERTY, check the appropriate box or boxes that describe your situation. This form assumes that you and your spouse have already divided most personal items. This is much easier than trying to cover all items in the **Agreement**. If you and your spouse are living separately, just be sure that you each have the personal property and household goods you each want and that you have separate bank accounts. If you are still living in the same household, get separate bank accounts and make a list of the items each of you will get when one or both of you moves out. The following subcategories will require you to fill in additional information.

- *Real property (real estate)*. If you do not own any real property, check the box for the first paragraph. If you have real property that one of you will keep, check the second box. You will need to fill in the name of the county where the property is located and the address of the property. The remaining blanks are to fill in either the word "Plaintiff" or "Defendant," whichever reflects your agreement. The person who will give up the property is the one who will execute a *quit claim deed*. The third box is for the situation wherein you agree to sell the property and divide the proceeds. Unless one of you can pay off the other, or get a mortgage to do so, sale may be the only option.

- *Automobiles, boats, etc*. This paragraph is to clearly identify which car each of you will keep. In the first blank, fill in the year, make, and model of the car the plaintiff will keep. Then fill in the "VIN #." This is the Vehicle Identification Number, which can be found on the vehicle and also on the vehicle registration certificate. The third and fourth blanks are for the same information regarding the vehicle the defendant will keep. For any other vehicle, such as a boat, RV, motorcycle, etc., be sure to transfer the title into the name of the person who will keep it before signing the **AGREEMENT**. (Or you can modify the **AGREEMENT** to include other vehicles in the same manner as the cars.)

◈ In the section on INSURANCE, check the box or boxes that reflect your agreement. The judge will probably be looking for some provision for medical insurance for any minor children.

◈ In the section on DEBTS, you will need to indicate which debts are to be each person's responsibility. Keep in mind that this agreement only affects responsibility for debts between you and your spouse. For example, suppose you have a car loan that is in both names. Your agreement says your spouse is to keep that car and be responsible for paying the loan. If your spouse does not pay, the bank can still come after you for payment. You would then have to take your spouse back to court for violating your agreement.

◈ The section on TAXES requires you to decide how you and your spouse will handle your income tax matters. The third paragraph simply follows federal law on this matter. The following information will help you complete this section.

• *Joint or separate return.* You must file individual returns for the year in which your final judgment is entered. However, if you are getting divorced early in the year and before you have filed your tax return for the previous year, you will need to check the box for the first paragraph to indicate whether you will file a joint return or separate returns for that year. Which way you file should be determined by such factors as whether you will save money by filing a joint return, whether you can trust your spouse to cooperate so you get your share of any refund, and whether your spouse's business dealings will increase your chances of an audit and penalties.

Any refund check will require both of your signatures to cash, so you had better be sure that your spouse will not try to keep the entire refund by getting your signature and then cashing the check, or by refusing to sign the check, thereby preventing either of you from getting it. Also, if your spouse is self-employed or has a habit of putting false information on tax returns, you would be liable for any interest and penalty charges in the event of an audit.

• *Responsibility for taxes.* The second paragraph is for the situation where taxes will, or may be, owed. Again, only check this box if you still need to file your return for the year prior to the year in which your final judgment will be entered. Simply check the box for who will be responsible to any tax which may be owed and fill in the applicable year.

◈ Each of you must sign and date the **AGREEMENT** before a notary public where indicated at the bottom and then file it with the clerk.

Additional Sample Provisions

Form 13 is a basic form that can be changed as needed to fit your situation and desires. You can either write in special provisions in form 13 itself, or type up your own settlement agreement using form 13 and the following examples as guidelines. A very important goal when writing your own settlement agreement provisions is to be clear and precise. *Be sure to read the entire agreement carefully before signing.* If there are any provisions you do not understand, or if there are special provisions needed that are not included (unless you feel comfortable modifying the **Agreement** to include them), you should consult an attorney.

Sample Optional Custody Provisions

There is no end to the possible variations of custody arrangements. The following are examples of custody provisions for you to consider.

Example: Sole Custody

The Plaintiff shall have temporary and permanent custody and control of the minor child(ren) being issue of this marriage, to wit: _____ *[type in names of children]*, and shall be denominated as the "Custodial Parent." The Defendant shall have the right of reasonable and liberal visitation with the child(ren) at times and places to be agreed upon by the parties, and shall be denominated as the "Noncustodial Parent." Should the parties be unable to agree upon reasonable visitation, the Defendant shall be entitled to visitation as follows: _____ *[type in an agreed-upon visitation schedule (see the following sample visitation provisions)].*

Example: Joint Custody

The Plaintiff and Defendant shall share "Joint Custody" of the minor child(ren), to wit: _____ *[type in names of children].* It is the intention of the parties in agreeing to this custodial arrangement that each of them shall have a full and active role in providing a sound moral, social, economic, religious, and educational environment for the child(ren). The parents shall consult with one another in substantial questions relating to religious upbringing, educational programs, significant changes in social environment, and non-emergency health care of the child(ren). In accepting the grant of privileges conferred by this custodial arrangement upon each of the parents, they specifically recognize that these powers shall not be exercised for the purpose of frustrating, denying, or controlling in any manner, the social development of the other parent. The parents shall exert their best efforts to work cooperatively in future plans consistent with the best interest of the child(ren) and in amicably resolving such disputes as may arise. For purposes of legal definition, the Wife shall have final decision-making authority and shall be considered to have primary physical custody of the child(ren), and the Husband shall be denominated as having secondary physical custody.

Sample Optional Visitation Provisions

There is no end to the possible variations of visitation arrangements. The following are examples of visitation provisions for you to consider.

Example: Visitation During Infancy

Until such time as the child(ren) shall have attained the child(ren)'s third birthday(s), all visitation will be at the residence of the Custodial Parent, subject to the following schedule: during the first and third weekends of each month from Saturday at 9:00 a.m. to 5:00 p.m. and Sunday from 1:00 p.m. to 5:00 p.m., provided the Noncustodial Parent shall give the Custodial Parent at least 24 hours' advance notice, written or oral, of any intention to exercise this right.

Example: Visitation After Infancy

After the child(ren) has attained the child(ren)'s third birthday, the visitation of the Noncustodial Parent shall be at such place of his or her choice, and such visitation shall be reasonable and liberal, but in the event that the parties are unable to agree to such visitation the agreed upon schedule shall be as follows:

(a)   During the first and third weekends of each month from Friday at 6:00 p.m. until Sunday at 6:00 p.m., provided that the Noncustodial Parent shall give the Custodial Parent at least 24 hours' advance notice, written or oral, of any intention not to exercise this right;

(b)   For any _____ weeks during summer vacation so long as the Noncustodial Parent does not interfere with or interrupt any of the child's school and further provided that the Noncustodial Parent shall give the Custodial Parent at least 14 days' advance notice, written or oral, of each summer visitation;

(c)   During even-numbered years, the Thanksgiving holiday, from 6:00 p.m. on the Wednesday before Thanksgiving to 6:00 p.m. on the Sunday following Thanksgiving, and the New Years holiday from December 27 at 6:00 p.m. to January 1 at 6:00 p.m., provided that the Noncustodial Parent shall give the Custodial Parent at least 14 days' advance notice of each intended visitation;

(d)   During odd-numbered years, the Christmas holiday from December 23 at 6:00 p.m. to December 27 at 6:00 p.m; the spring vacation specified by the child's school district, from the first day at 6:00 p.m. to the 7th day at 6:00 p.m. (the Custodial Parent shall give the Noncustodial Parent 30 days' notice as to the specified dates of the spring vacation); and the child(ren)'s birthdays, from 6:00 p.m. of the day preceding until 6:00 p.m. of birthday; all provided that the Noncustodial Parent shall give the Custodial Parent 14 days' advance notice of each intended visitation;

(e)   The Noncustodial Parent shall be responsible for transportation and promptness in each visitation. For each visitation, the Noncustodial Parent shall receive the child(ren) at the residence of the Custodial Parent, and after such visitation, shall return the child to the residence of the Custodial Parent. Holiday and vacation visitation is in lieu of, and not in addition to, regular visitation, and in the event of a conflict, the latter will control.

Example: Visitation with Geographical Separation

Notwithstanding the aforementioned, should the parties be domiciled more than one hundred miles apart, and the minor child be above the age of three years, the following minimum visitation shall apply:

(a)   The Noncustodial Parent shall be entitled to _____ days regular visitation per month. In no event shall the monthly visitation be cumulative, nor shall the regular visitation in any one month exceed _____ consecutive hours.

(b)   In addition, the Noncustodial Parent shall be entitled to _____ weeks of visitation to take place during the summer, or contemporaneously with the child's vacation, that may be exercised during any calendar year. The purpose of this visitation is to allow the Noncustodial Parent extended time with the minor child. This vacation visitation shall not exceed _____ consecutive days per visit and shall be in lieu of the regular visitation for the months in which vacation visitation is exercised. In the event that vacation visitation bridges two months, it shall be in lieu of the regular visitation for both months.

(c)   The Noncustodial Parent shall be responsible for the expenses of transporting the minor child to the residence of the Noncustodial Parent, and the Custodial Parent shall be responsible for the expenses of returning the child to the residence of the Custodial Parent.

NOTE: *The issue of geographic separation can be explosive. Often, after a divorce, one party moves—sometimes to another area of the country. The noncustodial parent no longer sees the children and feels cheated. However, in Georgia, the custodial parent has a pretty clear right to move. To be safe, he or she must notify the noncustodial parent prior to the move (sixty days is a good number). Generally, courts cannot order parties to stay in one place as a condition of custody; however, parties can agree between themselves that they will stay in the area as a condi-*

tion of being the primary custodial parent. If this is an issue in your case, get a lawyer's opinion. Also, keep in mind that this area of the law is changing rapidly, and could be amended by the General Assembly at any time.

Example: Visitation and Morals

Although the parties are establishing minimum visitation, it is the intention of the parties that either shall enjoy the right of reasonable and liberal visitation with said child(ren) at times and places to be agreed upon by the parties. Both parties agree to maintain a wholesome environment for the chid(ren) and covenant to not expose the child(ren) to illegal controlled substances, nor to excessive alcoholic consumption on the part of themselves or any guests, nor to immoral practices, including but not limited to, intimate and/or overnight associations with members of the opposite sex during periods of visitation. Violations of these conditions shall be grounds for the nonviolating party to ask the court for restrictions upon such visitation and shall entitle the non-violating party to such costs and fees incurred.

Sample Optional Child Support Provisions

The following are examples of optional child support provisions for you to consider.

Example: Child Support Annual Review and Adjustment

On the first anniversary of the date of this Agreement, and continuing with each successive anniversary date, the Noncustodial Parent shall provide to the Custodial parent a copy of his or her W-2, state, and federal returns for the previous year. The Noncustodial Parent's total gross annual income for the previous year shall then be determined from the aforementioned information and multiplied by ____% (as the applicable percentage of child support contribution), then divided by twelve, to obtain a monthly average for child support purposes. In the event this sum exceeds the original child support amounts, then the child support payments commencing thirty days from each said anniversary shall incorporate the new child support amounts.

Example: Child Support for Higher Education

The parties recognize and accept an obligation to support said child(ren) in pursuit of a college education. Therefore, each of the parties agrees to pay a pro rata share of the reasonable college tuition and room and board expenses for the child(ren), so long as said child(ren) are enrolled full time in a course of college study at an accredited college or university in pursuit of a bachelor's degree. The pro rata share of each of the parties shall be based upon the relative income of the parties as demonstrated by W-2, federal, and state tax documentation. The obligation created under this item shall not extend beyond the fifth year following the child(ren)'s graduation from high school nor exceed the cost of tuition for a full-time in-state student enrolled in a state college within 100 miles of the residence of the custodial parent.

NOTE: *Georgia Law does not provide a duty for parents to provide college for their children. Once a child is over the age of 18 and out of high school, there is no longer a duty of support. A judge cannot order college expenses to be paid as child support but the parties can agree to terms regarding college expenses.*

Example: Child Support Enforcement

Garnishment. The Noncustodial Parent is hereby notified that, pursuant to the provisions of O.C.G.A. § 19-6-30, whenever, in violation of the terms of this order, there shall have been a failure to make the support payments due hereunder so that the amount unpaid is equal to or greater than the amount payable for one month, the payments required to be made may be collected by the process of continuing garnishment for support, or income deduction order, at the election of the receiving spouse.

AFFIDAVIT REGARDING CUSTODY

The **AFFIDAVIT REGARDING CUSTODY** must be completed if you have minor children. (see form 15, p.249.) To complete the **AFFIDAVIT REGARDING CUSTODY**, do the following.

⬦ Complete the top portion according to the instructions in Chapter 6 on page 74.

⬦ In paragraph 1, type in the name, age, birth date, and present address of each child, and indicate with whom the child is living.

⬦ In paragraph 2, type in the addresses where each child has lived during the past five years. If a child is not yet five years old, type in the places the child has lived since birth. If the children have not lived with their parents, state with whom and where they have lived for the past five years.

⬦ Paragraphs 3, 4, and 5 require you to tell whether you have been involved in any other court cases involving the custody of, or visitation with, your children; and to tell if you know of any court case involving custody of, or visitation with, the children (even if you were not involved in the case). If there are no such cases, you do not need to do anything with paragraphs 4 or 5. If there are such cases, you need to describe the other case by giving the names of the parties, the name and location of the court, and the case number.

⬦ Take the form to a notary and sign it on the "Plaintiff" line before the notary.

ANSWER AND COUNTERCLAIM

The **ANSWER AND COUNTERCLAIM** (form 16, p.251) is only for very special circumstances. This form should only be used if all four of the following conditions apply to your situation:

✪ you and your spouse can agree on everything;

✪ both of you sign and file a settlement **AGREEMENT** (form 14);

✪ the husband is the Plaintiff; and,

✪ the wife wants her maiden name restored. (However, if the wife is the Plaintiff, she may simply ask for her maiden name to be restored in her **PETITION FOR DIVORCE**.)

– Warning –
Do not use form 16 in a contested divorce!

Complete the **ANSWER AND COUNTERCLAIM** as follows.

◈ Complete the top portion according to the instructions in Chapter 6 on page 74.

◈ Type in your spouse's name in the blank space in the first paragraph.

◈ Type in your spouse's name in paragraph 3.

◈ Have your spouse sign on the "Pro Se Defendant" line before a notary public.

◈ File this form with the clerk of the superior court within forty-five days of the filing of the **PETITION FOR DIVORCE**.

FINAL JUDGMENT AND DECREE

There are two **FINAL JUDGMENT AND DECREE** forms you can use. Form 17 will be used if you and your spouse have signed an **AGREEMENT**. Form 18 will be used if your spouse did not respond to the **PETITION FOR DIVORCE** or only signed an **ANSWER**. For form 18, see Chapter 8 for instructions.

Complete the **FINAL JUDGMENT AND DECREE** (form 17) as follows.

◈ Complete the top portion according to the instructions in Chapter 6 on page 74.

✧ The last (unnumbered) paragraph is for the judge to fill in on the date of the judgment. The judge will do this at the hearing.

If the judge tells you to change something major in the **FINAL JUDGMENT AND DECREE**, you will need to make a note of exactly what changes the judge requires or orders. Then go home and prepare the **FINAL JUDGMENT AND DECREE** the way the judge instructed. You will then need to take the revised form back to the judge for his or her signature.

You will also need to fill in a **REPORT OF DIVORCE, ANNULMENT OR DISSOLUTION OF MARRIAGE**. (form 25, p.271.) You will probably be given one of these by the clerk, but if not, use the form in Appendix C. Just fill in the information required for each box on the form.

If you need to prepare the **FINAL JUDGMENT AND DECREE** after the hearing, you will also complete a **CERTIFICATE OF SERVICE** (form 7, p.221), attach it to the **FINAL JUDGMENT AND DECREE**, and deliver it to the judge's secretary. Also give two extra copies to the secretary, along with a stamped envelope addressed to yourself and a stamped envelope addressed to your spouse. Ask the secretary whether you should sign and date the **CERTIFICATE OF SERVICE**. Sometimes the secretary will handle mailing the judgment after the judge signs it, in which case he or she may sign the **CERTIFICATE OF SERVICE**.

Contested Divorce

This book cannot turn you into a trial lawyer. It is very risky to try to handle a contested case yourself, although it has been done. There are several differences between a contested and an uncontested case.

PROCEDURE DIFFERENCES FROM UNCONTESTED DIVORCE

First, in an uncontested case the judge will usually go along with whatever you and your spouse have worked out. In a contested case, you need to prove that you are entitled to what you are asking for. This means you will need a longer time for the hearing, you will need to present papers as evidence, and you may need to have witnesses testify for you.

Second, you may have to do some extra work to get the evidence you need, such as sending out subpoenas (which are discussed in the next section of this chapter) or even hiring a private investigator. Third, the **FINAL JUDGMENT AND DECREE** form will be more complicated.

Also, you will need to pay extra attention to assure that your spouse is properly notified of any court hearings and that he or she is sent copies of any papers you file with the court clerk.

When it becomes apparent that you have a contested divorce, it is probably time to seriously consider hiring an attorney, especially if the issue of child custody is involved. If you are truly ready to go to war over custody, it shows that this is an extremely important matter for you, and you may want to get professional assistance. If the fight is too big, do not be afraid to bring in help. You can expect a contested case with near certainty when your spouse is seriously threatening to fight you every inch of the way or when he or she hires an attorney.

On the other hand, you should not assume that you need an attorney just because your spouse has hired one. Sometimes it will be easier to deal with the attorney than with your spouse. The attorney is not as emotionally involved and may see your settlement proposal as reasonable. So discuss things with your spouse's attorney first and see if things can be worked out. You can always hire your own lawyer if your spouse's is not reasonable. Just be very cautious about signing any papers until you are certain you understand what they mean. You may want to have an attorney review any papers prepared by your spouse's lawyer before you sign them.

Aside from deciding if you want a lawyer, there are three main differences in procedure between the uncontested and the contested divorce. First, you may need to prepare additional forms. Second, you will need to be more prepared for the hearing. Third, you will not prepare the **FINAL JUDGMENT AND DECREE** (form 18) until after the hearing with the judge. This is because you will not know what to put in the paperwork until the judge decides the various matters in dispute.

Forms   To begin a contested case, the following forms should be filed with the court clerk in all cases (see Chapter 6 for filing instructions):

✪   **DOMESTIC RELATIONS CASE FILING INFORMATION FORM** (form 9);

✪   **DISCLOSURE STATEMENT** (form 8);

✪   **PETITION FOR DIVORCE** (form 11);

✪   **DOMESTIC RELATIONS FINANCIAL AFFIDAVIT** (form 13);

✪   **Report of Divorce, Annulment, or Dissolution of Marriage** (form 25); and,

✪   **Sheriff's Entry of Service** (form 5), or **Acknowledgment of Service and Consent to Jurisdiction** (form 24).

The following forms will be prepared in advance, but will not be filed until the final hearing:

✪   **Final Judgment and Decree** (form 18);

✪   **Domestic Relations Case Final Disposition Information Form** (form 10); and,

✪   **Agreement** (form 14).

The instructions for preparing all of these forms, except the **Domestic Relations Financial Affidavit** (form 13), may be found in Chapter 7.

PETITION FOR DIVORCE

The **Petition for Divorce** (form 11, p.229) must be completed in all cases. This is simply the paper you file with the court to begin your case and to ask the judge to give you a divorce. The **Petition for Divorce** must be accompanied by your **Domestic Relations Financial Affidavit**, which gives the judge part of the financial information he or she will need. (see form 13, p.235.) The **Petition for Divorce** may also be accompanied by other affidavits, depending upon your situation. Together, these papers give the judge an idea of what your situation is and of what you want him or her to do.

Complete your **Petition for Divorce** as follows.

◈   Complete the top portion of the form according to the instructions in Chapter 6 on page 74.

◈   In paragraph 1, type your name after the word "Plaintiff" and the county name.

◈ In paragraph 2, check the first box if your spouse has signed an **Acknowledgment of Service and Consent to Jurisdiction** (form 24). Check the second box if your spouse will not sign form 4 and must be served by the sheriff. Type in your spouse's name after "Defendant." If you are going to require service by the sheriff, type in your spouse's address.

◈ In paragraph 3, type the date of your marriage and the date of separation.

◈ In paragraph 4, if you have no children, check the first box. If you have children, check the second box, and identify the children by name, age, and date of birth. If you have children, you will also need to fill in the employer and income information for you and your spouse. If you have children, be sure to include an **Affidavit Regarding Custody** (form 15, p.249), which is explained later in this chapter.

◈ Paragraph 5 is for you to indicate how your marital assets and debts are to be treated. If you have prepared an **Agreement** (form 13) or have no undivided marital assets, check the first box. If you need the judge to distribute the assets, check the second box, and the box in that paragraph before the phrase "An equitable division of the assets and liabilities of the parties." Also, check the second box if any of the matters in that paragraph need to be decided in your case and check the box or boxes for any of the matters that apply. If you and your spouse have not agreed upon the division of your marital assets and debts, you will need to read Chapter 8 about contested divorce procedures.

◈ Paragraph 6 is where you indicate the reason you want a divorce. In an uncontested case, you will use the language found in this paragraph. In a contested case, you may refer to the "fault" grounds previously discussed.

◈ Paragraph 7 is where the wife can request the restoration of her maiden name. Some judges require that if the husband files for divorce, the wife can only get her maiden name restored if she files an **Answer and Counterclaim** (form 16, p.251).

◈ At the bottom of the last page, type in your name, address, and telephone number under the heading "Name and address." Do not sign the form yet.

◈ Complete the Verification page. Type in the name of the county where you will sign the **PETITION FOR DIVORCE** after the words "COUNTY OF," and your name on the line in the main paragraph.

◈ Take this form to a notary and sign it before the notary on the line marked "Plaintiff, Pro Se."

DOMESTIC RELATIONS FINANCIAL AFFIDAVIT

In most courts, you and your spouse must each complete a separate **DOMESTIC RELATIONS FINANCIAL AFFIDAVIT**. (see form 13, p.253.) Generally, monthly guidelines are most appropriate, so try to figure each of the categories on a monthly basis. If you are paid weekly or every two weeks, you will need to convert your income to a monthly figure. The same conversion will be required for any of your expenses that are not paid monthly. To convert weekly amounts to monthly amounts, just take the weekly figure and multiply it by 4.3. (There are roughly 4.3 weeks to a month.) To convert from every two weeks, divide by 2, and then multiply by 4.3.

All you need to do is fill in all of the blank spaces on the **DOMESTIC RELATIONS FINANCIAL AFFIDAVIT** (form 13), then take it to a notary public before you sign it. You will sign it before the notary, then staple it to your petition (after you have made three copies). Make a blank copy for your spouse to complete. Most of the blanks on form 12 clearly indicate what information is to be filled in; however, the following may answer some questions.

◈ Complete the top portion of the form by filling in your name as "Affiant" (an *affiant* is a person who signs an affidavit) and your spouse's name as "Spouse." Type in your names, ages, and Social Security numbers. Fill in the date of your marriage, date of separation, and the number of times each of you has been married.

❖ Fill in the names and dates of birth of your children.

❖ Save paragraph 2 for last.

❖ In paragraph 3, type in your monthly salary, then add up all of your money over and above your salary (second jobs, commissions, etc.) on the next line. If you have earned any money in any other category, fill in those blanks and add the sums up on the line in 3.A for GROSS MONTHLY INCOME. Take this total and write it on line 2(a) as well. (See Chapter 5 for a discussion of what constitutes gross income.)

❖ In paragraph 3.B, identify your benefits, if applicable to your situation. In 3.C type in your net monthly income, only excluding state and federal taxes and FICA. Take this number and write it in line 2(b). Also indicate your pay period and the number of federal exemptions you will be eligible to claim on your tax return.

❖ Paragraph 4 simply asks for the items you have already identified in the **PROPERTY INVENTORY** (form 1). Fill in the categories and estimate what you think the present value is for each item and who has it. Total these figures at the bottom of the list.

❖ Paragraph 5 refers to AVERAGE MONTHLY EXPENSES. Simply refer to each item listed and estimate as best you can the amount you spend on that item in a month. If a particular item is an annual expense, such as auto insurance, convert it to a monthly amount. (If you are just guessing, place an asterisk (*) next to the figure.) Total these items at the bottom of the paragraph. Take this total and write it on the first line in 2(c).

❖ List your creditors (credit cards, car note, etc., which have not been entered previously) to complete paragraph 5.B. Write this number on the second line on 2(c). Add 5.A. and 5.B. together for 5.C. Write this number in the final line of 2(c).

❖ Now go back to paragraph 2. Subtract the last line of 2(c) from line 2(b), and write the answer in line 2(d). (That is, subtract the "Total monthly expenses and payments to creditors" from the "Net monthly income.")

◈ The last calculation, for line 2(e), requires you to go back to form 3 and calculate the guideline child support as a monthly amount. Write this monthly amount in 2(e). (See the **Child Support Guidelines Worksheet** (form 3, p.185).)

◈ Take the **Domestic Relations Financial Affidavit** form to a notary public and sign it before the notary on the line designated "Affiant." The notary will complete the part of the form directly opposite your signature.

If your spouse does not have a copy of this information, you will need to send him or her a copy. You will also need to complete a **Certificate of Service**. (see form 7, p.221.) On the form, fill in the name of the document as "Domestic Relations Financial Affidavit."

COLLECTING INFORMATION

The judge will require a **Domestic Relations Financial Affidavit** (form 13) from you and also one from your spouse. If your spouse has indicated that he or she will not cooperate at all and will not provide an affidavit, you may have to try to get the information yourself. You should first try to file a **Request for Production of Documents**.

Request for Production of Documents

Before you subpoena documents, the generally preferred practice is to file what is called a **Request for Production of Documents**. (see form 19, p.259.) Complete the form as follows.

◈ Complete the top portion according to the instructions in Chapter 6 on page 74.

◈ Type your spouse's name and address (or whoever you are requesting documents from) after the word "TO:"

◈ In the main paragraph, cross out either the word "Plaintiff" or "Defendant," whichever does not apply to you.

◈   In the main paragraph, type your address in the blank space.

◈   In the space after the main paragraph, describe the documents or information you want. Examples are:

• "All documents relating to _____."

• "Copies of any checks issued with respect to _____ _____."

• "All documents related to the payment of _____ to _____."

• "All payroll records indicating the annual and year-to-date income of _____."

◈   Fill in the date, sign your name on the last line, and type your name, address, and phone number below it. Also, below the signature line, cross out either the word "Plaintiff" or "Defendant," whichever does not apply to you.

Subpoenas   If your spouse refuses to cooperate, it may speed things up if you are able to get the information yourself and have it available at the hearing. This will require you to have subpoenas issued. To get a subpoena, go to the superior court clerk's office and ask for one. They cost about $1.00 each, depending upon the county.

Before you send a subpoena to your spouse's employer, bank, or accountant, you probably should let your spouse know what you are about to do. The thought that you are about to get these other people involved in your divorce may be enough to get your spouse to cooperate. If your spouse calls and says, "I'll give you the information," give him or her a few days to follow through. Ask when you can expect to receive the **Domestic Relations Financial Affidavit**, and offer to send your spouse another blank copy if he or she needs one.

If your spouse sends a completed **Domestic Relations Financial Affidavit** form, do not send the subpoena. If your spouse does not follow through, go ahead with the subpoena. You can send subpoenas to as many people or organizations as you need, but you will need to use the following procedure for each subpoena. If you were able to do a good job making copies of important papers while preparing to file for divorce, you should have the information you need to figure out where you need to send subpoenas. Your spouse's income information can be obtained from his or her employer. Stock and bond information can be obtained from his or her stockbroker, bank account balances from the bank, auto loan balances from the lender, etc.

You can have subpoenas issued to any or all of these places, but do not overdo it. Concentrate on income information (especially if you are asking for child support or expect to pay child support) and information on the major property items. It may not be necessary to send out subpoenas if you already have recent copies of the papers relating to these items. You can always show the judge the copies of your spouse's pay stubs, W-2 tax statements, or other papers at the hearing.

Fill out the subpoena (which you obtained from the court clerk) just as you have filled out other documents in your divorce. You are probably the Plaintiff, and you now know the court. Identify in the subpoena what documents you want to have. Next, have the sheriff or a process server personally serve the subpoena to the person or place named in the subpoena. The sheriff will need at least one extra copy of the subpoena and a check for the service fee. The employer, bank, etc., should send you the requested information.

If the employer calls you and says you must pay for copies, ask him or her how much they will cost and send a check or money order (if the amount is not too high and you do not already have some fairly recent income information). If the employer does not provide the information, you can try sending a letter to the employer saying, "Unless you provide the information requested in the subpoena in seven days, a motion for contempt will be filed with the circuit court." This may scare the employer into sending you the information.

The sheriff or process server will have also filed an affidavit verifying when the subpoena was served. There are more procedures you could go through to force the employer to give the information, but it probably is not worth the hassle, and you would probably need an attorney to help you with it. At the final hearing you can tell the judge that your spouse refused to provide income information and that the subpoena was not honored by the employer. The judge may do something to help you out, or he or she may advise you to see a lawyer.

There is also a procedure in which you send written questions to your spouse that he or she must answer in writing and under oath. These written questions are called *interrogatories*. If your spouse did not file a **Domestic Relations Financial Affidavit**, he or she probably will not answer the interrogatories either, which would leave you no better off. However, if you would like to try this, you may be able to locate the two forms you would need ("Plaintiff's First Interrogatories" and "Plaintiff's First Request for Production and Notice to Produce") at a law library in a forms book.

PROPERTY AND DEBTS

Generally, the judge will look at your property and debts and try to divide them *fairly*. This does not mean they will necessarily be divided fifty-fifty. What you want to do is offer the judge a reasonable solution that looks fair. Adultery or other misconduct on the part of one party may be used to justify an unequal division of property and debts, but there is no guarantee that a judge will completely strip an offending spouse of everything, so try not to expect it.

It is time to review the **Property Inventory** (form 1, p.181) and the **Debt Inventory** (form 2, p.183) you prepared earlier. For each item of property, note which of the following categories it fits into (it may fit into more than one):

- property you really want;

- property you would like to have;

- property you do not care about either way;

- property your spouse really wants;

- property your spouse would like to have; or,

- property your spouse does not care about either way.

Now start a list of what each of you should end up with, using the categories listed above. You will eventually end up with a list of things you can probably get with little difficulty (property you really want and your spouse does not care about), those that you will fight over (property you both really want), and those that need to be divided but can probably be easily divided equally (property you both do not really care about).

At the hearing the judge will probably try to get you to work out your disagreements, but he or she will not put up with arguing for very long. In the end he or she will arbitrarily divide the items you cannot agree upon, or order you to sell those items and divide the money you get equally. A judge will not decide ownership of each pot and pan!

On the few items that are really important to you, it may be necessary to prove why you should get them. It will help if you can convince the judge of one or more of the following:

- ✪ you paid for the item out of your own earnings or funds;

- ✪ you are the one who primarily uses the item;

- ✪ you use the item in your employment, business, or hobby;

- ✪ you are willing to give up something else you really want in exchange for the item (of course, you will try to give up something from your "do not care" or your "like to have" list); or,

- ✪ the item is needed for your children (assuming you will have custody).

Make up a list of how you think the property should be divided. Make it a reasonably fair and equal list, regardless of how angry you are at your spouse. Even if the judge changes some of it to appear fair to your spouse, you will most likely get more of what you want than if you do not offer a suggestion. This is not an exception to the negotiating rule of letting your spouse make the first offer, because at this point, you are no longer just negotiating with your spouse. You are now negotiating with the judge. You are trying to impress the judge with your fairness—not trying to convince your spouse.

Marital and Nonmarital Property

Special problems arise if a claim of nonmarital property becomes an issue. This may be in terms of your spouse trying to get your nonmarital property or you trying to get property you feel your spouse is wrongly claiming to be nonmarital. Basically, nonmarital property is property either of you had before you were married and kept separate.

Not every dime in the marriage is subject to division. If one party has received an inheritance and kept it completely separate, it may qualify as nonmarital property. Likewise, some future interests in business and property can be nonmarital. These rules are complex and may be worth a discussion with personal counsel. It is also a good idea to have any papers that prove the property you claim as nonmarital property is actually nonmarital property. These would be papers showing that:

- the item was purchased before you were married (such as dated sales receipts);

- the item was inherited as your own property (such as certified copies of wills and probate court papers); or,

- the item was exchanged for property you had before you got married, or for property you received as a gift or through an inheritance (such as a statement from the person you made the exchange with or some kind of receipt showing what was exchanged).

If you want to get at assets your spouse is claiming are nonmarital assets, you will need to collect the following types of evidence.

- Papers showing that you helped pay for the asset (such as a check that you wrote or bank statements showing that your money went into the same account that was used to make payments on the asset).

Example:

Suppose your spouse purchased a house before you got married. During your marriage you made some of the mortgage payments with your own checking account (you will have cancelled checks, hopefully with the mortgage account number on them, to prove this). At other times, you deposited some of your paychecks into your spouse's checking account, and your spouse wrote checks from that account to pay the mortgage (again, there should be some bank records and cancelled checks to show that this was done). Since you contributed to the purchase of the house, you can claim some of the value of the house as a marital asset.

❂   Papers showing you paid for repairs of the asset. If you paid for repairs on a home or car your spouse had before you were married, you can claim part of the value.

❂   Papers showing that the asset was improved or increased in value during your marriage.

Example 1:

Your spouse owned the house before you were married. During your marriage, you and your spouse added a family room to the house. This may enable you to make a claim for some of the value of the house.

Example 2:

Your spouse owned the house before you were married. The day before you got married, the house was worth $85,000. Now the house is appraised at $115,000. You could claim part of the $30,000 of increased value.

Final Judgment and Decree

During the hearing the judge will announce who gets which items. Make a list of this as the judge tells you. Then, complete the **FINAL JUDGMENT AND DECREE** (form 18, p.255) according to what the judge says. Once you have completed the decree form, make a copy and send it to your spouse. Send the original to the judge (not the court clerk), along with a completed **CERTIFICATE OF SERVICE** (form 7, p.221) stapled to it showing the date you sent a copy to your spouse. If your spouse does not object to how you have prepared the **FINAL JUDGMENT AND DECREE,** the judge will sign the judgment and return a copy to you. You should send the judge the original and two copies of the decree, along with two stamped envelopes (one addressed to yourself and the other addressed to your spouse).

Physical Relationships

Often contested situations resolve themselves into uncontested divorces, but the close proximity of the parties in many cases, a history of intimacy, and the loneliness that accompanies difficult situations routinely results in the parties having intimate physical relationships with each other. This can lead to some awkward legal issues, but the law is fairly clear. The parties are to have been separated in the legal and physical sense for thirty days prior to divorce.

No court has official *bedroom police*, and no one is going to take it upon themselves to inquire, but understand that if you are going to divorce, continuing a physical relationship is not a good tactical or strategic decision, regardless of how convenient it may be. On the other hand, advertising an intimate relationship with other parties is probably worse. As a general rule, a brief ignition of nearly forgotten flames will not destroy a divorce proceeding, but if you are going to act like husband and wife, why are you getting a divorce?

CHILD CUSTODY AND VISITATION

Generally, if you are the wife, the odds start out in favor of you getting custody—but do not depend upon the odds. Start out by reviewing the various factors the judge may consider in deciding the custody question. These can be found in Chapter 5. For each item listed in that section, write down an explanation of how that item applies to you. This will be your argument when you have your hearing with the judge.

Many custody battles revolve around the moral fitness of one or both of the parents. If you become involved in this type of a custody fight, you should consult a lawyer. Charges of moral unfitness (such as illegal drug use, child abuse, or immoral sexual conduct) can require long court hearings involving the testimony of many witnesses as well as possibly the employment of private investigators. For such a hearing you will require the help of an attorney who knows the law, what questions to ask witnesses, and the rules of evidence.

If the only question is whether you or your spouse has been the main caretaker of the child, you can always have a friend, neighbor, or relative come into the hearing (if they are willing to help you out) to testify on your behalf. Then it may not be necessary for you to have an attorney. However, if you need to subpoena an unwilling witness to testify, you should have an attorney.

The judge's decision regarding custody will have to be put into the **FINAL JUDGMENT AND DECREE**, but it will be more involved. Instructions on preparing this form are included later in this chapter.

CHILD SUPPORT

In Georgia, as in most states, the question of child support is mostly a matter of a mathematical calculation. Getting a fair child support amount depends upon the accuracy of the income information presented to the judge. If you feel fairly sure that the information your spouse presents is accurate, or that you have obtained accurate information about his or her income, there is not much to argue about. The judge will take the income information provided, use the formula to calculate the amount to be paid, and order that amount to be paid.

In most cases, there will not be much room to argue about the amount, so there usually is not a need to get an attorney. If you claim your spouse has not provided accurate income information, it will be up to you to prove this to the judge by showing the income information you have obtained from your spouse's employer or other source of income.

The only areas open for argument are whatever special needs are claimed by the party asking for child support. Once again, it will be necessary for that party to provide proof of the cost of these special needs by producing billing statements, receipts, or other papers to show the amount of these needs. The judge's decision regarding child support will have to be put into the **FINAL JUDGMENT AND DECREE** as well.

ALIMONY

A dispute over alimony may require a lawyer, especially if there is a request for permanent alimony because of a disability. Such a claim may require the testimony of expert witnesses (such as doctors, accountants, and actuaries), which requires the special skills of an attorney to present the case. A charge of adultery may also require a lawyer, and possibly a private investigator as well.

These alimony factors will be the subject of the court hearing on this question. You should determine what information (including papers and the testimony of witnesses) you will need to present to the judge to either support or refute the reasons alimony was requested.

For temporary (also called *rehabilitative*) alimony, the most common reason is that the person needs help until he or she can get training to enter the work force. The questions that will need to be answered include the following.

- ✪ What has the person been trained for in the past?

- ✪ What type of training is needed before the person can again be employable in that field?

- ✪ How long will this training take?

- ✪ What amount of income can be expected upon employment?

- ✪ How much money is required for the training?

Questions that may be asked in either a temporary or a permanent alimony situation include an examination of the situation of the parties during their marriage that led to the person not working, what contribution to the marriage that person made, and what improper conduct on the part of the other party makes an award of alimony appropriate. You should be prepared to present evidence regarding these questions.

Also remember that if you are receiving alimony, you generally will be required to pay taxes on it while the person who pays it can deduct it from his or her income. A good lawyer will sometimes use this aspect of the tax code to shift some money from property division or child support so that a highly taxed spouse can pay more money to a spouse in a lower tax bracket and increase the amount of support provided at the expense of the tax collectors. However, this is not for amateurs, and if you do not know what you are doing, do not try this without a professional.

TEMPORARY HEARING

In a contested case, the first hearing will be a temporary hearing. In many cases, however, the temporary hearing reflects what the judge would be inclined to do in a final hearing. If the judge has all of the information available at the temporary hearing, there is little point in coming back to argue the same points all over again. Therefore, it is common to have the **TEMPORARY ORDER** stand as the **FINAL JUDGMENT AND DECREE**. If this is the case, refer to the next section. However, if you think a **TEMPORARY ORDER** may be entered, a blank form is provided in Appendix C. (see form 26, p.253.) It will be handled the same as the **FINAL JUDGMENT AND DECREE**.

FINAL JUDGMENT AND DECREE

In a contested divorce, it is not possible to use the same **FINAL JUDGMENT AND DECREE** form as in an uncontested divorce. It is very likely that the judge will either prepare the **FINAL JUDGMENT AND DECREE** him- or herself, direct his or her clerk to prepare it, or appoint a lawyer to prepare it. However, you should be prepared to offer a **FINAL JUDGMENT AND DECREE** form to the judge at the hearing. (see form 18, p.255.) You should complete as much of the decree form as possible before the hearing. The **FINAL JUDGMENT AND DECREE** form is designed so that you can complete it at the hearing according to what the judge decides on each issue. You can complete ahead of time any items that you and your spouse have agreed upon.

You should give your spouse a copy of the **FINAL JUDGMENT AND DECREE** before the hearing so that he or she can tell the judge that he or she is aware of what it says and agrees with it.

Complete the **FINAL JUDGMENT AND DECREE** (form 18) as follows.

⟡ Complete the top portion according to the instructions in Chapter 6 on page 74.

⟡ Check each of the paragraphs that apply to your situation according to the following guidelines. If a paragraph or provision does not apply to your situation, simply leave it blank.

⟡ Paragraph 1: If the wife will have her former name restored, type her restored name in the blank.

⟡ Paragraph 2: Type in the date that any settlement agreement was filed with the court.

⟡ Paragraph 3: Fill in the blank for gross income for "father" or "mother," whichever one will be paying child support.

⟡ Paragraph 4: Type in the amount of the support payment, how often it will be paid (weekly, monthly, etc.), and the date the first payment is due. If the amounts are outside of the guidelines in paragraph 3, explain why.

⟡ Paragraph 5: Check whichever statement applies to your situation.

⟡ Paragraph 6: This paragraph is a statement about failure to pay support.

⟡ The judge will fill in the date of the judgment and sign it at the hearing.

Be sure to review the section in the previous chapter concerning preparing the **FINAL JUDGMENT AND DECREE** after the hearing if the judge directs you to make changes.

DHR Report   Prior to getting a divorce finalized, the Georgia Department of Human Resources **REPORT OF DIVORCE, ANNULMENT OR DISSOLUTION OF MARRIAGE** must be filed. (see form 25, p.271.) The form is self-explanatory and is given to the clerk of the court, usually on the day of the divorce becoming final.

Negotiating Agreements

It is beyond the scope and ability of this book to fully present a course in negotiation techniques. However, a few basic rules may be of some help.

Ask for More than You Want

Start by asking for more than you want. This always gives you some room to compromise by giving up a few things and ending up with close to what you really want. With property division, this means you will review your **PROPERTY INVENTORY** (form 1, p.181) and decide which items you really want, would like to have, and do not care much about. Also try to figure out which items your spouse really wants, would like to have, and does not care much about.

At the beginning you will say that you want certain things. Your list will include:

- ✪ everything you really want;

- ✪ almost everything you would like to have;

- ✪ some of the things you do not care about; and,

- ✪ some of the things you think your spouse really wants or would like to have.

Once you find out what is on your spouse's list, you can begin trading items. Usually you try to give your spouse things he or she really wants and you do not care about in return for your spouse giving you the items you really care about and would like to have.

Child Custody and Support

Generally, child custody tends to be something that cannot be negotiated. It is more often used as a threat by one of the parties in order to get something else, such as more of the property or lower child support. If the real issue is one of these other matters, do not be concerned by a threat of a custody fight. In these cases the other party probably does not really want custody and will not fight for it. If the real issue is custody, you will not be able to negotiate for it and will end up letting the judge decide anyway.

If you will be receiving child support, you should first work out what you think the judge will order based upon the child support guidelines discussed in Chapter 5. Then you should ask for more and negotiate down to what the guidelines call for. If your spouse will not settle for something close to the guidelines, give up trying to work it out and let the judge decide.

Let Your Spouse Start the Bidding

The general thought in negotiations is the first person to mention a dollar figure loses. Whether it is a child support figure or the value of a piece of property, try to get your spouse to name the amount he or she thinks it should be first. If your spouse starts with a figure close to what you had in mind, it will be much easier to get to your figure. If your spouse begins with a figure far from yours, you know how far in the other direction to begin your bid.

Give Your Spouse Time to Think and Worry

Your spouse probably is just as afraid as you about the possibility of losing to the judge's decision and would like to settle. Do not be afraid to state your final offer, and then walk away. Give your spouse a day or two to think it over. Maybe he or she will call back and make a better offer. If not, you can always reconsider and make a different offer in a few days, but do not be too willing to do this or your spouse may think you will give in even more.

Know Your Bottom Line

Before you begin negotiating, you should try to set a point that you will not go beyond. If you have decided that there are four items of property that you absolutely must have, and your spouse is only willing to agree to let you have three, it is time to end the bargaining session and go home.

Remember what You have Learned

By the time you have read this far you should be aware of two things:

1. the judge will roughly divide your property equally and

2. the judge will probably follow the child support guidelines.

This awareness should give you an approximate idea of how things will turn out if the judge is asked to decide these issues, which should help you set your bottom line on them.

The Court Hearing

Keep in mind that, in Georgia, if your case is contested, the first hearing is a *temporary hearing*, and the judge's decision will be in the form of a **TEMPORARY ORDER**. The temporary hearing is primarily concerned with child custody, child support, and who gets the marital residence. You are usually only allowed one witness at a temporary hearing. You may be entitled to submit affidavits. If affidavits are important to your case, an attorney might be a good idea. In any event, if the judge's temporary decision in the temporary hearing is satisfactory, and the parties agree to all of the issues, then you will not need a final hearing. You may simply agree with your spouse to let the **TEMPORARY ORDER** become final. If one of the parties wants to try for a better deal in the final, an attorney is going to just about be a necessity.

PREPARATION

One of the first things you will need to do is schedule a hearing date. (See Chapter 6 for instructions on setting a hearing date.)

Now that you have got a hearing date set with the judge, you will need to notify your spouse of when the hearing will be. Even if you can easily call your spouse on the phone and notify him or her of the hearing, it is proper to send a formal **RULE NISI** (notice of hearing) (form 6). Complete the form according to the instructions in Chapter 6. Make three copies of the **RULE NISI** form and mail one copy to your spouse. File the original with the court clerk and keep two copies for yourself.

What Papers to Bring

Bring your copies (if available) of the following papers to the hearing:

○ your **PETITION FOR DIVORCE** and the affidavits you attached to it;

○ any papers you may have showing that your spouse was properly notified of the divorce (although the sheriff's affidavit of serving papers should be in the court file, and you may not have a copy);

○ any papers you may have to support what is in your **DOMESTIC RELATIONS FINANCIAL AFFIDAVIT** (this should include copies of your most recent pay stub, federal income tax return, and W-2 forms);

○ any papers showing your spouse's income or property;

○ your settlement agreement, if you have one that has not yet been filed with the court; and,

○ the **FINAL JUDGMENT AND DECREE** (form 17) and **DOMESTIC RELATIONS CASE FINAL DISPOSITION INFORMATION FORM** (form 10).

Civil Case Disposition Form. Complete the **DOMESTIC RELATIONS CASE FINAL DISPOSITION INFORMATION FORM** as follows.

◈ Type in the name of the county on the line after the word "County."

◈ Type in your name, and whether you are the petitioner or respondent after the words "Reporting Party."

◈ Check the box "Pro Se."

◈ Check all the boxes that apply under "Type of Disposition," "Relief Granted," and "ADR."

THE HEARING

Your hearing will probably take place in a large courtroom like you see on TV or in the movies. It may also be in what looks more like a conference room. If so, the judge will be at the head of a table, with you and your spouse on either side.

The judge may start the hearing by summarizing what you are there for and then ask you and your spouse if you have any additional evidence to present. He or she may then ask each of you any questions he or she may have. The judge will review the papers you filed with the clerk and will probably ask you whether you understand and agree with what is in the papers. He will also ask you to explain why your marriage is *irretrievably broken*. Just tell the judge why you are getting divorced.

Example 1:

We just do not have any interests in common anymore and have drifted apart.

Example 2:

My husband has had several affairs.

If you have any information that is significantly different and more current than what is in the **DOMESTIC RELATIONS FINANCIAL AFFIDAVIT**, you should mention to the judge that you have more current information. You will then give a copy of whatever papers you have to show the changed situation (such as a current pay stub showing an increase in pay or a current bank statement showing a new balance).

The judge may ask to see any papers you have to prove what you have put in your **DOMESTIC RELATIONS FINANCIAL AFFIDAVIT**. Your basic job at the hearing is to answer the judge's questions and to give the information needed for a divorce.

If there are any items that you and your spouse have not yet agreed upon, tell the judge what these items are. Refer to Chapter 8, relating to the contested divorce, for more information about how to handle these unresolved issues. Be prepared to make a suggestion as to how these matters should be settled and to explain to the judge why your suggestion is the best solution.

If the judge asks for any information that you have not brought with you, tell the judge that you do not have it with you but will be happy to provide the information by the end of the following day. Just be sure you get the papers to the judge.

At the end of the hearing, the judge will tell you whether he or she is going to grant you a divorce and accept your settlement agreement. It would be very unusual not to grant the divorce and accept your agreement. You will then tell the judge that you have prepared a proposed judgment, and hand him or her the original. (Refer to Chapters 7 and 8 regarding the **FINAL JUDGMENT AND DECREE**.)

You will need two extra copies of the **FINAL JUDGMENT AND DECREE**—one for yourself and one for your spouse. You should also bring two stamped envelopes, with one addressed to yourself and one addressed to your spouse. This is in case the judge wants to review the **FINAL JUDGMENT AND DECREE** and mail it to you later instead of signing it at the hearing.

If the judge wants you to make any changes in the decree form, make a careful note of exactly what the judge wants (ask him or her to explain it again if you did not understand the first time). Then tell the judge you will make the corrections and deliver the judgment the following day. If the change requested is a small one, you might even be able to write in the change by hand at the hearing.

If child support or alimony is to be paid, you will also need to bring a third copy of the **FINAL JUDGMENT AND DECREE**. Each county has a procedure for income deduction from employers (sometimes called *income deduction orders*), and these procedures are handled through the *Child Support Recovery Office*. If you want your child support handled through the county office, call and ask for the appropriate forms.

When the hearing is over, thank the judge and leave. The judge will sign the original **FINAL JUDGMENT AND DECREE** and send it to the court clerk's office to be entered in the court's file. Take the copies of the **FINAL JUDGMENT AND DECREE** and income deduction order (if appropriate) to the judge's secretary. The secretary will write in the date and use a stamp with the judge's name on each copy to authenticate them.

If any serious problems develop at the hearing (such as your spouse's attorney starts making a lot of technical objections, or the judge gives you a hard time), just tell the judge you would like to *continue* (postpone) the hearing so you can retain an attorney. Then go get one!

COLLECTING SUPPORT PAYMENTS

The *Child Support Recovery Office* is the agency (called a *depository*) that processes the child support and alimony payments. This is frequently a division of the court clerk's office. The spouse responsible to pay the support (or his or her employer) will make payments to the depository. The depository then cashes that check and issues a check to the spouse entitled to receive support or alimony. Sometimes the judge's secretary or the court clerk will take an extra copy of the **FINAL JUDGMENT AND DECREE** and send it to the central depository. The central depository keeps the official records of what has and has not been paid.

Child Support Enforcement Office

The *Child Support Enforcement Office* is responsible for enforcing the payment of child support to custodial parents receiving welfare (Aid to Families with Dependent Children) and others who request their services. If you are to receive support and would like to use the enforcement services of this office, you will need to contact your local Child Support Enforcement Office. This may not be necessary if your spouse goes on an income deduction order immediately and keeps his or her job. However, if some payments are missed, you may call the Child Support Enforcement office at any time and ask for their assistance.

Income Deduction Order

You may also request payment of child support through an **INCOME DEDUCTION ORDER**. (see form 27, p.275.) The information to be filled in on each blank line is described immediately after each line. To make the process of obtaining an income deduction order easier, you may put a provision in the child support paragraph of your **AGREEMENT** that states, "The parent receiving support shall have the right to submit an income deduction order at his or her sole election." (You will note that such a provision is already contained in form 14.) This may result in the court simply approving your **INCOME DEDUCTION ORDER** without the need for any further court hearings.

Notice to Payor

Send the **INCOME DEDUCTION ORDER** to the judge who signed your original divorce judgment along with a copy of your agreement or order that gives you the right to request payment through income deduction (you may even want to highlight that provision). Even if that judge is no longer there, his or her replacement may sign the order and return it to you. Once you receive the signed order, send it to your spouse's employer by certified, return-receipt mail along with a **NOTICE TO PAYOR**. (see form 28, p.277.) You should soon begin receiving support payment directly from the employer.

The **NOTICE TO PAYOR** gives the employer important information about the employer's rights and responsibilities connected with the order. As with the **INCOME DEDUCTION ORDER**, there is a notation after each blank line on the **NOTICE TO PAYOR** describing what information needs to be filled in on that line. The notice needs to be submitted to the judge for signature along with the **INCOME DEDUCTION ORDER**. Once signed by the judge and returned to you, it needs to be sent to the employer along with the **INCOME DEDUCTION ORDER**.

When You Cannot Find Your Spouse

Your spouse has run off, and you have no idea of where he or she might be. So how do you have the sheriff deliver a copy of your **PETITION FOR DIVORCE** to your spouse? The answer is, you cannot use the sheriff. Instead of personal service, you will use a method of giving notice called *service by publication*. This is one of the most complicated procedures in the legal system. You will need to follow the steps listed below very carefully.

THE DILIGENT SEARCH

The court will only permit publication when you cannot locate your spouse. This also includes the situation when the sheriff has tried several times to personally serve your spouse, but it appears that your spouse is hiding to avoid being served. First, you will have to show that you cannot locate your spouse by letting the court know what you have done to try to find him or her. In making this search you should try the following:

- ✪ check the phone book and directory assistance in the area where you live;

- ✪ check directory assistance in the area where you last knew your spouse to be;

- ✪ ask friends and relatives who might know where your spouse might be;

- ✪ check with the post office where he or she last lived to see if there is a forwarding address (you can ask by mail if it is too far away);

- ✪ check records of the tax collector and property assessor to see if your spouse owns property;

- ✪ write to the Department of Motor Vehicles to see if your spouse has any car registrations; and,

- ✪ check with any other sources you know that may lead you to a current address (such as landlords, prior employers, etc.).

If you do come up with a current address, go back to personal service by the sheriff, but if not, continue with this procedure.

PREPARING AND FILING COURT PAPERS

Once you have made your search you need to notify the court. This is done by filing the **AFFIDAVIT OF PUBLICATION AND DILIGENT SEARCH**. (see form 20, p.261.) This form tells the court what you have done to try to locate your spouse, and asks for permission to publish your notice. (If your spouse lives in another state and you do have his or her address, this procedure may not be appropriate, and it is probably advisable to seek counsel. Georgia has a *long-arm statute* that the court may require to be used in your circumstances. In any event, since this is fairly complicated, you may want to call the sheriff in the county and state where your spouse lives and arrange for personal service by the sheriff.)

Complete the **AFFIDAVIT OF PUBLICATION AND DILIGENT SEARCH** as follows.

◈ Complete the top portion of the form according to the instructions in Chapter 6 on page 74.

◈ Fill in the blanks with what you have done to find your spouse. Use more space if necessary.

◈ Type in your name, address, and phone number on the lines below the "Affiant Signature" line.

◈ Sign your name on the "Affiant Signature" line and fill in the date before a notary public.

You can first try simply mailing the affidavit to the clerk of superior court for filing along with the blank **ORDER OF PUBLICATION** (form 21, p.263) and a partially completed **NOTICE OF PUBLICATION** (form 22, p.265). If that does not work, you will need to have a hearing. Some judges may let you file this action by a motion, and some will require a hearing. For safety's sake, you may want to seek counsel to determine the best process. To partially complete the **NOTICE OF PUBLICATION**, you need to do the following.

◈ Complete the top portion according to the instructions in Chapter 6 on page 74.

◈ Type in your spouse's name after the word "TO:".

◈ Leave blank the spaces in the first and second lines of the main paragraph. On the fourth line, type in the word "Divorce."

◈ In the sixth line, type in your address. The judge and clerk will complete the other parts of form.

THE CLERK'S JOB

If the judge issues an order, then the clerk will fill in the remaining blanks on the **NOTICE OF PUBLICATION** (form 22) and return two copies to you. If the clerk finds any errors in your papers, he or she will notify you about what needs to be corrected. You should provide the clerk with a self-addressed, stamped envelope when you deliver or send him or her these papers.

PUBLISHING

Your next step is to have a newspaper publish your **NOTICE OF PUBLICATION**. Check the Yellow Pages listings under "Newspapers" and call several of the smaller ones in your county (making sure it is in the same county as the court) and ask if they are approved for legal announcements. If they are, ask how much they charge to publish a **NOTICE OF PUBLICATION** that does not involve property. What you are searching for is the cheapest paper. Some metropolitan Atlanta counties have a paper that specializes in the publishing of legal announcements at a much cheaper rate than the regular daily newspapers. If you look around the courthouse you may be able to find a copy of this paper.

Once you have found the paper you want, send them a copy of the **NOTICE OF PUBLICATION** and the **ORDER OF PUBLICATION** along with a short cover letter stating:

> Enclosed is a Notice of Publication for publication as required by law.
>
> Please take notice of the return date in the Notice of Publication and ensure that the date of first publication is at least 60 days before the return date. If you cannot comply with this requirement, please notify me immediately so I may obtain a revised Notice of Publication.

Be sure to include a check for the cost of publication or to comply with whatever other payment arrangements you make with the paper.

The **NOTICE OF PUBLICATION** will be published once a week for four weeks. Get a copy of the paper the first time it appears and check to be sure it was printed correctly. If you find an error, notify the newspaper immediately.

Also, look at the date the clerk put in the **NOTICE OF PUBLICATION** in the blank space after the words "Answer in writing within sixty

(60) days of." You must make sure that this date is at least sixty days after the date the newspaper first published the **NOTICE OF PUBLICATION**. If this requirement is not met, notify the newspaper of its mistake. Remind them of your cover letter if necessary. You will also need to prepare a new **ORDER OF PUBLICATION** and **NOTICE OF PUBLICATION** for the clerk to sign, and then go through this procedure again. If the newspaper made the mistake, they should not charge you for the second publication.

As indicated in the **NOTICE OF PUBLICATION**, your spouse has until a certain date to respond. If your spouse responds to the notice published in the newspaper, proceed with either the uncontested or contested procedure as necessary. If your spouse does not respond by the date indicated in the **NOTICE OF PUBLICATION**, proceed with the uncontested divorce procedure as discussed in Chapter 7.

Special Circumstances

This chapter covers some of the special circumstances that come up. Some of the issues discussed here may affect your divorce case; others may play no part at all. The issues discussed include:

- ✪ when you cannot afford court costs;

- ✪ protecting yourself, your children, and your property;

- ✪ tax matters;

- ✪ pension plans;

- ✪ military divorces;

- ✪ paternity;

- ✪ name changes;

- ✪ adoption; and,

- ✪ grandparent issues.

WHEN YOU CANNOT AFFORD COURT COSTS

Use an **AFFIDAVIT OF INDIGENCE** when you cannot afford to pay the filing fee and other costs associated with the divorce. (see form 23, p.267.) In order to qualify for a waiver of the filing fee, you must be *indigent*. If you are indigent, your income is probably low enough for you to qualify for public assistance.

– Caution –

If you decide to use this form, you will probably be asked for more information to prove that you meet the requirements for being declared indigent, and therefore, eligible to have the filing and service fees waived. Before you file this form, you may want to see if the court clerk will give you any information on what is required to be declared indigent. You should also be aware that you can be held in contempt of court for giving false information on this form.

Complete the **AFFIDAVIT OF INDIGENCE** as follows.

◈ Complete the top portion according to the instructions in Chapter 6 on page 74.

◈ Do not sign this form yet. Do type in your name, address, and phone number where indicated under the line marked "Affiant."

◈ Take this form to a notary and sign it before the notary on the line marked "Affiant." The notary will then date and sign the form. This form is now ready for filing.

PROTECTING YOURSELF, YOUR CHILDREN, AND YOUR PROPERTY

Families must be aware of signs of abuse and know that resources, such as the temporary protective order, exist to provide legal remedies to families in crisis. If your partner gets angry easily, controls all the family spending and requires you to account for every amount you spend, or discourages your relationships with family and friends, then you may be in a relationship in which domination and control are substituted for love and affection. Many times counseling is a good idea before patterns get too firmly established.

Sometimes this dominance and control manifests itself through verbal assaults or physical abuse. If so, it is important that you understand that as a victim of family violence you have legal rights you can pursue. Keep in mind, though, that each personal circumstance will determine whether you qualify to use tools such as the *temporary protective order* (TPO) to correct the violent situation. Before exercising legal rights, it may be advisable to discuss your situation with relatives, an attorney, a member of the Family Violence Center in your area, or any other trusted individual. Some referral numbers are provided on pages 140–141.

A temporary protective order is a court order that grants victims of family violence certain legal rights. If you are eligible, the TPO can provide various protective resources such as:

- ✪ order the person to cease violent acts;

- ✪ order the batterer to refrain from harassing or interfering with you;

- ✪ order temporary custody (with possible temporary visitation rights) for minor children;

- ✪ order temporary child support for minor children and the spouse;

- ✪ award you sole possession of the residence or require the batterer to provide a suitable alternative for you and the minor children; and,

- ✪ require the batterer to pay attorney's fees and court costs.

If the abuser disobeys a court order, that person may be arrested. Therefore, this legal device is invaluable for families dealing with domestic violence.

City or County	*Program*	*Contact #*
Albany	Liberty House	229-439-7094
Athens	Project Safe	706-543-3331
	Family Counseling Service	706-549-7755
Augusta	Safe Homes	706-736-2499
Avondale Estates	Tapestri, Inc.	404-299-2185
Blairsville	S.A.F.E.	706-379-3000
	Support in Abusive Family Emergencies	706-379-1901
Blue Ridge	Mountain Crisis Network	706-632-8400
Brunswick	Glynn Community	
	Crisis Center/Amity House	912-264-4357
Calhoun	Council on Battered Women	706-629-6065
Canton	Cherokee Family Violence Center	770-479-1804
Carroll County	Emergency Shelter	770-834-1141
Cartersville	Tranquility House	770-386-8779
Catoosa County	Family Crisis Center	706-375-7630
Chattanooga County	Family Crisis Center	706-375-7630
Clarkston	Refugee Family Services	404-299-6217
Clayton	Fight Abuse in the Home	706-782-1338
Clayton County	Association on Battered Women	770-961-7233
	Rainbow House	770-478-6905
Cobb County	YWCA	770-427-3390
College Park	Women's Crisis Center	770-969-6423
Columbus	Alliance for Battered Women	706-324-3850
Conley	Safe Haven Transitional	404-241-8740
Conyers	Project Renewal	770-860-1666
Cornelia	Circle of Hope Women's Center	706-776-4673
Dade County	Family Crisis Center	706-375-7630
Decatur	International Women's House, Inc.	770-413-5557
	Women Moving On	404-688-9436
Dahlonega	No One Alone (NOA's Ark)	706-864-1986
Dallas	Shepherd's Rest Ministries	770-443-5213
Dalton	Family Crisis Center	706-278-5586
Douglasville	Share House	770-949-0626
Effingham County	Victim Assistance Program	912-754-7460
Fayette County	Council on Domestic Violence	404-460-1604
Forsyth County	Family Haven	770-887-1121
	Victim Assistance Program	770-205-2268

City or County	Program	Contact #
Fulton County	Victim Witness Assistance	404-865-8135
	Jewish Family Services	770-677-9300
	Partership Against Violence	404-873-1766
Greensboro	Circle of Love Center, Inc.	706-453-4017
Hall County	Gateway House	770-536-5860
Hapeville	Odyssey Family Counseling	404-669-3462
Hartwell	Council on Domestic Violence	706-376-7111
Hinesville	Tri-County Protective Agency, Inc.	912-368-9200
LaGrange	Project LOVE	706-882-1000
Laurens County	TLC CASA	478-275-8100
	Wings	478-272-8000
Lawrenceville	Partnership Against Domestic Violence	770-963-9799
Macon	Salvation Army Safe House	478-738-9800
	Central Georgia CASA	478-238-6318
	Crisis Line	478-745-9292
	Family Counseling Center	912-745-2811
McDonough	Haven House	770-954-9229
Milledgeville	Georgia's Porch	478-445-1783
Polk County	Our House Women's Shelter	770-748-2800
Rome	Hospitality House for Women, Inc.	706-235-4673
Saint Marys	Camden Crisis Center, Inc.	912-882-7858
Savannah	SAFE Shelter	912-629-8888
Statesboro	Citizens Against Violence, Inc.	912-764-4605
Thomasville	Halcyon Home	229-226-6666
Tifton	Ruth's Cottage	229-387-9697
Valdosta	The Haven	229-244-1765
Walker County	Family Crisis Center	706-375-7630
	Four Points, Inc.	706-638-1555
Warner Robins	Salvation Army Safe House	478-923-6294
Waycross	Magnolia House	912-285-5850
Wayne County	Fair Haven	912-588-0382
	Protective Agency	912-588-9999
Winder	Peace Place	770-586-0927

NOTE: *A temporary protective order is sometimes used in emotionally charged circumstances if the parents separate and one parent wishes to obtain sole custody of a minor child. By definition, this relief is temporary, and ultimately any custodial parent must petition the court for legal custody. The court will then look to the best interest of the child to determine which parent should be awarded custody.*

Temporary Protective Orders

Regrettably, family violence has become very common, even in situations when uncontested divorces may be appropriate. In recent years temporary protective orders have been accepted as the legal solution to this problem, and it is not unusual to see them filed by individuals. A **PETITION FOR RELIEF UNDER THE FAMILY VIOLENCE ACT** can be filed if you are the victim of family violence. (see form 30, p.289.)

By statute, if you take this document to a county courthouse for filing, you will receive assistance in filling out the forms and there are no costs for filing. You need to be aware that this can produce immediate and very dramatic results and is not to be taken lightly. The first time a spouse applies for protection from abuse, the system is incredibly sympathetic. However, even though it may seem unfair, if the process is repeated several times, the system tends to address the problems with less urgency.

If the judge believes that domestic violence has occurred and protection is necessary, he or she will fill out and issue a **FAMILY VIOLENCE EX PARTE PROTECTIVE ORDER**. (see form 32a, p.299.) As you can see, the court can order immediate relief (for example, taking the person out of the home), but many courts are very careful about taking these steps without having a hearing.

In Georgia, a person may have to wait between ten and thirty days to defend him- or herself from the results of this order, so it is very important to judges that the order is fair and comprehensive. Often, the parties will reconcile, be counseled, or will otherwise wish to withdraw the charges. If the court allows them to do so, the parties can submit a **DISMISSAL OF TEMPORARY PROTECTIVE ORDER**. (see form 31, p.297.)

Finally, after a temporary order has been entered, any party can make it a final order by requesting a hearing within six months. The decision of the court will be effective for an extended period of time—from three years all the way to perhaps permanently. A **Three Year or Permanent Family Violence Protective Order** will be entered. (see form 32b, p.305.)

Protecting Your Property

If you genuinely fear that your spouse will try to remove money from bank accounts and try to hide important papers showing what property you own, you may want to take this same action before your spouse can. However, you can make a great deal of trouble for yourself with the judge if you do this to try to get these assets for yourself. So, make a complete list of any property you do take and be sure to include these items in your **Domestic Relations Financial Affidavit**. (see form 13, p.235.) You may need to convince the judge that you only took these items temporarily in order to preserve them until a **Final Judgment and Decree** is entered.

Do not spend any cash you take from a bank account, or sell or give away any items of property you take. Any cash should be placed in a separate bank account, without your spouse's name on it, and kept separate from any other cash you have. Any papers, such as deeds, car titles or stock or bond certificates, should be placed in a safe-deposit box without your spouse's name on it. The idea is not to take these things for yourself but to get them in a safe place so your spouse cannot hide them and deny they ever existed.

If your spouse is determined and resourceful, there is no guaranteed way to prevent the things discussed in this section from happening. All you can do is put as many obstacles in his or her way as possible, so he or she may suffer legal consequences for acting improperly.

Temporary Support and Custody

If your spouse has left you with the children, the mortgage, and monthly bills and is not helping you financially, you need to ask the clerk to be sure that a **Rule Nisi** (form 6) and the **Domestic Standing Order** (form 33) are served along with the **Petition for Divorce**.

NOTE: *Each superior court clerk's office has its own Standing Order of the Court. Check with them before using form 33.*

The Rule Nisi will give you a temporary hearing date at which you may ask the court to order the payment of support for you and the children during the divorce procedure. Of course, if you were the only person bringing in income and have been paying all the bills, it is difficult to be awarded much support. There are also criminal charges that can be brought if the breadwinner leaves the family without support for at least thirty days.

TAXES

As you are no doubt aware, the United States' income tax code is complicated and ever-changing. For this reason, it is impossible to give detailed information with respect to taxes in a book such as this. It is strongly recommended that you consult your accountant, lawyer, or whomever prepares your tax return about the tax consequences of a divorce. A few general concerns are discussed in this chapter to give you an idea of some of the tax questions that can arise.

Property Division and Taxes

You and your spouse may be exchanging the title of property as a result of your divorce. Generally, there will not be any tax to pay as the result of such a transfer. However, whoever gets a piece of property will be responsible to pay any tax that may become due upon sale. This amount may be substantial in regard to transfers of property or investments.

The Internal Revenue Service (IRS) has issued numerous rulings about how property is to be treated in divorce situations. You need to be especially careful if you are transferring any tax shelters or other complicated financial arrangements. Be sure to read the following section on alimony, because fancy property settlements are asking for tax problems.

Alimony and Taxes

Alimony can cause the most tax problems of any aspect of divorce. The IRS is always making new rulings on whether an agreement is really alimony or property division. The basic rule is that alimony is treated as income to the person receiving it and as a deduction for the person paying it. Therefore, in order to manipulate the tax consequences, many couples try to show something as part of the property settlement instead of as alimony, or the reverse.

If you are simply talking about the regular, periodic payment of cash, the IRS will probably not question that it is alimony. However, if you try to call it property settlement, you may run into problems. The important thing is to consult a tax expert if you are considering any unusual or creative property settlement or alimony arrangements.

Child Support and Taxes

There are simple tax rules regarding child support.

✪ Whoever has custody gets to claim the children on his or her tax return, both for a deduction and for any new tax credit (unless both parents file a special IRS form agreeing to a different arrangement each year).

✪ The parent receiving child support does not need to report it as income.

✪ The parent paying child support cannot deduct it.

If you are sharing physical custody, the parent with whom the child lives for the most time during the year is entitled to claim the child as a dependent.

The IRS form to reverse this must be filed each year. Therefore, if you and your spouse have agreed that you will get to claim the children (even though you do not have custody), you should have your spouse sign an open-ended form that you can file each year. A phone call to the IRS can help you get answers to questions on this point.

PENSION PLANS

Pension plans and retirement plans are marital assets. They may be very valuable assets. If you and your spouse are young and have not been working very long, you may not have pension plans worth worrying about. Also, if you have both worked and have similar pensions plans, it may be best just to include a provision in your settlement agreement that "each party shall keep his or her own pension plan." However, if you have been married a long time and your spouse worked while you stayed home to raise the children, your spouse's pension plan may be worth a lot of money and may be necessary to see you through retirement. If you and your spouse cannot agree on how to divide a pension plan, you should see an attorney. The valuation of pension plans and how they are to be divided is a complicated matter that you should not attempt.

Be sure to include all three types of pension accounts in your negotiations (if you have all three). IRAs are fairly simple, but defined contribution plans—401(k)s and Keoghs—and defined benefit plans (retirement accounts) are extremely complicated matters. Expect to pay $500 and up for a CPA or lawyer to determine the division of these.

MILITARY DIVORCES

This can be a topic for an entire book, but a military divorce has separate issues to resolve. First, it is often unclear where the divorce needs to be filed. Second, the federal government has established procedures that are addressed in dividing military pensions. Finally, even beginning a divorce proceeding against a servicemember may trigger the *Servicemembers Civil Relief Act*.

Servicemembers Civil Relief Act

Congress recognized that military service places servicemembers at a disadvantage in some situations. For example, it can be difficult for a service member to defend a lawsuit if his or her military duties prevent him or her from appearing in court. For this reason, Congress enacted the Servicemembers Civil Relief Act. This law provides certain protections to persons who are on active duty in the armed forces. The purpose of this act is to enable servicemembers to devote themselves to the defense of the country by relieving them of the fear that someone will take advantage of them during their period of service. However, the statute does not permit a servicemember to avoid his or her legal obligations, nor does it discharge or relieve those obligations.

The Servicemembers Civil Relief Act provides for the temporary suspension of civil (*not* criminal) legal proceedings when a servicemember's ability to prosecute or defend that action is adversely affected by military duties. For example, if you are sued in another state and cannot get leave to attend the trial, you should be able to get the case delayed until you can get leave. On the other hand, civil proceedings will normally not be delayed when military duties have no impact; therefore, if the only reason you cannot attend court is that you cannot afford the plane fare, a delay is unlikely to be granted. (The act also provides for the appointment of an attorney to protect the servicemember's interests when the member cannot appear.)

The Servicemembers Civil Relief Act also provides the following rights to servicemembers:

- ✪ protection from foreclosure and repossession on debts incurred prior to military service;

- ✪ reduction of interest rates to 6% on debts incurred prior to military service;

- ✪ right to terminate a lease made prior to military service;

- ✪ protection of dependents from eviction (only under very limited circumstances);

- ✪ payment of life insurance premiums by the government, when the servicemember is unable to do so;

- ✪ relief from taxation by a state where a servicemember is stationed pursuant to military orders; and,

- ✪ protection from default judgments. When a servicemember's military duties affect his or her ability to either prosecute or defend a lawsuit, the Servicemembers Civil Relief Act provides some relief.

Military Personnel Stationed in Georgia

In divorce, child custody, and paternity cases, the courts are extremely reluctant to issue a lengthy stay or set aside a judgment, but assistance in this area is regularly provided by the military lawyers on base. Generally, if the soldier has been stationed in Georgia for at least one year, you can file in any county that borders the military base to which he or she is assigned. If he or she has been transferred out of the country, it is the county bordering the military base to which he or she was last assigned.

NOTE: *In Georgia, parties can generally agree to a county to file in if one of them has lived there for more than six months preceding the filing of the divorce.*

PATERNITY

Paternity can be established voluntarily through a *paternity affidavit* in which the natural father admits paternity. If the alleged father disputes paternity, there are two tests available to him:

1. traditional blood testing and

2. DNA fingerprinting, which compares the genetic material of alleged father, mother, and child.

While neither test can conclusively establish paternity, they will be given considerable weight by the court and will probably suffice to establish paternity in the absence of compelling evidence to the contrary. Both tests are capable of conclusively disproving paternity. The Child Support Enforcement Agency can set up a blood test if the father is willing to take one.

NAME CHANGES

Name changes in Georgia are done through the courts. When taken in conjunction with a divorce, the wife can ask to have her maiden name restored at no additional charge. This free service does not apply to changing the name of minor children. If a name change is likely, this is the appropriate time to take advantage of the opportunity because it can cost several hundred dollars to legally change your name outside of the divorce process.

Georgia also has a law providing that the name of the child can be changed if the father has no contact with the child and is not paying support. Ask a local attorney for the particulars because this can be tricky.

ADOPTION

If you and your spouse adopted a child, that child has all the same rights as a natural born child, and you and your spouse must follow all of the same child custody, support, and visitation rules you must follow with any natural born child. If the adoption is being done by a stepparent, the adoption confers upon the adoptive parent all of the rights and obligations of the natural parent, and terminates the rights and obligations of the affected natural parent. Thus, the natural parent no longer is under an obligation to support the child and also loses any visitation rights. The child is no longer his or her natural heir.

NOTE: *A stepparent has no legal right to name a guardian for a child, which can be inconvenient if the custodial natural parent dies. A stepparent adoption can avoid this difficulty.*

Because of its significant consequences, the consent of the natural parent(s) whose rights are being terminated is usually required. The adoption of foreign nationals can be a particularly complicated matter, not only because of the problems related to the adoption but also because of immigration issues.

The complexities of the adoption process almost always require the assistance of an attorney, but it is possible for the process to cost as little as $500.

GRANDPARENT VISITATION AND CUSTODY

Under Georgia law, it is very difficult for grandparents to be awarded visitation, even when it is in the best interests of the child. However, it is possible for grandparents (and other third parties) to get custody of the children when it is in their best interest. If grandparent visitation or custody issues applies to you, talk to an attorney about the rules that are currently in effect.

Glossary

A

acknowledgment. A statement, written or oral, made before a person authorized by law to administer oaths (such as a notary public).

adult. A person 18 years of age or older.

affiant. The legal term for the person who signs an affidavit.

affidavit. A person's written statement of facts, signed under oath before a person authorized to administer oaths (such as a notary public or court clerk).

alimony. Money paid by one spouse to help support the other spouse.

annulment. A legal procedure by which a marriage is declared invalid.

answer. The title of a legal pleading that responds to a petition, usually by either admitting or denying the allegations in the petition.

C

counterpetition. A response to a petition that seeks some relief from the court rather than merely admitting or denying the allegations in the petition.

creditor. A person or institution to whom money is owed.

D

debtor. A person or institution who owes money.

deposition. The posing of verbal questions to one party who is required to answer verbally under oath, usually before a court reporter.

dissolution of marriage. The legal term for divorce used in Georgia (as well as in some other states).

E

equitable distribution. A way to divide marital property, the goal of which is to treat the parties fairly under the circumstances.

execute. To sign a legal document, in the legally required manner (e.g., before witnesses or a notary public), thereby making it effective.

F

final judgment. The order of the court at the end of a trial or pursuant to a settlement agreement.

H

homestead. Real estate that is a person's primary place of residence. The homestead is given special treatment for property tax purposes, and is exempt from the claims of creditors (other than a creditor holding a mortgage on the homestead property).

I

instrument. A legal term for a document.

interrogatories. Written questions sent by one party to the other that must be answered in writing under oath.

irretrievably broken. A legal way of saying that a marriage is broken and cannot be repaired.

J

joint custody. Where both parents share the responsibility of making decisions regarding their child.

joint tenancy. A way for two or more people to own property, so that when one owner dies, his or her interest in the property passes automatically to the remaining owner(s).

M

marital assets. Assets that are considered the property of both parties to a marriage.

motion. A party's written or oral request that the judge take certain action.

N

nonmarital assets. Assets that are considered the separate property of only one party to a marriage. Generally these are assets that were acquired before the marriage, or acquired by one party as a separate gift or inheritance.

notary public. A person who is legally authorized by the state to acknowledge signatures on legal documents.

P

pay-on-death account. A financial account, such as a bank account or certificate of deposit, which is payable to a certain person upon the death of the account holder.

personal property. All property other than land and things permanently attached to the land (such as buildings).

petition. The title of the legal pleading that begins a divorce case.

R

recording. The process of filing a deed, mortgage, or other legal document affecting title to land, with the court clerk's office.

S

separate maintenance. Another phrase, used in some states, for alimony.

separate property. Another phrase, used in some states, for nonmarital property.

served. To be given official, legal notice of lawsuit papers.

service. To give official, legal notice of legal papers to a person.

service by publication. When a person is given official, legal notice of legal papers by publication of a notice in a newspaper. This is only done when the person cannot be found and given personal service.

service of process. To be served with a summons or a subpoena.

shared custody. Another term for joint custody.

sole custody. Where one parent is given the sole legal right to make decisions regarding his or her child.

subpoena. An order from a court that a person appear before the court or at a deposition and give testimony.

subpoena duces tecum. A particular type of subpoena that requires the person to bring certain specified documents, records, or other items to the court or deposition.

T

tenancy by the entirety. This is essentially the same as joint tenancy, but it can only occur between a husband and wife. Upon the death of one spouse, the property automatically passes to the surviving spouse.

tenancy in common. A way for two or more people to own property, whereby if one of the owners dies, his or her interest in the property passes to his or her heirs (not to the other co-owners).

title. A document that proves ownership of property.

V

verified complaint. A complaint that has been signed by a party under oath (such as before a notary public or the court clerk).

Appendix A: Superior Court Clerks

Appling County
F. Floyd Hunter
P.O. Box 269
Baxley, GA 31513
912-367-8126

Atkinson County
Wilson Paulk
P.O. Box 6
Pearson, GA 31642
912-422-3343

Bacon County
Sherry Tillman
P.O. Box 376
Alma, GA 31510
912-632-4915

Baker County
Betty Bush
P.O. Box 10
Newton, GA 31770
229-734-3004

Baldwin County
Rosemary Fordham
Phillips
P.O. Box 987
Milledgeville, GA 31059
912-445-6324

Banks County
Tim Harper
P.O. Box 337
Homer, GA 30547
706-677-6240

Barrow County
Gloria M. Wall
P.O. Box 1280
Winder, GA 30680
770-307-3035

Bartow County
Gary Bell
135 West Cherokee Avenue
Suite 233
Cartersville, GA 30120
770-387-5025

Ben Hill County
Laverne D. Wheeler
P.O. Box 1104
Fitzgerald, GA 31750
229-426-5135

Berrien County
Carol Ross
101 East Marion Avenue
Suite 3
Nashville, GA 31639
912-686-5506

Bibb County
Dianne Brannen
P.O. Box 1015
Macon, GA 31202
478-621-6527

Bleckley County
Dianne C. Brown
306 S.E. Second Street
Cochran, GA 31014
478-934-3210

Brantley County
Tony Ham
P.O. Box 1067
Nahunta, GA 31553
912-462-6280

Brooks County
Ginger Shiver
P.O. Box 630
Quitman, GA 31643
229-263-4747

Bryan County
Rebecca G. Crowe
P.O. Box 670
Pembroke, GA 31321
912-653-3872

Bulloch County
Sherri A. Atkins
20 Siebald Street
Statesboro, GA 30458
912-764-9009

Burke County
Sherrie J. Cochran
P.O. Box 803
Waynesboro, GA 30830
706-554-2279

Butts County
Rhonda T. Waits
P.O. Box 320
Jackson, GA 30233
770-775-8215

Calhoun County
James C. Shippey
P.O. Box 69
Morgan, GA 31766-0069
229-849-2715

Camden County
Susan Waldron
P.O. Box 550
Woodbine, GA 31569
912-576-5622

Candler County
Linda F. Sewell
P.O. Drawer 830
Metter, GA 30439
912-685-5257

Carroll County
Kenneth Skinner
P.O. Box 1620
Carrollton, GA 30112
770-830-5830

Catoosa County
Norman L. Stone
875 Lafayette Street
Ringgold, GA 30736
706-935-4202

Charlton County
Kay Carter
P.O. Box 760
Folkston, GA 31537
912-496-2354

Chatham County
Daniel Massey
P.O. Box 10227
Savannah, GA 31412
912-652-7200

Chattahoochee County
Laura Marion
P.O. Box 120
Cusseta, GA 31805
706-989-3424

Chattooga County
Sam L. Cordle, Jr.
P.O. Box 159
Summerville, GA 30747-0159
706-857-0706

Cherokee County
Patricia Baker
90 North Street
Suite G-170
Canton, GA 30114
678-493-6511

Clarke County
Beverly Logan
P.O. Box 1805
Athens, GA 30603
706-613-3190

Clay County
Deanna Bertrand
P.O. Box 550
Fort Gaines, GA 39851
229-768-2631

Clayton County
Linda T. Miller
9151 Tara Boulevard
Jonesboro, GA 30236
770-477-3401

Clinch County
Daniel V. Leccese
P.O. Box 433
Homerville, GA 31634
912-487-5854

Cobb County
Jay C. Stephenson
P.O. Box 3490
Marietta, GA 30061
770-528-1300

Coffee County
Angela Spell
P.O. Box 10
Douglas, GA 31534
912-384-2865

Colquitt County
Carolyn Brazel
P.O. Box 2827
Moultrie, GA 31776
229-616-7420

Columbia County
Cindy Mason
P.O. Box 2930
Appling, GA 30809
706-312-7139

Cook County
Chlois Lollis
212 North Hutchinson Avenue
Adel, GA 31620
229-896-7717

Coweta County
Cindy G. Brown
P.O. Box 943
Newman, GA 30264
770-254-2690

Crawford County
John D. Castleberry
P.O. Box 1037
Roberta, GA 31078
478-836-3328

Crisp County
Jean H. Rogers
P.O. Box 747
Cordele, GA 31010
229-276-2616

Dade County
Kathy D. Page
P.O. Box 417
Trenton, GA 30752
706-657-4778

Dawson County
Becky V. McCord
25 Tucker Avenue
Suite 106
Dawsonville, GA 30534
706-344-3510

Decatur County
Rebecca McCook
P.O. Box 336
Bainbridge, GA 39818
229-248-3026

Dekalb County
Linda Carter
556 North McDonough Street Suite 207
Decatur, GA 30030
404-371-2836

Dodge County
Rhett Walker
P.O. Drawer 4276
Eastman, GA 31023
478-374-2817

Dooly County
Betty Colter
P.O. Box 326
Vienna, GA 31092
229-268-4234

Dougherty County
Evonne Mull
P.O. Box 1827
Albany, GA 31702
229-431-2198

Douglas County
Cindy Chaffin
8700 Hospital Drive
Douglasville, GA 30134
770-920-7252

Early County
India E. Thompson
P.O. Box 849
Blakely, GA 31723
229-723-3033

Echols County
Paula Goss
P.O. Box 213
Statenville, GA 31648
229-559-5642

Effingham County
Elizabeth Z. Hursey
P.O. Box 387
Springfield, GA 31329
912-754-2118

Elbert County
Pat V. Anderson
P.O. Box 619
Elberton, GA 30635
706-283-2005

Emanuel County
J. Carlton Lawson
P.O. Box 627
Swainsboro, GA 30401
478-237-8911

Evans County
Gail B. McCooey
P.O. Box 845
Claxton, GA 30417
912-739-3868

Fannin County
Dana Chastain
P.O. Box 1300
Blue Ridge, GA 30513
706-632-2039

Fayette County
Sheila Studdard
P.O. Box 130
Fayetteville, GA 30214
770-716-4290

Floyd County
Joe E. Johnston
P.O. Box 1110
Rome, GA 30162
706-291-5190

Forsyth County
Douglas Sorrells
100 Courthouse Square
Room 010
Cumming, GA 30040
770-781-2120

Franklin County
Melissa Blakely Holbrooke
P.O. Box 70
Carnesville, GA 30521
706-384-2514

Fulton County
Cathlene Robinson
136 Pryor Street, S.W.
Room 106
Atlanta, GA 30303
404-730-5313

Gilmer County
Glenda Sue Johnson
1 Westside Square
Ellijay, GA 30540
706-635-4462

Glascock County
Carla Stevens
P.O. Box 231
Gibson, GA 30810
706-598-2084

Glynn County
Lola Jamsky
P.O. Box 1355
Brunswick, GA 31521
912-554-7272

Gordon County
Brian Brannon
100 Wall Street
Suite 102
Calhoun, GA 30701
706-629-9533

Grady County
Annette H. Alred
250 North Broad Street
Box 8
Cairo, GA 39828
229-377-2912

Greene County
Deborah D. Jackson
113 East North Main Street
Suite 109
Greensboro, GA 30642
706-453-3340

Gwinnett County
Tom Lawler
P.O. Box 880
Lawrenceville, GA 30046
770-822-8100

Habersham County
David Wall
555 Monroe Street
Unit 35
Clarkesville, GA 30523
706-754-2923

Hall County
Dwight S. Wood
P.O. Box 336
Gainesville, GA 30503
770-531-7025

Hancock County
Leroy S. Wiley
P.O. Box 451
Sparta, GA 31087
706-444-6644

Haralson County
Dorthy Parker
P.O. Drawer 849
Buchanan, GA 30113
770-646-2005

Harris County
Staci K. Haralson
P.O. Box 528
Hamilton, GA 31811
706-628-4944

Hart County
William E. Holland, III
P.O. Box 386
Hartwell, GA 30643
706-376-7189

Heard County
Bryan Owensby
P.O. Box 249
Franklin, GA 30217
706-675-3301

Henry County
Judy Lewis
One Courthouse Square
McDonough, GA 30253
770-954-2121

Houston County
Carolyn V. Sullivan
201 Perry Parkway
Perry, GA 31069
478-218-4720

Irwin County
Nancy Ross
113 North Irwin Avenue
Ocilla, GA 31774
229-468-5356

Jackson County
Camie W. Thomas
P.O. Box 7
Jefferson, GA 30549
706-387-6255

Jasper County
Dan Jordan
126 West Green Street
Suite 110
Monticello, GA 31064
706-468-4901

Jeff Davis County
Myra Murphy
P.O. Box 429
Hazelhurst, GA 31539
912-375-6615

Jefferson County
Michael R. Jones
P.O. Box 151
Louisville, GA 30434
478-625-7922

Jenkins County
Elizabeth T. Landing
P.O. Box 659
Millen, GA 30442
478-982-4683

Johnson County
Patricia Glover
P.O. Box 321
Wrightsville, GA 31096
478-864-3484

Jones County
Bart W. Jackson
P.O. Box 39
Gray, GA 31032
478-986-6671

Lamar County
Robert F. Abbott
326 Thomaston Street
Box 7
Barnesville, GA 30204
770-358-5145

Lanier County
Martha B. Neugent
100 Main Street
Lakeland, GA 31635
229-482-3594

Laurens County
Allen Thomas
P.O. Box 2028
Dublin, GA 31040
478-272-3210

Lee County
Sondra Cook
P.O. Box 49
Leesburg, GA 31763
229-759-6018

Liberty County
F. Barry Wilkes
100 Main Street
Courthouse Square
Hinesville, GA 31313
912-876-3625

Lincoln County
Bruce C. Beggs
P.O. Box 340
Lincolnton, GA 30817
706-359-5505

Long County
Frank S. Middleton
P.O. Box 458
Ludowici, GA 31316
912-545-2123

Lowndes County
Sara L. Crow
P.O. Box 1349
Valdosta, GA 31603
229-333-5126

Lumpkin County
Edward E. Tucker
99 Courthouse Hill
Suite D
Dahlonega, GA 30533
706-864-3736

Macon County
Juanita Laidler
P.O. Box 337
Ogelthorpe, GA 31068
478-472-7661

Madison County
Michelle H. Strickland
P.O. Box 247
Danielsville, GA 30633
706-795-6310

Marion County
Joy Smith
P.O. Box 41
Buena Vista, GA 31803
229-649-7321

McDuffie County
Connie H. Cheatham
P.O. Box 158
Thomson, GA 30824
706-595-2134

McIntosh County
Bootie W. Goodrich
P.O. Box 1661
Darien, GA 31305
912-437-6641

Meriwether County
Louise T. Garrett
P.O. Box 160
Greenville, GA 30222
706-672-4416

Miller County
Annie L. Middleton
P.O. Box 66
Colquitt, GA 31737
229-758-4102

Mitchell County
Adayna B. Broome
P.O. Box 427
Camilla, GA 31730
229-336-2022

Monroe County
Lynn W. Ham
P.O. Box 450
Forsyth, GA 31029
478-994-7022

Montgomery County
Keith Hamilton
P.O. Box 311
Mount Vernon, GA 30445
912-583-4401

Morgan County
Jody M. Moss
P.O. Drawer 551
Madison, GA 30650
706-342-3605

Murray County
Loreine P. Matthews
P.O. Box 1000
Chatsworth, GA 30705
706-695-2932

Muscogee County
Linda Pierce
P.O. Box 2145
Columbus, GA 31902
706-653-4353

Newton County
Linda Dalton Hays
1132 Usher Street
Room 338
Covington, GA 30014
770-784-2035

Oconee County
Angie Watson
P.O. Box 1099
Watkinsville, GA 30677
706-769-3940

Oglethorpe County
Geneva G. Stamey
P.O. Box 68
Lexington, GA 30648
706-743-5731

Paulding County
Treva Shelton
11 Courthouse Square
Room G-3
Dallas, GA 30132
770-443-7527

Peach County
Joe Wilder
P.O. Box 389
Fort Valley, GA 31030
478-825-5331

Pickens County
Gail Brown
P.O. Box 130
Jasper, GA 30143
706-253-8763

Pierce County
Thomas W. Sauls
P.O. Box 588
Blackshear, GA 31516
912-449-2020

Pike County
Carolyn Williams
P.O. Box 10
Zebulon, GA 30295
770-567-2000

Polk County
Sheila Wells
P.O. Box 948
Cedartown, GA 30125
770-749-2114

Pulaski County
Peggy G. Fauscett
P.O. Box 60
Hawkinsville, GA 31036
478-783-1911

Putnam County
Sheila H. Layson
100 South Jefferson Avenue
Suite 236
Eatonton, GA 31024
706-485-4501

Quitman County
Rebecca S. Fendley
P.O. Box 307
Georgetown, GA 39854
229-334-2578

Rabun County
Holly Henry-Perry
25 Courthouse Square
Suite 105
Clayton, GA 30525
706-782-3615

Randolph County
Kay Arnold
P.O. Box 98
Cuthbert, GA 38840
229-732-2216

Richmond County
Elaine C. Johnson
P.O. Box 2046
Augusta, GA 30903
706-821-2460

Rockdale County
Joanne P. Caldwell
P.O. Box 937
Conyers, GA 30012
770-929-4021

Schley County
Kathy S. Royal
P.O. Box 7
Ellaville, GA 31806
229-937-5581

Screven County
Janis Reddick
P.O. Box 156
Sylvania, GA 30467
912-564-2614

Seminole County
Earlene Bramlett
P.O. Box 672
Donalsonville, GA 39845
229-524-2525

Spalding County
Marcia L. Norris
P.O. Box 1046
Griffin, GA 30224
770-467-4356

Stephens County
Aubre Grafton
205 North Alexander Street
Room 202
Toccoa, GA 30577
706-886-9496

Stewart County
Patti Smith
P.O. Box 910
Lumpkin, GA 31815
912-838-6220

Sumter County
Nancy Smith
P.O. Box 333
Americus, GA 31709
229-928-4537

Talbot County
Penny Dillingham-Mahone
P.O. Box 325
Talbotton, GA 31827
706-665-3239

Taliaferro County
Sandra S. Greene
P.O. Box 182
Crawfordville, GA 30631
706-456-2123

Tatnall County
Debbie Crews
P.O. Box 39
Reidsville, GA 30453
912-557-6716

Taylor County
Robert Taunton Jr.
P.O. Box 248
Butler, GA 31006
478-862-5594

Telfair County
Gene Johnson
128 East Oak Street Suite 2
McRae, GA 31055
229-868-6525

Terrell County
Louise B. Darley
513 South Main Street
Dawson, GA 31742
229-995-2631

Thomas County
David Hutchings Jr.
P.O. Box 1995
Thomasville, GA 31799
229-225-4108

Tift County
Gwen C. Pate
P.O. Box 354
Tifton, GA 31793
229-386-7816

Toombs County
Chess Fountain
P.O. Drawer 530
Lyons, GA 30436
912-526-3501

Towns County
Cecil Ray Dye
48 River Street
Suite E
Hiawassee, GA 30546
706-896-2130

Treutlen County
Curtis Rogers, Jr.
203 Second Street South
Suite 307
Sooperton, GA 30457
912-529-4515

Troup County
Jackie Taylor
P.O. Box 866
LaGrange, GA 30241
706-883-1740

Turner County
Linda House
P.O. Box 106
Ashburn, GA 31714
229-567-2011

Twiggs County
Patti H. Grimsley
P.O. Box 234
Jeffersonville, GA 31044
478-945-3350

Union County
Allen Conley
114 Courthouse Street
Suite 5
Blairsville, GA 30512
706-439-6022

Upson County
Nancy B. Adams
P.O. Box 469
Thomaston, GA 30286
706-647-7835

Walker County
Bill McDaniel
P.O. Box 448
LaFayette, GA 30728
706-638-1742

Walton County
Kathy K. Trost
303 South Hammond Drive
Suite 335
Monroe, GA 30655
770-267-1307

Ware County
Melba H. Fiveash
P.O. Box 776
Waycross, GA 31502
912-287-4340

Warren County
Shirley Cheeley
P.O. Box 227
Warrenton, GA 30828
706-465-2262

Washington County
Joy H. Conner
P.O. Box 231
Sandersville, GA 31082
478-552-3186

Wayne County
Stetson Bennett Jr.
P.O. Box 918
Jessup, GA 31598
912-427-5930

Webster County
Tina Blankenship
P.O. Box 117
Preston, GA 31824
229-828-3525

Wheeler County
Michael Morrison
P.O. Box 38
Alamo, GA 30411
912-568-7137

White County
Dena M. Adams
59 South Main Street
Suite B
Cleveland, GA 30528
706-865-2613

Whitfield County
Melica Kendrick
205 North Selvidge Street
Dalton, GA 30720
706-275-7450

Wilcox County
Wanda F. Hawkins
103 North Broad Street
Abbeville, GA 31001
229-467-2442

Wilkes County
Mildred Peeler
23 East Court Street
Room 205
Washington, GA 30673
706-678-2423

Wilkinson County
Cinda S. Bright
P.O. Box 250
Irwinton, GA 31042
229-946-2221

Worth County
Joann Powell
201 North Main Street
Room 13
Sylvester, GA 31791
229-776-8205

Appendix B:
Georgia Code
Divorce Provisions

This appendix contains some of the provisions from the Georgia Code that are most applicable to divorce situations.

Senate Bill 382
By: Senators Harp of the 29th and Hill of the 32nd
AS PASSED
AN ACT

To amend Titles 5, 7, and 19 of the Official Code of Georgia Annotated, relating respectively to appeal and error, banking and finance, and domestic relations, so as to change provisions relating to the calculation of child support; to clarify the appeal process in certain domestic relations cases; to clarify the calculation of the amount of interest on arrearage of child support; to clarify definitions; to provide guidelines for determining the amount of child support to be paid; to change provisions relating to guidelines for calculating child support; to reorganize Code Section 19-6-15, relating to guidelines for calculating child support, to provide more clarity on the application of such child support; to allow a jury to determine gross income and deviations; to provide calculation of parenting time; to provide for definitions; to provide for headings to better structure the Code section; to provide for the Child Support Obligation Table; to change certain provisions relating to the duties of the Georgia Child Support Commission; to correct cross-references; to amend an Act amending Titles 5, 7, and 19 of the Official Code of Georgia Annotated so as to state legislative findings, change provisions relating to calculation of child support, and make other related changes, approved April 22, 2005 (Ga. L. 2005, p. 224), so as to change the effective date of said Act; to state legislative intent; to provide for related matters; to provide for applicability and an effective date; to repeal conflicting laws; and for other purposes.

BE IT ENACTED BY THE
GENERAL ASSEMBLY OF GEORGIA:
SECTION 1.
Title 5 of the Official Code of Georgia Annotated, relating to appeal and error, is amended by striking subsection (a) of Code Section 5-6-34, relating to judgments and rulings deemed directly appealable, and inserting in lieu thereof the following: "5-6-34. (a) Appeals may be taken to the Supreme Court and the Court of Appeals from the

following judgments and rulings of the superior courts, the constitutional city courts, and such other courts or tribunals from which appeals are authorized by the Constitution and laws of this state:

(1) All final judgments, that is to say, where the case is no longer pending in the court below, except as provided in Code Section 5-6-35;

(2) All judgments involving applications for discharge in bail trover and contempt cases;

(3) All judgments or orders directing that an accounting be had;

(4) All judgments or orders granting or refusing applications for receivers or for interlocutory or final injunctions;

(5) All judgments or orders granting or refusing applications for attachment against fraudulent debtors;

(5.1) Any ruling on a motion which would be dispositive if granted with respect to a defense that the action is barred by Code Section 16-11-184;

(6) All judgments or orders granting or refusing to grant mandamus or any other extraordinary remedy, except with respect to temporary restraining orders;

(7) All judgments or orders refusing applications for dissolution of corporations created by the superior courts; and

(8) All judgments or orders sustaining motions to dismiss a caveat to the probate of a will."

SECTION 2.

Title 7 of the Official Code of Georgia Annotated, relating to banking and finance, is amended by striking in its entirety Code Section 7-4-12.1, relating to interest on arrearage of child support, and inserting in lieu thereof the following: "7-4-12.1.

(a) All awards of child support expressed in monetary amounts shall accrue interest at the rate of 7 percent per annum commencing 30 days from the day such award or payment is due. This Code section shall apply to all awards, court orders, decrees, and judgments rendered pursuant to Title 19. It shall not be necessary for the party to whom the child support is due to reduce any such award to judgment in order to recover such interest. The court shall have discretion in applying or waiving past due interest. In determining whether to apply, waive, or reduce the amount of interest owed, the Court shall consider whether:

(1) Good cause existed for the nonpayment of the child support;

(2) Payment of the interest would result in substantial and unreasonable hardship for the parent owing the interest;

(3) Applying, waiving, or reducing the interest would enhance or detract from the parent's current ability to pay child support, including the consideration of the regularity of payments made for current child support of those dependents for whom support is owed; and

(4) The waiver or reduction of interest would result in substantial and unreasonable hardship to the parent to whom interest is owed.

(b) This Code section shall not be construed to abrogate the authority of a IV-D agency to waive, reduce, or negotiate a settlement of unreimbursed public assistance in accordance with subsection

(b) of Code Section 19-11-5."

SECTION 3.

Title 19 of the Official Code of Georgia Annotated, relating to domestic relations, is amended by striking subsection (c) of Code Section 19-5-12, relating to form of judgment and decree in divorce actions, and inserting in lieu thereof a new subsection (c) to read as follows:

"(c) In any case which involves the determination of child support, the form of the judgment shall also include provisions indicating both parents' income, the number of children for which support is being provided, the presumptive amount of child support award calculation, and, if the presumptive amount of child support is rebutted, the award amount and the basis for the rebuttal award. The final judgment shall have attached to it the child support worksheet containing the calculation of the final award of child support and Schedule E pertaining to deviations. The final judgment shall specify a sum certain amount of child support to be paid."

SECTION 4.

Said title is further amended by striking in its entirety Code Section 19-6-15, relating to guidelines for calculating child support, and inserting in lieu thereof a new Code Section 19-6-15 to read as follows: "19-6-15.

(a) *Definitions.* As used in this Code section, the term:

(1) 'Adjusted Child Support Obligation' means the Basic Child Support Obligation adjusted by the Parenting Time Adjustment, if applicable, Health Insurance, and Work Related Child Care Costs.

(2) 'Adjusted Income' means the determination of a Parent's monthly income, calculated by deducting from that Parent's monthly Gross Income one-half of the amount of any applicable selfemployment taxes being paid by the Parent, any Preexisting Order for current child support which is being paid by the Parent, and any Theoretical Child Support Order for other Qualified Children, if allowed by the Court. For further reference see paragraph (5) of subsection (f) of this Code section.

(3) 'Basic Child Support Obligation' means the amount of support displayed on the Child Support Obligation Table which corresponds to the Combined Adjusted Income of the Custodial Parent and the Noncustodial Parent and the number of children for whom child support is being determined. This amount is rebuttably presumed to be the appropriate amount of child support to be provided by the Custodial Parent and the Noncustodial Parent prior to consideration of percentage of income, Health Insurance, Work Related Child Care Costs, and Deviations.

(4) 'Child' means child or children.

(5) 'Child Support Enforcement Agency' means the Child Support Enforcement Agency within the Department of Human Resources.

(6) 'Child Support Obligation Table' means the chart which displays the dollar amount of the Basic Child Support Obligation corresponding to various levels of Combined Adjusted Income of the children's Parents and the number of children for whom a child support order is being established or modified. The Child Support Obligation Table shall be used to calculate the Basic Child Support Obligation according to the provisions of this Code section. For further reference see subsections (n) and (o) of this Code section.

(7) 'Combined Adjusted Income' means the amount of Adjusted Income of the Custodial Parent added to the amount of Adjusted Income of the Noncustodial Parent.

(8) 'Court' means a judge of any Court of record or an administrative law judge of the Office of State Administrative Hearings.

(9) 'Custodial Parent' means the Parent with whom the Child resides more than 50 percent of the time. Where a Custodial Parent has not been designated or where a Child resides with both Parents an equal amount of time, the Court shall designate the Custodial Parent as the Parent with the lesser support obligation and the other Parent as the Noncustodial Parent. Where the Child resides equally with both Parents and neither Parent can be determined as owing a greater amount than the other, the Court shall determine which Parent to designate as the Custodial Parent for the purpose of this Code section.

(10) 'Deviation' means an increase or decrease from the Presumptive Amount of Child Support if the presumed order is rebutted by evidence and the required findings of fact are made by the Court pursuant to subsection (i) of this Code section.

(11) 'Final Child Support Order' means the Presumptive Amount of Child Support adjusted by any Deviations.

(12) 'Gross Income' means all income to be included in the calculation of child support as set forth in subsection (f) of this Code section.

(13) 'Health Insurance' means any general health or medical policy. For further reference see paragraph (2) of subsection (h) of this Code section.

(14) 'Noncustodial Parent' means the Parent with whom the Child resides less than 50 percent of the time or the Parent who has the greater payment obligation for child support. Where the Child resides equally with both Parents and neither Parent can be determined as owing a lesser amount than the other, the Court shall determine which Parent to designate as the Noncustodial Parent for the purpose of this Code section.

(15) 'Nonparent Custodian' means an individual who has been granted legal custody of a Child, or an individual who has a legal right to seek, modify, or enforce a child support order.

(16) 'Parent' means a person who owes a Child a duty of support pursuant to Code Section 19-7-2.

(17) 'Parenting Time Adjustment' means an adjustment to the Noncustodial Parent's portion of the Basic Child Support Obligation based upon the Noncustodial Parent's court ordered visitation with the Child. For further reference see subsection (g) of this Code section.

(18) 'Preexisting Order' means:

(A) An order in another case that requires a Parent to make child support payments for another Child, which child support the Parent is actually paying, as evidenced by documentation as provided in division (f)(5)(B)(iii) of this Code section; and

(B) That the date of filing of the initial order for each such other case is earlier than the date of filing of the initial order in the case immediately before the Court, regardless of the age of any Child in any of the cases.

(19) 'Presumptive Amount of Child Support' means the Basic Child Support Obligation including Health Insurance and Work Related Child Care Costs.

(20) A 'Qualified Child' or 'Qualified Children' means any Child:

(A) For whom the Parent is legally responsible and in whose home the Child resides; (B) That the Parent is actually supporting;

(C) Who is not subject to a Preexisting Child Support Order; and

(D) Who is not before the Court to set, modify, or enforce support in the case immediately under consideration. Qualified Children shall not include stepchildren or other minors in the home that the Parent has no legal obligation to support.

(21) 'Split Parenting' can occur in a child support case only if there are two or more children of the same Parents, where one Parent is the Custodial Parent for at least one Child of the Parents, and the other Parent is the Custodial Parent for at least one other Child of the Parents. In a Split Parenting case, each Parent is the Custodial Parent of any Child spending more than 50 percent of the time with that Parent and is the Noncustodial Parent of any Child spending more than 50 percent of the time with the other Parent. A Split Parenting situation shall have two Custodial Parents and two Noncustodial Parents, but no Child shall have more than one Custodial Parent or Noncustodial Parent.

(22) 'Theoretical Child Support Order' means a hypothetical child support order for Qualified Children calculated as set forth in subparagraph (f)(5)(C) of this Code section which allows the Court to determine the amount of child support as if a child support order existed.

(23) 'Uninsured Health Care Expenses' means a Child's uninsured medical expenses including, but not limited to, Health Insurance copayments, deductibles, and such other costs as are reasonably necessary for orthodontia, dental treatment, asthma treatments, physical therapy, vision care, and any acute or chronic medical or health problem or mental health illness, including counseling and other medical or mental health expenses, that are not covered by insurance. For further reference see paragraph (3) of subsection (h) of this Code section.

(24) 'Work Related Child Care Costs' means expenses for the care of the Child for whom support is being determined which are due to employment of either Parent. In an appropriate case, the Court may consider the child care costs associated with a Parent's job search or the training or education of a Parent necessary to obtain a job or enhance earning potential, not to exceed a reasonable time as determined by the Court, if the Parent proves by a preponderance of the evidence that the job search, job training, or education will benefit the Child being supported. The term shall be projected for the next consecutive 12 months and averaged to obtain a monthly amount. For further reference see paragraph (1) of subsection (h) of this Code section.

(25) 'Worksheet' or 'Child Support Worksheet' means the Worksheet used to record information necessary to determine and calculate child support. In Child Support Enforcement Agency cases in which neither Parent prepared a Worksheet, the Court may rely solely on the Worksheet prepared by the Child Support Enforcement Agency as a basis for its order. For further reference see subsection (m) of this Code section.

(b) *Process of calculating child support.* Pursuant to this Code section, the determination of child support shall be calculated as follows:

(1) Determine the monthly Gross Income of both the Custodial Parent and the Noncustodial Parent. Gross Income may include imputed income, if applicable. Gross Income shall be calculated on a monthly basis. The determination of monthly Gross Income shall be entered on the Child Support Schedule A – Gross Income;

(2) Adjust each Parent's monthly Gross Income by deducting the following from the Parents' monthly Gross Income, and entering it on the Child Support Schedule B – Adjusted Income if any of the following apply:

(A) One-half of the amount of self-employment taxes;

(B) Preexisting Orders; and

(C) Theoretical Child Support Order for Qualified Children, if allowed by the Court;

(3) Add each Parent's Adjusted Income together to compute the Combined Adjusted Income;

(4) Locate the Basic Child Support Obligation by referring to the Child Support Obligation Table. Using the figure closest to the amount of the Combined Adjusted Income, locate the amount of the Basic Child Support Obligation in the column underneath the number of children for whom support is being determined. If the Combined Adjusted Income falls between the amounts shown in the table, then the Basic Child Support Obligation shall be based on the income bracket most closely matched to the Combined Adjusted Income;

(5) Calculate the pro rata share of the Basic Child Support Obligation for the Custodial Parent and the Noncustodial Parent by dividing the Combined Adjusted Income into each Parent's Adjusted Income to arrive at each Parent's pro rata percentage of the Basic Child Support Obligation;

(6) Find the Adjusted Child Support Obligation amount by adding the additional expenses of the costs of Health Insurance and Work Related Child Care Costs, prorating such expenses in accordance with each Parent's pro rata share of the obligation and adding such expenses to the pro rata share of the obligation. The monthly cost of health insurance premiums and Work Related Child Care Costs shall be entered on the Child Support Schedule D – Additional Expenses. The pro rata share of the Basic Child Support Obligation and the pro rata share of the combined additional expenses shall be added together to create the Adjusted Child Support Obligation;

(7) Determine the Presumptive Amount of Child Support for the Custodial Parent and the Noncustodial Parent resulting in a sum certain single payment due to the Custodial Parent by assigning or deducting credit for actual payments for Health Insurance and Work Related Child Care Costs;

(8) In accordance with subsection (i) of this Code section, deviations subtracted from or increased to the Presumptive Amount of Child Support are applied, if applicable, and if supported by the required findings of fact and application of the best interest of the child standard. The proposed Deviations shall be entered on the Child Support Schedule E – Deviations. In the Court's or the jury's discretion, Deviations may include, but are not limited to, the following:

(A) High income;

(B) Low income;

(C) Other health related insurance;

(D) Child and dependent care tax credit;

(E) Travel expenses;

(F) Alimony;

(G) Mortgage;

(H) Permanency plan or foster care plan;

(I) Extraordinary expenses;

(J) Nonspecific deviations; and

(K) Parenting time;

(9) The Final Child Support Order shall be the Presumptive Amount of Child Support as increased or decreased by Deviations. The final child support amount for each Parent shall be entered on the Child Support Worksheet, together with the information from each of the utilized schedules;

(10) In addition, the Parents shall allocate the Uninsured Health Care Expenses which shall be based on the pro rata responsibility of the Parents or as otherwise ordered by the Court. Each Parent's pro rata responsibility for Uninsured Health Care Expenses shall be entered on the Child Support Worksheet; and

(11) In a Split Parenting case, there shall be a separate calculation and Final Child Support Order for each Parent.

(c) *Applicability and required findings.*

(1) The child support guidelines contained in this Code section are a minimum basis for determining the amount of child support and shall apply as a rebuttable presumption in all legal proceedings involving the child support responsibility of a Parent. This Code section shall be used when the Court enters a temporary or permanent child support order in a contested or noncontested hearing. The rebuttable Presumptive Amount of Child Support provided by this Code section may be increased according to the best interest of the Child for whom support is being considered, the circumstances of the parties, the grounds for Deviation set forth in subsection (i) of this Code section, and to achieve the state policy of affording to children of unmarried Parents, to the extent possible, the same economic standard of living enjoyed by children living in intact families consisting of Parents with similar financial means.

(2) The provisions of this Code section shall not apply with respect to any divorce case in which there are no minor children, except to the limited extent authorized by subsection (e) of this Code section. In the final judgment or decree in a divorce case in which there are minor children, or in other cases which are governed by the provisions of this Code section, the Court shall:

(A) Specify in what sum certain amount and from which Parent the Child is entitled to permanent support as determined by use of the Worksheet;

(B) Specify as required by Code Section 19-5-12 in what manner, how often, to whom, and until when the support shall be paid;

(C) Include a written finding of the Parent's Gross Income as determined by the Court or the jury;

(D) Determine whether Health Insurance for the Child involved is reasonably available at a reasonable cost to either Parent. If the Health Insurance is reasonably available at a reasonable cost to the Parent, then the Court may order that the Child be covered under such Health Insurance;

(E) Include written findings of fact as to whether one or more of the Deviations allowed under this Code section are applicable, and if one or more such Deviations are applicable as determined by the Court or the jury, the written findings of fact shall further set forth:

(i) The reasons the Court or the jury deviated from the Presumptive Amount of Child Support;

(ii) The amount of child support that would have been required under this Code section if the
Presumptive Amount of Child Support had not been rebutted; and

(iii) A finding that states how the Court's or the jury's application of the child support guidelines would be unjust or inappropriate considering the relative ability of each Parent to provide support and how the best interest of the Child who is subject to the child support determination is served by Deviation from the Presumptive Amount of Child Support;

(F) Specify the amount of the Noncustodial Parent's parenting time as set forth in the order of visitation; and

(G) Specify the percentage of Uninsured Health Care Expenses for which each Parent shall be responsible.

(3) When child support is ordered, the party who is required to pay the child support shall not be liable to third persons for necessaries furnished to the Child embraced in the judgment or decree. In all cases, the parties shall submit to the Court their Worksheets and schedules and the presence or absence of other factors to be considered by the Court pursuant to the provisions of this Code section.

(4) In any case in which the Gross Income of the Custodial Parent and the Noncustodial Parent is determined by a jury, the Court shall charge the provisions of this Code section applicable to the determination of Gross Income. The jury shall be required to return a special interrogatory determining Gross Income. Based upon the jury's verdict as to Gross Income, the Court shall determine the Presumptive Amount of Child Support in accordance with the provisions of this Code section. The Court shall inform the jury of the Presumptive Amount of Child Support and the identity of the Custodial and Noncustodial Parents. In the final instructions to the jury, the Court shall charge the provisions of this Code section applicable to the determination of Deviations and the jury shall be required to return a special interrogatory as to Deviations and the final award of child support. The Court shall include its findings and the jury's verdict on the Child Support Worksheet in accordance with this Code section and Code Section 19-5-12.

(5) Nothing contained within this Code section shall prevent the parties from entering into an enforceable agreement contrary to the Presumptive Amount of Child Support which may be made the order of the Court pursuant to review by the Court of the adequacy of the child support amounts negotiated by the parties, including the provision for medical expenses and Health Insurance; provided, however, that if the agreement negotiated by the parties does not comply with the provisions contained in this Code section and does not contain findings of fact as required to support a Deviation, the Court shall reject such agreement.

(6) In any case filed pursuant to Chapter 11 of this title, relating to the 'Child Support Recovery Act,' the 'Uniform Reciprocal Enforcement of Support Act,' or the 'Uniform Interstate Family Support Act,' the Court shall make all determinations of fact, including Gross Income and Deviations, and a jury shall not hear any issue related to such cases.

(d) *Nature of guidelines; Court's discretion.* In the event of a hearing or trial on the issue of child support, the guidelines enumerated in this Code section are intended by the General Assembly to be guidelines only and any Court so applying these guidelines shall not abrogate its responsibility in making the final determination of child support based on the evidence presented to it at the time of the hearing or trial.

(e) *Duration of child support responsibility.* The duty to provide support for a minor Child shall continue until the Child reaches the age of majority, dies, marries, or becomes emancipated, whichever first occurs; provided, however, that, in any temporary, final, or modified order for child support with respect to any proceeding for divorce, separate maintenance, legitimacy, or paternity entered on or after July 1, 1992, the Court, in the exercise of sound discretion, may direct either or both Parents to provide financial assistance to a Child who has not previously married or become emancipated, who is enrolled in and attending a secondary school, and who has attained the age of majority before completing his or her secondary school education, provided that such financial assistance shall not be required after a Child attains 20 years of age. The provisions for child support provided in this subsection may be enforced by either Parent, by any Nonparent Custodian, by a guardian appointed to receive child support for the Child for whose benefit the child support is ordered, or by the Child for whose benefit the child support is ordered.

(f) *Gross Income.*

(1) INCLUSION TO GROSS INCOME.

(A) *ATTRIBUTABLE INCOME.* Gross Income of each Parent shall be determined in the process of setting the Presumptive Amount of Child Support and shall include all income from any source, before deductions for taxes and other deductions such as Preexisting Orders for child support and credits for other Qualified Children, whether earned or unearned, and includes, but is not limited to, the following:

(i) Salaries;

(ii) Commissions, fees, and tips;

(iii) Income from self-employment;

(iv) Bonuses;

(v) Overtime payments;

(vi) Severance pay;

(vii) Recurring income from pensions or retirement plans including, but not limited to, Veterans' Administration, Railroad Retirement Board, Keoghs, and individual retirement accounts;

(viii) Interest income;

(ix) Dividend income;

(x) Trust income;

(xi) Income from annuities;

(xii) Capital gains;

(xiii) Disability or retirement benefits that are received from the Social Security Administration pursuant to Title II of the federal Social Security Act;

(xiv) Workers' compensation benefits, whether temporary or permanent;

(xv) Unemployment insurance benefits;

(xvi) Judgments recovered for personal injuries and awards from other civil actions;

(xvii) Gifts that consist of cash or other liquid instruments, or which can be converted to cash;

(xviii) Prizes;

(xix) Lottery winnings;

(xx) Alimony or maintenance received from persons other than parties to the proceeding before the Court; and

(xxi) Assets which are used for the support of the family.

(B) *SELF-EMPLOYMENT INCOME.* Income from self-employment includes income from, but not limited to, business operations, work as an independent contractor or consultant, sales of goods or services, and rental properties, less ordinary and reasonable expenses necessary to produce such income. Income from self-employment, rent, royalties, proprietorship of a business, or joint ownership of a partnership, limited liability company, or closely held corporation is defined as gross receipts minus ordinary and necessary expenses required for selfemployment or business operations. Ordinary and reasonable expenses of self-employment or business operations necessary to produce income do not include:

(i) Excessive promotional, travel, vehicle, or personal living expenses, depreciation on equipment, or costs of operation of home offices; or

(ii) Amounts allowable by the Internal Revenue Service for the accelerated component of depreciation expenses, investment tax credits, or any other business expenses determined by the Court or the jury to be inappropriate for determining Gross Income. In general, income and expenses from self-employment or operation of a business should be carefully reviewed by the Court or the jury to determine an appropriate level of Gross Income available to the Parent to satisfy a child support obligation. Generally, this amount will differ from a determination of business income for tax purposes.

(C) *FRINGE BENEFITS.* Fringe benefits for inclusion as income or 'in kind' remuneration received by a Parent in the course of employment, or operation of a trade or business, shall be counted as income if the benefits significantly reduce personal living expenses. Such fringe benefits might include, but are not limited to, use of a company car, housing, or room and board. Basic allowance for housing and subsistence and variable housing allowances for members of the armed services shall be considered income for the purposes of determining child support. Fringe benefits do not include employee benefits that are typically added to the salary, wage, or other compensation that a Parent may receive as a standard added benefit, including, but not limited to, employer paid portions of Health Insurance premiums or employer contributions to a retirement or pension plan.

(D) *VARIABLE INCOME.* Variable income such as commissions, bonuses, overtime pay, and dividends shall be averaged by the Court or the jury over a reasonable period of time consistent with the circumstances of the case and added to a Parent's fixed salary or wages to determine Gross Income. When income is received on an irregular, nonrecurring, or one-time basis, the Court or the jury may, but is not required to, average or prorate the income over a reasonable specified period of time or require the Parent to pay as a one-time support amount a percentage of his or her nonrecurring income, taking into consideration the percentage of recurring income of that Parent.

(2) EXCLUSIONS FROM GROSS INCOME. Excluded from Gross Income are the following:

(A) Child support payments received by either Parent for the benefit of a Child of another relationship;

(B) Benefits received from means-tested public assistance programs such as, but not limited to:

(i) PeachCare for Kids Program, temporary assistance for needy families, or similar programs in other states or territories under Title IV-A of the federal Social Security Act;

(ii) Food stamps or the value of food assistance provided by way of electronic benefits transfer procedures by the Department of Human Resources;

(iii) Supplemental security income received under Title XVI of the federal Social Security Act;

(iv) Benefits received under Section 402(d) of the federal Social Security Act for disabled adult children of deceased disabled workers; and

(v) Low income heating and energy assistance program payments; and

(C) A Nonparent Custodian's Gross Income.

(3) SOCIAL SECURITY BENEFITS.

(A) Benefits received under Title II of the federal Social Security Act by a Child on the obligor's account shall be counted as child support payments and shall be applied against the Final Child Support Order to be paid by the obligor for the Child.

(B) After calculating the obligor's monthly Gross Income, including the countable Social Security benefits as specified in division (1)(A)(xiii) of this subsection, and after calculating the amount of child support, if the Presumptive Amount of Child Support is greater than the Social Security benefits paid on behalf of the Child on the obligor's account, the obligor shall be required to pay the amount exceeding the Social Security benefit as part of the Final Child Support Order in the case.

(C) After calculating the obligor's monthly Gross Income, including the countable Social Security benefits as specified in division (1)(A)(xiii) of this subsection, and after calculating the amount of child support, if the Presumptive Amount of Child Support is equal to or less than the Social Security benefits paid to the Nonparent Custodian or Custodial Parent on behalf of the Child on the obligor's account, the child support responsibility of that Parent is met and no further child support shall be paid.

(D) Any benefit amounts under Title II of the federal Social Security Act as determined by the Social Security Administration sent to the Nonparent Custodian or Custodial Parent by the Social Security Administration for the Child's benefit which are greater than the Final Child Support Order shall be retained by the Nonparent Custodian or Custodial Parent for the Child's benefit and shall not be used as a reason for decreasing the Final Child Support Order or reducing arrearages.

(E) The Court shall make a written finding of fact in the Final Child Support Order regarding the use of Social Security benefits in the calculation of the child support.

(4) RELIABLE EVIDENCE OF INCOME.

(A) *IMPUTED INCOME.* When establishing the amount of child support, if a Parent fails to produce reliable evidence of income, such as tax returns for prior years, check stubs, or other information for determining current ability to pay child support or ability to pay child support in prior years, and the Court or the jury has no other reliable evidence of the Parent's income or income potential, Gross Income for the current year shall be determined by imputing Gross

Income based on a 40 hour workweek at minimum wage.

(B) *MODIFICATION.* When cases with established orders are reviewed for modification and a Parent fails to produce reliable evidence of income, such as tax returns for prior years, check stubs, or other information for determining current ability to pay child support or ability to pay child support in prior years, and the Court has no other reliable evidence of that Parent's income or income potential, the Court may enter an order to increase the child support of the Parent failing or refusing to produce evidence of income by an increment of at least 10 percent per year of that Parent's pro rata share of the Basic Child Support Obligation for each year since the Final Child Support Order was entered or last modified.

(C) *REHEARING.* If income is imputed pursuant to subparagraph (A) of this paragraph, the party believing the income of the other party is higher than the amount imputed may provide within 90 days, upon motion to the Court, evidence necessary to determine the appropriate amount of child support based upon reliable evidence. A hearing shall be scheduled after the motion is filed. The Court may increase, decrease, or the amount of current child support may remain the same from the date of filing of either Parent's initial filing or motion for reconsideration. While the motion for reconsideration is pending, the obligor shall be responsible for the amount of child support originally ordered. Arrearages entered in the original child support order based upon imputed income shall not be forgiven. When there is reliable evidence to support a motion for reconsideration of the amount of income imputed, the party shall not be required to demonstrate the existence of a significant variance or other such factors required for modification of an order pursuant to subsection (k) of this Code section.

(D) *WILLFUL OR VOLUNTARY UNEMPLOYMENT OR UNDEREMPLOYMENT.* In determining whether a Parent is willfully or voluntarily unemployed or underemployed, the Court or the jury shall ascertain the reasons for the Parent's occupational choices and assess the reasonableness of these choices in light of the Parent's responsibility to support his or her Child and whether such choices benefit the Child. A determination of willful or voluntary unemployment or underemployment shall not be limited to occupational choices motivated only by an intent to avoid or reduce the payment of child support but can be based on any intentional choice or act that affects a Parent's income. In determining willful or voluntary unemployment or underemployment, the Court may examine whether there is a substantial likelihood that the Parent could, with reasonable effort, apply his or her education, skills, or training to produce income. Specific factors for the Court to consider when determining willful or voluntary unemployment or underemployment include, but are not limited to:

(i) The Parent's past and present employment;

(ii) The Parent's education and training;

(iii) Whether unemployment or underemployment for the purpose of pursuing additional training or education is reasonable in light of the Parent's responsibility to support his or her Child and, to this end, whether the training or education may ultimately benefit the Child in the case immediately under consideration by increasing the Parent's level of support for that Child in the future;

(iv) A Parent's ownership of valuable assets and resources, such as an expensive home or automobile, that appear inappropriate or unreasonable for the income claimed by the Parent;

(v) The Parent's own health and ability to work outside the home; and

(vi) The Parent's role as caretaker of a Child of that Parent, a disabled or seriously ill Child of that Parent, or a disabled or seriously ill adult Child of that Parent, or any other disabled or seriously ill relative for whom that Parent has assumed the role of caretaker, which eliminates or substantially reduces the Parent's ability to work outside the home, and the need of that Parent to continue in the role of caretaker in the future. When considering the income potential of a Parent whose work experience is limited due to the caretaker role of that Parent, the Court shall consider the following factors:

(I) Whether the Parent acted in the role of full-time caretaker immediately prior to separation by the married parties or prior to the divorce or annulment of the marriage or dissolution of another relationship in which the Parent was a full-time caretaker;

(II) The length of time the Parent staying at home has remained out of the workforce for this purpose;

(III) The Parent's education, training, and ability to work; and

(IV) Whether the Parent is caring for a Child who is four years of age or younger. If the Court or the jury determines that a Parent is willfully or voluntarily unemployed or underemployed, child support shall be calculated based on a determination of earning capacity, as evidenced by educational level or previous work experience. In the absence of any other reliable evidence, income may be imputed to the Parent pursuant to a determination that Gross Income for the current year is based on a 40 hour workweek at minimum wage. A determination of willful and voluntary unemployment or underemployment shall not be made when an individual is activated from the National Guard or other armed forces unit or enlists or is drafted for full-time service in the armed forces of the United States.

(5) ADJUSTMENTS TO GROSS INCOME.

(A) *SELF-EMPLOYMENT.* One-half of the self-employment and Medicare taxes shall be calculated as follows:

(i) Six and one-quarter percent of self-employment income up to the maximum amount to which federal old age, survivors, and disability insurance (OASDI) applies; plus

(ii) One and forty-five one-hundredths of a percent of self-employment income for Medicare and this amount shall be deducted from a self-employed Parent's monthly Gross Income.

(B) *PREEXISTING ORDERS.* An adjustment to the Parent's monthly Gross Income shall be made on the Child Support Schedule B – Adjusted Income for current Preexisting Orders actually being paid under an order of support for a period of not less than 12 consecutive months immediately prior to the date of the hearing or such period that an order has been in effect if less than 12 months prior to the date of the hearing before the Court to set, modify, or enforce child support.

(i) In calculating the adjustment for Preexisting Orders, the Court shall include only those Preexisting Orders where the date of entry of the initial support order precedes the date of entry of the initial order in the case immediately under consideration;

(ii) The priority for Preexisting Orders shall be determined by the date of the initial order in each case. Subsequent modifications of the initial support order shall not affect the priority position established by the date of the initial order. In any modification proceeding, the Court rendering the decision shall make a specific finding of the date of the initial order of the case;

(iii) Adjustments shall be allowed for current preexisting support only to the extent that the payments are actually being paid as evidenced by documentation including, but not limited to, payment history from a court clerk, a IV-D agency, as defined in Code Section 19-6-31, the Child Support Enforcement Agency's computer data base, the child support payment history, or canceled checks or other written proof of payments paid directly to the other Parent. The maximum credit allowed for a Preexisting Order is an average of the amount of current support actually paid under the Preexisting Order over the past 12 months prior to the hearing date;

(iv) All Preexisting Orders shall be entered on the Child Support Schedule B – Adjusted Income for the purpose of calculating the total amount of the credit to be included on the Child Support Worksheet; and

(v) Payments being made by a Parent on any arrearages shall not be considered payments on Preexisting Orders or subsequent orders and shall not be used as a basis for reducing Gross Income.

(C) *THEORETICAL CHILD SUPPORT ORDERS.* In addition to the adjustments to monthly Gross Income for self-employment taxes provided in subparagraph (A) of this paragraph and for Preexisting Orders provided in subparagraph (B) of this paragraph, credits for either Parent's other Qualified Child living in the Parent's home for whom the Parent owes a legal duty of support may be considered by the Court for the purpose of reducing the Parent's Gross Income. To consider a Parent's other Qualified Children for determining the Theoretical Child Support Order, a Parent shall present documentary evidence of the Parent-Child relationship to the Court. Adjustments to income pursuant to this paragraph may be considered in such circumstances in which the failure to consider a Qualified Child would cause substantial hardship to the Parent; provided, however, that such consideration of an adjustment shall be based upon the best interest of the Child for whom child support is being awarded. If the Court, in its discretion, decides to apply the Qualified Child adjustment, the Basic Child Support Obligation of the Parent for the number of other Qualified Children living with such Parent shall be determined based upon that Parent's monthly Gross Income. Except for self-employment taxes paid, no other amounts shall be subtracted from the Parent's monthly Gross Income when calculating a Theoretical Child Support Order under this subparagraph. The Basic Child Support Obligation for such Parent shall be multiplied by 75 percent and the resulting amount shall be subtracted from such Parent's monthly Gross Income and entered on the Child Support Schedule B – Adjusted Income.

(D) *PRIORITY OF ADJUSTMENTS.* In multiple family situations, the adjustments to a Parent's monthly Gross Income shall be calculated in the following order:

(i) Preexisting Orders according to the date of the initial order; and

(ii) After applying the deductions on the Child Support Schedule B – Adjusted Income for Preexisting Orders, if any, in subparagraph (A) of paragraph (4) of this subsection, any credit for a Parent's other Qualified Children may be considered using the procedure set forth in subparagraph (B) of this paragraph.

(g) *Parenting Time Adjustment.* The Court or the jury may deviate from the Presumptive Amount of Child Support as set forth in subparagraph (i)(2)(K) of this Code section.

(h) *Adjusted support obligation.* The Child Support Obligation Table does not include the cost of the Parent's Work Related Child Care Costs, Health Insurance premiums, or Uninsured Health Care Expenses. The additional expenses for the Child's Health Insurance premium and Work Related Child Care Costs shall be included in the calculations to determine child support. A Nonparent Custodian's expenses for Work Related Child Care Costs and Health Insurancepremiums shall be taken into account when establishing a Final Child Support Order.

(1) WORK RELATED CHILD CARE COSTS.

(A) Work Related Child Care Costs necessary for the Parent's employment, education, or vocational training that are determined by the Court to be appropriate, and that are appropriate to the Parents' financial abilities and to the lifestyle of the Child if the Parents and Child were living together, shall be averaged for a monthly amount and entered on the Child Support Worksheet in the column of the Parent initially paying the expense. Work Related Child Care Costs of a Nonparent Custodian shall be considered when determining the amount of this expense.

(B) If a child care subsidy is being provided pursuant to a means-tested public assistance program, only the amount of the child care expense actually paid by either Parent or a Nonparent Custodian shall be included in the calculation.

(C) If either Parent is the provider of child care services to the Child for whom support is being determined, the value of those services shall not be an adjustment to the Basic Child Support Obligation when calculating the support award.

(D) If child care is provided without charge to the Parent, the value of these services shall not be an adjustment to the Basic Child Support Obligation. If child care is or will be provided by a person who is paid for his or her services, proof of actual cost or payment shall be shown to the Court before the Court includes such payment in its consideration.

(E) The amount of Work Related Child Care Costs shall be determined and added as an adjustment to the Basic Child Support Obligation as 'additional expenses' whether paid directly by the Parent or through a payroll deduction.

(F) The total amount of Work Related Child Care Costs shall be divided between the Parents pro rata to determine the Presumptive Amount of Child Support and shall be included in the Worksheet and written order of the Court.

(2) COST OF HEALTH INSURANCE PREMIUMS.

(A)(i) The amount that is, or will be, paid by a Parent for Health Insurance for the Child for whom support is being determined shall be an adjustment to the Basic Child Support Obligation and prorated between the Parents based upon their respective incomes. Payments made by a

Parent's employer for Health Insurance and not deducted from the Parent's wages shall not be included. When a Child for whom support is being determined is covered by a family policy, only the Health Insurance premium actually attributable to that Child shall be added.

(ii) The amount of the cost for the Child's Health Insurance premium shall be determined and added as an adjustment to the Basic Child Support Obligation as 'additional expenses' whether paid directly by the Parent or through a payroll deduction.

(iii) The total amount of the cost for the Child's Health Insurance premium shall be divided between the Parents pro rata to determine the total Presumptive Amount of Child Support and shall be included in the Child Support Schedule D – Additional Expenses and written order of the Court together with the amount of the Basic Child Support Obligation.

(B)(i) If Health Insurance that provides for the health care needs of the Child can be obtained by a Parent at reasonable cost, then an amount to cover the cost of the premium shall be added as an adjustment to the Basic Child Support Obligation. A Health Insurance premium paid by a Nonparent Custodian shall be included when determining the amount of Health Insurance expense. In determining the amount to be added to the order for the Health Insurance cost, only the amount of the Health Insurance cost attributable to the Child who is the subject of the order shall be included.

(ii) If coverage is applicable to other persons and the amount of the Health Insurance premium attributable to the Child who is the subject of the current action for support is not verifiable, the total cost to the Parent paying the premium shall be prorated by the number of persons covered so that only the cost attributable to the Child who is the subject of the order under consideration is included. The amount of Health Insurance premium shall be determined by dividing the total amount of the insurance premium by the number of persons covered by the insurance policy and multiplying the resulting amount by the number of children covered by the insurance policy. The monthly cost of Health Insurance premium shall be entered on the Child Support Schedule D – Additional Expenses in the column of the Parent paying the premium.

(iii) Eligibility for or enrollment of the Child in Medicaid or PeachCare for Kids Program shall not satisfy the requirement that the Final Child Support Order provide for the Child's healthcare needs. Health coverage through PeachCare for Kids Program and Medicaid shall not prevent a Court from ordering either or both Parents to obtain other Health Insurance.

(3) UNINSURED HEALTH CARE EXPENSES.

(A) The Child's Uninsured Health Care Expenses shall be the financial responsibility of both Parents. The Final Child Support Order shall include provisions for payment of the Uninsured Heath Care Expenses; provided, however, that the Uninsured Health Care Expenses shall not be used for the purpose of calculating the amount of child support. The Parents shall divide the Uninsured Health Care Expenses pro rata, unless otherwise specifically ordered by the Court.

(B) If a Parent fails to pay his or her pro rata share of the Child's Uninsured Health Care Expenses, as specified in the Final Child Support Order, within a reasonable time after receipt of evidence documenting the uninsured portion of the expense:

(i) The other Parent or the Nonparent Custodian may enforce payment of the expense by any means permitted by law; or

(ii) The Child Support Enforcement Agency shall pursue enforcement of payment of such unpaid expenses only if the unpaid expenses have been reduced to a judgment in a sum certain amount.

(i) *Grounds for Deviation.*

(1) GENERAL PRINCIPLES.

(A) The amount of child support established by this Code section and the Presumptive Amount of Child Support are rebuttable and the Court or the jury may deviate from the Presumptive Amount of Child Support in compliance with this subsection. In deviating from the Presumptive Amount of Child Support, primary consideration shall be given to the best interest of the Child for whom support under this Code section is being determined. A Nonparent Custodian's expenses may be the basis for a Deviation.

(B) When ordering a Deviation from the Presumptive Amount of Child Support, the Court or the jury shall consider all available income of the Parents and shall make written findings or special interrogatory findings that an amount of child support other than the amount calculated is reasonably necessary to provide for the needs of the Child for whom child support is being determined and the order or special interrogatory shall state:

(i) The reasons for the Deviation from the Presumptive Amount of Child Support;

(ii) The amount of child support that would have been required under this Code section if the Presumptive Amount of Child Support had not been rebutted; and

(iii) How, in its determination:

(I) Application of the Presumptive Amount of Child Support would be unjust or inappropriate; and

(II) The best interest of the Child for whom support is being determined will be served by Deviation from the Presumptive Amount of Child Support.

(C) No Deviation in the Presumptive Amount of Child Support shall be made which seriously mpairs the ability of the Custodial Parent to maintain minimally adequate housing, food, and clothing for the Child being supported by the order and to provide other basic necessities, as determined by the Court or the jury.

(2) SPECIFIC DEVIATIONS.

(A) *HIGH INCOME.* For purposes of this subparagraph, Parents are considered to be high income Parents if their Combined Adjusted Income exceeds $30,000.00 per month. For high income Parents, the Court shall set the Basic Child Support Obligation at the highest amount allowed by the Child Support Obligation Table but the Court or the jury may consider upward Deviation to attain an appropriate award of child support for high-income Parents which is consistent with the best interest of the Child.

(B) *LOW INCOME.* For purposes of this subparagraph, 'low income person' means a Parent whose annual Gross Income is at or below $1,850.00 per month.

(i) If the Noncustodial Parent is a low income person and requests a Deviation on such basis, the Court or the jury shall determine if the Noncustodial Parent will be financially able to pay the child support order and maintain at least a minimum standard of living by calculating a selfsupport reserve as set forth in division (ii) of this subparagraph. The Court or the jury shall take into account all nonexcluded sources of income available to each Parent and all reasonable expenses of each Parent, ensuring that such expenses are actually paid by the Parent and are clearly justified expenses. The Court or the jury shall also consider the financial impact that a reduction in the amount of child support paid to the Custodial Parent would have on the Custodial Parent's household. Under no circumstances shall the amount of child support awarded to the Custodial Parent impair the ability of the Custodial Parent to maintain minimally adequate housing, food, and clothing and provide for other basic necessities for the child being supported by the court order.

(ii) To calculate the self-support reserve for the Noncustodial Parent, the Court or the jury shall deduct $900.00 from the Noncustodial Parent's Adjusted Income. If the resulting amount is less than the Noncustodial Parent's pro rata responsibility of the Presumptive Amount of Child Support, the Court or the jury may deviate from the amount of support provided for in the Child Support Obligation Table to the resulting amount. If the child support award amount would be less than $75.00, then the minimum child support order amount shall be $75.00.

(iii) If the Custodial Parent is a low income person, the Court or the jury shall subtract $900.00 from the Custodial Parent's Adjusted Income. If the resulting amount is less than the Custodial Parent's pro rata responsibility of the Presumptive Amount of Child Support, the Court or the jury shall not deviate from the amount of support required to be paid by the Noncustodial Parent as provided for in the Child Support Obligation Table.

(iv) The self-support reserve calculation described in this subparagraph shall apply only to the current child support amount and shall not prohibit an additional amount being ordered to reduce an obligor's arrears.

(v) The Court shall make a written finding in its order or the jury shall find by special interrogatory that the low income Deviation from the Presumptive Amount of Child Support is clearly justified based upon the considerations and calculations described in this subparagraph.

(C) *OTHER HEALTH-RELATED INSURANCE.* If the Court or the jury finds that either Parent has vision or dental insurance available at a reasonable cost for the Child, the Court may deviate from the Presumptive Amount of Child Support for the cost of such insurance.

(D) *LIFE INSURANCE.* In accordance with Code Section 19-6-34, if the Court or the jury finds that either Parent has purchased life insurance on the life of either Parent or the lives of both Parents for the benefit of the Child, the Court may deviate from the Presumptive Amount of Child Support for the cost of such insurance by either adding or subtracting the amount of the premium.

(E) *CHILD AND DEPENDENT CARE TAX CREDIT.* If the Court or the jury finds that one of the Parents is entitled to the Child and Dependent Care Tax Credit, the Court or the jury may deviate from the Presumptive Amount of Child Support in consideration of such credit.

(F) *TRAVEL EXPENSES.* If court ordered visitation related travel expenses are substantial due to the distance between the Parents, the Court may order the allocation of such costs or the jury may by a finding in its special interrogatory allocate such costs by Deviation from the Presumptive Amount of Child Support, taking into consideration the circumstances of the respective Parents as well as which Parent moved and the reason for such move.

(G) *ALIMONY.* Actual payments of alimony shall not be considered as a deduction from Gross Income but may be considered as a Deviation from the Presumptive Amount of Child Support. If the Court or the jury considers the actual payment of alimony, the Court shall make a written finding of such consideration or the jury in its special interrogatory of such consideration as a basis for Deviation from the Presumptive Amount of Child Support.

(H) *MORTGAGE.* If the Noncustodial Parent is providing shelter, such as paying the mortgage of the home, or has provided a home at no cost to the Custodial Parent in which the Child resides, the Court or the jury may allocate such costs or an amount equivalent to such costs by Deviation from the Presumptive Amount of Child Support, taking into consideration the circumstances of the respective Parents and the best interest of the Child.

(I) *PERMANENCY PLAN OR FOSTER CARE PLAN.* In cases where the Child is in the legal custody of the Department of Human Resources, the child protection or foster care agency of another state or territory, or any other child-caring entity, public or private, the Court or the jury may consider a Deviation from the Presumptive Amount of Child Support if the Deviation will assist in accomplishing a permanency plan or foster care plan for the Child that has a goal of returning the Child to the Parent or Parents and the Parent's need to establish an adequate household or to otherwise adequately prepare herself or himself for the return of the Child clearly justifies a Deviation for this purpose.

(J) *EXTRAORDINARY EXPENSES.* The Child Support Obligation Table includes average child rearing expenditures for families given the Parents' Combined Adjusted Income and number of children. Extraordinary expenses are in excess of average amounts estimated in the Child Support Obligation Table and are highly variable among families. Extraordinary expenses shall be considered on a case-by-case basis in the calculation of support and may form the basis for Deviation from the Presumptive Amount of Child Support so that the actual amount of the expense is considered in the calculation of the Final Child Support Order for only those families actually incurring the expense. Extraordinary expenses shall be prorated between the Parents.

(i) *Extraordinary educational expenses.* Extraordinary educational expenses may be a basis for Deviation from the Presumptive Amount of Child Support. Extraordinary educational expenses include, but are not limited to, tuition, room and board, lab fees, books, fees, and other reasonable and necessary expenses associated with special needs education or private elementary and secondary schooling that are appropriate to the Parent's financial abilities and to the lifestyle of the Child if the Parents and the Child were living together.

(I) In determining the amount of Deviation for extraordinary educational expenses, scholarships, grants, stipends, and other cost-reducing programs received by or on behalf of the Child shall be considered; and

(II) If a Deviation is allowed for extraordinary educational expenses, a monthly average of the extraordinary educational expenses shall be based on evidence of prior or anticipated expenses and entered on the Child Support Schedule E – Deviations.

(ii) *Special expenses incurred for child rearing.* Special expenses incurred for child rearing, including, but not limited to, quantifiable expense variations related to the food, clothing, and hygiene costs of children at different age levels, may be a basis for a Deviation from the Presumptive Amount of Child Support. Such expenses include, but are not limited to, summer camp; music or art lessons; travel; school sponsored extracurricular activities, such as band, clubs, and athletics; and other activities intended to enhance the athletic, social, or cultural development of a Child but not otherwise required to be used in calculating the Presumptive Amount of Child Support as are Health Insurance premiums and Work Related Child Care Costs. A portion of the Basic Child Support Obligation is intended to cover average amounts of special expenses incurred in the rearing of a Child. In order to determine if a Deviation for special expenses is warranted, the Court or the jury shall consider the full amount of the special expenses as described in this division; and when these special expenses exceed 7 percent of the Basic Child Support Obligation, then the additional amount of special expenses shall be considered as a Deviation to cover the full amount of the special expenses.

(iii) *Extraordinary medical expenses.* In instances of extreme economic hardship involving extraordinary medical expenses not covered by insurance, the Court or the jury may consider a Deviation from the Presumptive Amount of Child Support for extraordinary medical expenses. Such expenses may include, but are not limited to, extraordinary medical expenses of the Child, a Parent, or a Child of a Parent's current family; provided, however, that any such Deviation:

(I) Shall not act to leave a Child unsupported; and

(II) May be ordered for a specific period of time measured in months. When extraordinary medical expenses are claimed, the Court or the jury shall consider the resources available for meeting such needs, including sources available from agencies and other adults.

(K) *PARENTING TIME.*

(i) The Child Support Obligation Table is based upon expenditures for a Child in intact households. The Court may order or the jury may find by special interrogatory a Deviation from the Presumptive Amount of Child Support when special circumstances make the Presumptive Amount of Child Support excessive or inadequate due to extended parenting time or when the Child resides with both Parents equally.

(ii) If the Court or the jury determines that a parenting time Deviation is applicable, then such Deviation shall be applied to the Noncustodial Parent's Basic Child Support Obligation.

(iii) In accordance with subsection (d) of Code Section 19-11-8, if any action or claim for parenting time is brought under this subparagraph, it shall be an action or claim solely between the Custodial Parent and the Noncustodial Parent, and not any third parties, including the Child Support Enforcement Agency.

(3) NONSPECIFIC DEVIATIONS. Deviation from the Presumptive Amount of Child Support may be appropriate for reasons in addition to those established under this subsection when the Court or the jury finds it is in the best interest of the Child. If the circumstances which supported the Deviation cease to exist, the Final Child Support Order may be modified as set forth in subsection (k) of this Code section to eliminate the Deviation.

(j) *Involuntary loss of income.*

(1) In the event a Parent suffers an involuntary termination of employment, has an extended involuntary loss of average weekly hours, is involved in an organized strike, incurs a loss of health, or similar involuntary adversity resulting in a loss of income of 25 percent or more, then the portion of child support attributable to lost income shall not accrue from the date of the service of the petition for modification, provided that service is made on the other Parent. It shall not be considered an involuntary termination of employment if the Parent has left the employer without good cause in connection with the Parent's most recent work.

(2) In the event a modification action is filed pursuant to this subsection, the Court shall make every effort to expedite hearing such action.

(3) The Court may, at its discretion, phase in the new child support award over a period of up to one year with the phasing in being largely evenly distributed with at least an initial immediate adjustment of not less than 25 percent of the difference and at least one intermediate adjustment prior to the final adjustment at the end of the phase-in period. In the new child support award over a period of up to two years with the phasing in being largely evenly distributed with at least an initial immediate adjustment of not less than 25 percent of the difference and at least one intermediate adjustment prior to the final adjustment at the end of the phase-in period.

(k) *Modification.*

(1) Except as provided in paragraph (2) of this subsection, a Parent shall not have the right to petition for modification of the child support award regardless of the length of time since the establishment of the child support award unless there is a substantial change in either Parents' income and financial status or the needs of the Child.

(2) No petition to modify child support may be filed by either Parent within a period of two years rom the date of the final order on a previous petition to modify by the same Parent except where:

(A) A Noncustodial Parent has failed to exercise the court ordered visitation;

(B) A Noncustodial Parent has exercised a greater amount of visitation than was provided in the court order; or

(C) The motion to modify is based upon an involuntary loss of income as set forth in subsection (j) of this Code section.

(3)(A) If there is a difference of at least 15 percent but less than 30 percent between a new award and a Georgia child support order entered prior to January 1, 2007, the Court may, at its discretion, phase in the new child support award over a period of up to one year with the phasing in being largely evenly distributed with at least an initial immediate adjustment of not less than 25 percent of the difference and at least one intermediate adjustment prior to the final adjustment at the end of the phase-in period.

(B) If there is a difference of 30 percent or more between a new award and a Georgia child support order entered prior to January 1, 2007, the Court may, at its discretion, phase in the new child support award over a period of up to two years with the phasing in being largely evenly distributed with at least an initial immediate adjustment of not less than 25 percent of the difference and at least one intermediate adjustment prior to the final adjustment at the end of the phase-in period.

(C) All IV-D case reviews and modifications shall proceed and be governed by Code Section 19-11-12. Subsequent changes to the Child Support Obligation Table shall be a reason to request a review for modification from the IV-D agency to the extent that such changes are consistent with the requirements of Code Section 19-11-12.

(4) A petition for modification shall be filed and returnable under the same rules of procedure applicable to divorce proceedings. A jury may be demanded on a petition for modification but the jury shall only be responsible for determining a Parent's Gross Income and any Deviations. In the hearing upon a petition for modification, testimony may be given and evidence introduced relative to the change of circumstances, income and financial status of either Parent, or in the needs of the Child. After hearing both parties and the evidence, the Court may modify and revise the previous judgment, in accordance with the changed circumstances, income and financial status of either Parent, or in the needs of the Child, if such change or changes are satisfactorily proven so as to warrant the modification and revision and such modification and revisions are in the Child's best interest. The Court shall enter a written order specifying the basis for the modification, if any, and shall include all of the information set forth in paragraph (2) of subsection (c) of this Code section.

(5) In proceedings for the modification of a child support award pursuant to the provisions of this Code section, the Court may award attorney's fees, costs, and expenses of litigation to the prevailing party as the interests of justice may require. Where a Custodial Parent prevails in an upward modification of child support based upon the Noncustodial Parent's failure to be available and willing to exercise court ordered visitation, reasonable and necessary attorney's fees and expenses of litigation shall be awarded to the Custodial Parent.

(l) *Split Parenting.* In cases of Split Parenting, a Worksheet shall be prepared separately for the Child for whom the father is the Custodial Parent and for the Child for whom the mother is the Custodial Parent, and that Worksheet shall be filed with the clerk of court. For each Split Parenting custodial situation, the Court shall determine:

(1) Which Parent is the obligor;

(2) The Presumptive Amount of Child Support;

(3) The actual award of child support, if different from the Presumptive Amount of Child Support;

(4) How and when the sum certain amount of child support owed shall be paid; and

(5) Any other child support responsibilities for each Parent.

(m) *Worksheets.*

(1) The Child Support Worksheet is used to record information necessary to determine and calculate child support. Schedules and Worksheets shall be prepared by the parties for purposes of calculating the amount of child support. Information from the schedules shall be entered on the Child Support Worksheet. The Child Support Worksheet and Schedule E shall be attached to the final court order or judgment, and any schedules completed by the parties shall be filed with the clerk of court.

(2) The Child Support Worksheet and schedules shall be promulgated by the Georgia Child Support Commission.

(n) *Child Support Obligation Table.* The Child Support Obligation Table shall be proposed by the Georgia Child Support Commission and shall be as codified in subsection (o) of this Code section.

(o) *Georgia Schedule of Basic Child Support Obligations.*

NOTE: TABLE APPEARS IN ITS ENTIRETY IN FORM 3 FOUND IN APPENDIX C. THE TABLE WAS REMOVED HERE FOR SPACE REASONS.

SECTION 5.

Said title is further amended by striking subsection (b) of Code Section 19-6-34, relating to inclusion of life insurance in an order of support, and inserting in lieu thereof the following:

"(b) The amount of the premium for such life insurance may be considered as a deviation to the presumptive amount of child support pursuant to the provisions of Code Section 19-6-15, provided that the court shall review the amount of the premium for reasonableness under the circumstances of the case and the best interest of the child."

SECTION 6.

Said title is further amended by striking subsection (a) of Code Section 19-6-53, relating to the duties of the Georgia Child Support Commission, and inserting in lieu thereof the following:

"(a) The commission shall have the following duties:

(1) To study and evaluate the effectiveness and efficiency of Georgia's child support guidelines;

(2) To evaluate and consider the experiences and results in other states which utilize child support guidelines;

(3)(A) To create and recommend to the General Assembly a child support obligation table consistent with Code Section 19-6-15. Prior to January 1, 2006, the commission shall produce the child support obligation table and provide an explanation of the underlying data and assumptions to the General Assembly by delivering copies to the President Pro Tempore of the Senate and the Speaker of the House of Representatives.

(B)(i) The child support obligation table shall include deductions from a parent's gross income for the employee's share of the contributions for the first 6.2 percent in Federal Insurance Contributions Act (FICA) and 1.45 percent in medicare taxes.

(ii) FICA tax withholding for high-income persons may vary during the year. Six and twotenths percent is withheld on the first $90,000.00 of gross earnings. After the maximum $5,580.00 is withheld, no additional FICA taxes shall be withheld.

(iii) Self-employed persons are required by law to pay the full FICA tax of 12.4 percent up to the $90,000.00 gross earnings limit and the full medicare tax rate of 2.9 percent on all earned income.

(iv) The percentages and dollar amounts established or referenced in this subparagraph with respect to the payment of self-employment taxes shall be adjusted by the commission, as necessary, as relevant changes occur in the federal tax laws;

(4) To determine periodically, and at least every two years, if the child support obligation table results in appropriate presumptive awards;

(5) To identify and recommend whether and when the child support obligation table or child support guidelines should be modified;

(6) To develop, publish, and update the child support obligation table and worksheets and schedules associated with the use of such table;

(7) To develop or cause to be developed software and a calculator associated with the use of the child support obligation table and child support guidelines;

(8) To develop training manuals and information to educate judges, attorneys, and litigants on the use of the child support obligation table and child support guidelines;

(9) To collaborate with the Institute for Continuing Judicial Education, the Institute of Continuing Legal Education, and other agencies for the purpose of training persons who will be utilizing the child support obligation table and child support guidelines;

(10) To make recommendations for proposed legislation;

(11) To study the appellate courts' acceptance of discretionary appeals in domestic relations cases and the formulation of case law in the area of domestic relations;

(12) To study alternative programs, such as mediation, collaborative practice, and pro se assistance programs, in order to reduce litigation in child support and child custody cases; and

(13) To study the impact of having parenting time serve as a deviation to the presumptive amount of child support and make recommendations concerning the utilization of the parenting time adjustment."

SECTION 7.

Said title is further amended by striking Code Section 19-7-2, relating to parents' obligations to child, and inserting in lieu thereof the following: "19-7-2.

It is the joint and several duty of each parent to provide for the maintenance, protection, and education of his or her child until the child reaches the age of majority, dies, marries, or becomes emancipated, whichever first occurs, except as otherwise authorized and ordered pursuant to subsection (e) of Code Section 19-6-15 and except to the extent that the duty of the parents is therwise or further defined by court order."

SECTION 8.

An Act amending Titles 5, 7, and 19 of the Official Code of Georgia Annotated so as to state legislative findings, change provisions relating to calculation of child support, and make other related changes, approved April 22, 2005 (Ga. L. 2005, p. 224), is amended by striking Section 13 and inserting in its place a new Section 13 to read as follows: "SECTION 13. Section 11 of this Act shall become effective upon its approval by the Governor or upon its becoming law without such approval, and the remaining sections of this Act shall become effective on January 1, 2007."

SECTION 9.

It is the intention of this Act to delay for six months the effectiveness of the provisions of 2005 Act No. 52 of the General Assembly, excepting only those provisions of 2005 Act No. 52 creating the Georgia Child Support Commission which went into effect upon approval of that Act by the Governor.

SECTION 10.

(a) This section and Sections 8, 9, and 11 of this Act shall become effective upon their approval by the Governor or upon becoming law without such approval. (b) Sections 1 through 7 of this Act shall become effective on January 1, 2007, and shall apply to all pending civil actions on or after January 1, 2007.

SECTION 11.

All laws and parts of laws in conflict with this Act are repealed.

Live Broadcast | Legislative Search | Find Your Legislator | Picture Book | FAQ | Help | Previous Sessions 2005 Summary of General Statutes | Georgia Code | State Departments

This information is provided in electronic format by the Georgia general Assembly as a public service. This information does not constitute an official record of the General Assembly and no warranty or guarantee of any kind is provided.

Appendix C: Blank Forms

Most of the forms you need to complete your divorce are included in this appendix. However, you should know that many counties have their own forms that you can use. In some counties, you may be required to use their forms, so always check with the county clerk to be sure the forms in this book will work for your situation.

Instructions for completing the forms are found throughout the book. You will not need to use all of the forms in this appendix. The forms are listed on the following page, both by number and title. The page number given is where each form begins.

While these forms are perforated for your use, you may also want to make copies of the blanks to use as practice worksheets.

Table of Forms

Where to find additional forms. This book is designed for the most typical of divorce situations. In unusual situations there are numerous forms that can be filed to obtain various results. These include forms for such matters as protection from domestic violence, ordering drug testing, the appointment of a guardian ad litem for your children, counseling and psychological examinations, mediation, preventing the removal of children from the state and denial of passport services, and dismissing a divorce case due a reconciliation with your spouse.

There are two basic sources of legal forms. The first is the law library. Ask the librarian where to find divorce form books. There are specific guides to divorce matters that will contain forms, and there are also general legal form books containing forms on all kinds of legal matters. (See the section in Chapter 2 on legal research for the titles of some of these books.) The second source is the court clerk, who may have standardized forms for certain matters.

PROPERTY INVENTORY

(1) N-M	(2) DESCRIPTION	(3) ID#	(4) VALUE	(5) BALANCE OWED	(6) EQUITY	(7) OWNER H-W-J	(8) H	(9) W

This page intentionally blank.

DEBT INVENTORY

(1) N-M	(2) CREDITOR	(3) ACCOUNT NO.	(4) NOTES	(5) MONTHLY PAYMENT	(6) BALANCE OWED	(7) DATE	(8) OWNER H-W-J	(9) H	(10) W

This page intentionally blank.

Downloadable Child Support Guidelines Calculator

User Guide

General Information

The Downloadable Child Support Guidelines Calculator is a Microsoft Excel™ file (.xls). All of the functionality of Microsoft Excel™ is present in the file, but the worksheets have been protected so that you may only modify the input fields, which are highlighted in yellow. **It is recommended that you print a copy of this Guide to refer to as you use this calculator.**

Contents of the Calculator

The Calculator contains ten workbook tabs that are labled as indicated below:

(1) Start Here
(2) BCSO (the Basic Child Support Obligation Table)
(3) CS Worksheet (the Child Support Worksheet)
(4) Schedule A (Gross Income)
(5) Schedule B (Adjusted Income)
(6) Schedule C (RESERVED FOR FUTURE USE)
(7) Schedule D (Additional Expenses)
(8) Schedule D Supplemental Tables (Additional Supplemental Tables 2, 3 & 4)
(9) Schedule E (Deviation Special Circumstances)
(10) Schedule E Supplemental Tables (Additional Supplemental Tables 2, 3 & 4)

You may navigate between these worksheets using the tabs at the bottom of the screen.

Saving the File

After you open the Calculator in Excel™ to begin calculating child support for a case, it is recommended that you save the file. To do so, you should always select 'Save As' from the 'File' menu located at the upper left of the screen. Select a location to save the file and always give the file a new name, perhaps using the case number for the file name. Be sure to always save as an Excel™ workbook (.xls) file to avoid overwriting the original template file. If you do overwrite this file, it may be to your best benefit to download the file again.

A few other things to know...

For fields that use a drop-down menu, such as the County and Court fields, you must place your cursor or mouse over the field and click to reveal a drop down box. Click the down arrow button and selections will appear. Choose from the information contained in the drop down box.

Updating fields where boxes appear. Place your cursor or mouse over the box and click to reveal a drop down box. Click the down arrow button to show the selections. For fields with an X or ☐ as the options in the drop-down box, choosing X makes your selection Active, and choosing ☐ makes your selection Inactive.

Calculations will occur automatically as yellow fields are updated with dollar amounts.

ATTENTION First Time Users

Make sure your version of Microsoft Excel™ is using the Analysis Tool Pak. How? Click on Tools and select Add-Ins - Check the box for the Analysis ToolPak and click OK to make this feature active. If this feature is not active, the Georgia Basic Child Support Obligation Table will not import amounts into the Excel™ Child Support Guidelines Calculator.

Step 1 – Begin by clicking the CS Worksheet tab

Click the Court and County boxes and select an option from the drop down box .

Type in names of Plaintiff, Defendant, Mother, Father and Nonparent Custodian, if involved in action, in appropriate fields provided.

Type Civil Action Case No. and IV-D Case No., if one applies, in appropriate fields provided.

Select Initial Action or Modification by selecting X option from the drop down box.

For Modification actions enter "Date of the Initial Support Order".

To add children, Click box to the left of child's name field.

Choose X for each child to identify children involved in action.

Total Number of Children will automatically populate.

Type name and date of birth for each child in appropriate fields provided.

Type in name of person submitting Worksheet.

Select Noncustodial Parent as Mother or Father by clicking the box to the left Mother and Father fields.
If case includes Nonparent Custodian, select Nonparent Custodian and select Mother and Father as Noncustodial Parents.

If Social Security Amount applies, enter amount.

Step 2 - Schedule A

Select TANF for a Parent if that Parent receives a monthly grant for Temporary Assistance for Needy Families.
Do not include income for a Nonparent Custodian.
Enter Income amounts.

Enter Income amounts.

Step 3 - Schedule B

If Self Employment applies, enter the amount on Line 2 for the appropriate Parent.

If Pre-Existing Support Orders apply, enter the information and amounts starting at Line 7(a).

If after reading Questions A – E, Qualified Children Apply, enter the required information on Line 10. Select the box under "Mark X if Mother (or Father) is Claiming Credit" to indicate applicable parent.

Select X under the Date of Birth Column for the Total number of QUALIFIED children for whom adjustment is being claimed. If this box is not selected with an X, a calculation will not occur for this section.

Step 4 - Schedule D

Enter Health Insurance Premiums Paid for the Children on Line 2

Enter Work Related Child Care for each Parent and/or the Nonparent Custodian in the Supplemental Table 1 .
 Use Schedule D Supplemental Tables Tab for 4 or more.

Step 5 - Schedule E

Enter High Income and Other amounts that apply to the case.

Enter Parenting Time Deviation that apply to the case.
This amount should be entered only as a positive dollar amount on Line 13.

Extraordinary Educational, Medical and Special Expenses for Child Rearing are entered on Supplemental Table 1.
Use Schedule E Supplemental Tables Tab for 4 or more children.

The Deviation total appears on Line 14.

Step 6 - CS Worksheet

Review CS Worksheet -The Amount on Line 13 is the Final Child Support Amount

Indicate Schedules attached to Worksheet by selecting Checkmark option from the drop-down box under Attached columns.

Indicate Schedules Not Applicable to the case by selecting Checkmark option from the drop-down box under Not Applicable column.

Georgia
Schedule of Basic Child Support Obligations

COMBINED ADJUSTED GROSS INCOME		ONE CHILD	TWO CHILDREN	THREE CHILDREN	FOUR CHILDREN	FIVE CHILDREN	SIX CHILDREN
$ 800.00		$ 197.00	$ 283.00	$ 330.00	$ 367.00	$ 404.00	$ 440.00
$ 850.00		$ 208.00	$ 298.00	$ 347.00	$ 387.00	$ 425.00	$ 463.00
$ 900.00		$ 218.00	$ 313.00	$ 364.00	$ 406.00	$ 447.00	$ 486.00
$ 950.00		$ 229.00	$ 328.00	$ 381.00	$ 425.00	$ 468.00	$ 509.00
$ 1,000.00		$ 239.00	$ 343.00	$ 398.00	$ 444.00	$ 489.00	$ 532.00
$ 1,050.00		$ 250.00	$ 357.00	$ 415.00	$ 463.00	$ 510.00	$ 554.00
$ 1,100.00		$ 260.00	$ 372.00	$ 432.00	$ 482.00	$ 530.00	$ 577.00
$ 1,150.00		$ 270.00	$ 387.00	$ 449.00	$ 501.00	$ 551.00	$ 600.00
$ 1,200.00		$ 280.00	$ 401.00	$ 466.00	$ 520.00	$ 572.00	$ 622.00
$ 1,250.00		$ 291.00	$ 416.00	$ 483.00	$ 539.00	$ 593.00	$ 645.00
$ 1,300.00		$ 301.00	$ 431.00	$ 500.00	$ 558.00	$ 614.00	$ 668.00
$ 1,350.00		$ 311.00	$ 445.00	$ 517.00	$ 577.00	$ 634.00	$ 690.00
$ 1,400.00		$ 321.00	$ 459.00	$ 533.00	$ 594.00	$ 654.00	$ 711.00
$ 1,450.00		$ 331.00	$ 473.00	$ 549.00	$ 612.00	$ 673.00	$ 733.00
$ 1,500.00		$ 340.00	$ 487.00	$ 565.00	$ 630.00	$ 693.00	$ 754.00
$ 1,550.00		$ 350.00	$ 500.00	$ 581.00	$ 647.00	$ 712.00	$ 775.00
$ 1,600.00		$ 360.00	$ 514.00	$ 597.00	$ 665.00	$ 732.00	$ 796.00
$ 1,650.00		$ 369.00	$ 528.00	$ 612.00	$ 683.00	$ 751.00	$ 817.00
$ 1,700.00		$ 379.00	$ 542.00	$ 628.00	$ 701.00	$ 771.00	$ 838.00
$ 1,750.00		$ 389.00	$ 555.00	$ 644.00	$ 718.00	$ 790.00	$ 860.00
$ 1,800.00		$ 398.00	$ 569.00	$ 660.00	$ 736.00	$ 809.00	$ 881.00
$ 1,850.00		$ 408.00	$ 583.00	$ 676.00	$ 754.00	$ 829.00	$ 902.00
$ 1,900.00		$ 418.00	$ 596.00	$ 692.00	$ 771.00	$ 848.00	$ 923.00
$ 1,950.00		$ 427.00	$ 610.00	$ 708.00	$ 789.00	$ 868.00	$ 944.00
$ 2,000.00		$ 437.00	$ 624.00	$ 723.00	$ 807.00	$ 887.00	$ 965.00
$ 2,050.00		$ 446.00	$ 637.00	$ 739.00	$ 824.00	$ 906.00	$ 986.00
$ 2,100.00		$ 455.00	$ 650.00	$ 754.00	$ 840.00	$ 924.00	$ 1,006.00
$ 2,150.00		$ 465.00	$ 663.00	$ 769.00	$ 857.00	$ 943.00	$ 1,026.00
$ 2,200.00		$ 474.00	$ 676.00	$ 783.00	$ 873.00	$ 961.00	$ 1,045.00
$ 2,250.00		$ 483.00	$ 688.00	$ 798.00	$ 890.00	$ 979.00	$ 1,065.00
$ 2,300.00		$ 492.00	$ 701.00	$ 813.00	$ 907.00	$ 997.00	$ 1,085.00
$ 2,350.00		$ 501.00	$ 714.00	$ 828.00	$ 923.00	$ 1,016.00	$ 1,105.00
$ 2,400.00		$ 510.00	$ 727.00	$ 843.00	$ 940.00	$ 1,034.00	$ 1,125.00
$ 2,450.00		$ 519.00	$ 740.00	$ 858.00	$ 956.00	$ 1,052.00	$ 1,145.00
$ 2,500.00		$ 528.00	$ 752.00	$ 873.00	$ 973.00	$ 1,070.00	$ 1,165.00
$ 2,550.00		$ 537.00	$ 765.00	$ 888.00	$ 990.00	$ 1,089.00	$ 1,184.00
$ 2,600.00		$ 547.00	$ 778.00	$ 902.00	$ 1,006.00	$ 1,107.00	$ 1,204.00
$ 2,650.00		$ 556.00	$ 791.00	$ 917.00	$ 1,023.00	$ 1,125.00	$ 1,224.00
$ 2,700.00		$ 565.00	$ 804.00	$ 932.00	$ 1,039.00	$ 1,143.00	$ 1,244.00
$ 2,750.00		$ 574.00	$ 816.00	$ 947.00	$ 1,056.00	$ 1,162.00	$ 1,264.00
$ 2,800.00		$ 583.00	$ 829.00	$ 962.00	$ 1,073.00	$ 1,180.00	$ 1,284.00
$ 2,850.00		$ 592.00	$ 842.00	$ 977.00	$ 1,089.00	$ 1,198.00	$ 1,303.00
$ 2,900.00		$ 601.00	$ 855.00	$ 992.00	$ 1,106.00	$ 1,216.00	$ 1,323.00
$ 2,950.00		$ 611.00	$ 868.00	$ 1,006.00	$ 1,122.00	$ 1,234.00	$ 1,343.00
$ 3,000.00		$ 620.00	$ 881.00	$ 1,021.00	$ 1,139.00	$ 1,253.00	$ 1,363.00
$ 3,050.00		$ 629.00	$ 893.00	$ 1,036.00	$ 1,155.00	$ 1,271.00	$ 1,383.00
$ 3,100.00		$ 638.00	$ 906.00	$ 1,051.00	$ 1,172.00	$ 1,289.00	$ 1,402.00
$ 3,150.00		$ 647.00	$ 919.00	$ 1,066.00	$ 1,188.00	$ 1,307.00	$ 1,422.00
$ 3,200.00		$ 655.00	$ 930.00	$ 1,079.00	$ 1,203.00	$ 1,323.00	$ 1,440.00
$ 3,250.00		$ 663.00	$ 941.00	$ 1,092.00	$ 1,217.00	$ 1,339.00	$ 1,457.00
$ 3,300.00		$ 671.00	$ 952.00	$ 1,104.00	$ 1,231.00	$ 1,355.00	$ 1,474.00
$ 3,350.00		$ 679.00	$ 963.00	$ 1,117.00	$ 1,246.00	$ 1,370.00	$ 1,491.00
$ 3,400.00		$ 687.00	$ 974.00	$ 1,130.00	$ 1,260.00	$ 1,386.00	$ 1,508.00

Georgia
Schedule of Basic Child Support Obligations

COMBINED ADJUSTED GROSS INCOME		ONE CHILD	TWO CHILDREN	THREE CHILDREN	FOUR CHILDREN	FIVE CHILDREN	SIX CHILDREN
$ 3,450.00		$ 694.00	$ 985.00	$ 1,143.00	$ 1,274.00	$ 1,402.00	$ 1,525.00
$ 3,500.00		$ 702.00	$ 996.00	$ 1,155.00	$ 1,288.00	$ 1,417.00	$ 1,542.00
$ 3,550.00		$ 710.00	$ 1,008.00	$ 1,168.00	$ 1,303.00	$ 1,433.00	$ 1,559.00
$ 3,600.00		$ 718.00	$ 1,019.00	$ 1,181.00	$ 1,317.00	$ 1,448.00	$ 1,576.00
$ 3,650.00		$ 726.00	$ 1,030.00	$ 1,194.00	$ 1,331.00	$ 1,464.00	$ 1,593.00
$ 3,700.00		$ 734.00	$ 1,041.00	$ 1,207.00	$ 1,345.00	$ 1,480.00	$ 1,610.00
$ 3,750.00		$ 741.00	$ 1,051.00	$ 1,219.00	$ 1,359.00	$ 1,495.00	$ 1,627.00
$ 3,800.00		$ 749.00	$ 1,062.00	$ 1,231.00	$ 1,373.00	$ 1,510.00	$ 1,643.00
$ 3,850.00		$ 756.00	$ 1,072.00	$ 1,243.00	$ 1,386.00	$ 1,525.00	$ 1,659.00
$ 3,900.00		$ 764.00	$ 1,083.00	$ 1,255.00	$ 1,400.00	$ 1,540.00	$ 1,675.00
$ 3,950.00		$ 771.00	$ 1,093.00	$ 1,267.00	$ 1,413.00	$ 1,555.00	$ 1,691.00
$ 4,000.00		$ 779.00	$ 1,104.00	$ 1,280.00	$ 1,427.00	$ 1,569.00	$ 1,707.00
$ 4,050.00		$ 786.00	$ 1,114.00	$ 1,292.00	$ 1,440.00	$ 1,584.00	$ 1,724.00
$ 4,100.00		$ 794.00	$ 1,125.00	$ 1,304.00	$ 1,454.00	$ 1,599.00	$ 1,740.00
$ 4,150.00		$ 801.00	$ 1,135.00	$ 1,316.00	$ 1,467.00	$ 1,614.00	$ 1,756.00
$ 4,200.00		$ 809.00	$ 1,146.00	$ 1,328.00	$ 1,481.00	$ 1,629.00	$ 1,772.00
$ 4,250.00		$ 816.00	$ 1,156.00	$ 1,340.00	$ 1,494.00	$ 1,643.00	$ 1,788.00
$ 4,300.00		$ 824.00	$ 1,167.00	$ 1,352.00	$ 1,508.00	$ 1,658.00	$ 1,804.00
$ 4,350.00		$ 831.00	$ 1,177.00	$ 1,364.00	$ 1,521.00	$ 1,673.00	$ 1,820.00
$ 4,400.00		$ 839.00	$ 1,188.00	$ 1,376.00	$ 1,534.00	$ 1,688.00	$ 1,836.00
$ 4,450.00		$ 846.00	$ 1,198.00	$ 1,388.00	$ 1,548.00	$ 1,703.00	$ 1,853.00
$ 4,500.00		$ 853.00	$ 1,209.00	$ 1,400.00	$ 1,561.00	$ 1,718.00	$ 1,869.00
$ 4,550.00		$ 861.00	$ 1,219.00	$ 1,412.00	$ 1,575.00	$ 1,732.00	$ 1,885.00
$ 4,600.00		$ 868.00	$ 1,230.00	$ 1,425.00	$ 1,588.00	$ 1,747.00	$ 1,901.00
$ 4,650.00		$ 876.00	$ 1,240.00	$ 1,437.00	$ 1,602.00	$ 1,762.00	$ 1,917.00
$ 4,700.00		$ 883.00	$ 1,251.00	$ 1,449.00	$ 1,615.00	$ 1,777.00	$ 1,933.00
$ 4,750.00		$ 891.00	$ 1,261.00	$ 1,461.00	$ 1,629.00	$ 1,792.00	$ 1,949.00
$ 4,800.00		$ 898.00	$ 1,271.00	$ 1,473.00	$ 1,642.00	$ 1,807.00	$ 1,966.00
$ 4,850.00		$ 906.00	$ 1,282.00	$ 1,485.00	$ 1,656.00	$ 1,821.00	$ 1,982.00
$ 4,900.00		$ 911.00	$ 1,289.00	$ 1,493.00	$ 1,664.00	$ 1,831.00	$ 1,992.00
$ 4,950.00		$ 914.00	$ 1,293.00	$ 1,496.00	$ 1,668.00	$ 1,835.00	$ 1,997.00
$ 5,000.00		$ 917.00	$ 1,297.00	$ 1,500.00	$ 1,672.00	$ 1,839.00	$ 2,001.00
$ 5,050.00		$ 921.00	$ 1,300.00	$ 1,503.00	$ 1,676.00	$ 1,844.00	$ 2,006.00
$ 5,100.00		$ 924.00	$ 1,304.00	$ 1,507.00	$ 1,680.00	$ 1,848.00	$ 2,011.00
$ 5,150.00		$ 927.00	$ 1,308.00	$ 1,510.00	$ 1,684.00	$ 1,852.00	$ 2,015.00
$ 5,200.00		$ 930.00	$ 1,312.00	$ 1,514.00	$ 1,688.00	$ 1,857.00	$ 2,020.00
$ 5,250.00		$ 934.00	$ 1,316.00	$ 1,517.00	$ 1,692.00	$ 1,861.00	$ 2,025.00
$ 5,300.00		$ 937.00	$ 1,320.00	$ 1,521.00	$ 1,696.00	$ 1,865.00	$ 2,029.00
$ 5,350.00		$ 940.00	$ 1,323.00	$ 1,524.00	$ 1,700.00	$ 1,870.00	$ 2,034.00
$ 5,400.00		$ 943.00	$ 1,327.00	$ 1,528.00	$ 1,704.00	$ 1,874.00	$ 2,039.00
$ 5,450.00		$ 947.00	$ 1,331.00	$ 1,531.00	$ 1,708.00	$ 1,878.00	$ 2,044.00
$ 5,500.00		$ 950.00	$ 1,335.00	$ 1,535.00	$ 1,711.00	$ 1,883.00	$ 2,048.00
$ 5,550.00		$ 953.00	$ 1,339.00	$ 1,538.00	$ 1,715.00	$ 1,887.00	$ 2,053.00
$ 5,600.00		$ 956.00	$ 1,342.00	$ 1,542.00	$ 1,719.00	$ 1,891.00	$ 2,058.00
$ 5,650.00		$ 960.00	$ 1,347.00	$ 1,546.00	$ 1,724.00	$ 1,896.00	$ 2,063.00
$ 5,700.00		$ 964.00	$ 1,352.00	$ 1,552.00	$ 1,731.00	$ 1,904.00	$ 2,071.00
$ 5,750.00		$ 968.00	$ 1,357.00	$ 1,558.00	$ 1,737.00	$ 1,911.00	$ 2,079.00
$ 5,800.00		$ 971.00	$ 1,363.00	$ 1,564.00	$ 1,744.00	$ 1,918.00	$ 2,087.00
$ 5,850.00		$ 975.00	$ 1,368.00	$ 1,570.00	$ 1,750.00	$ 1,925.00	$ 2,094.00
$ 5,900.00		$ 979.00	$ 1,373.00	$ 1,575.00	$ 1,757.00	$ 1,932.00	$ 2,102.00
$ 5,950.00		$ 983.00	$ 1,379.00	$ 1,581.00	$ 1,763.00	$ 1,939.00	$ 2,110.00
$ 6,000.00		$ 987.00	$ 1,384.00	$ 1,587.00	$ 1,770.00	$ 1,947.00	$ 2,118.00
$ 6,050.00		$ 991.00	$ 1,389.00	$ 1,593.00	$ 1,776.00	$ 1,954.00	$ 2,126.00
$ 6,100.00		$ 995.00	$ 1,394.00	$ 1,599.00	$ 1,783.00	$ 1,961.00	$ 2,133.00

Georgia
Schedule of Basic Child Support Obligations

COMBINED ADJUSTED GROSS INCOME		ONE CHILD	TWO CHILDREN	THREE CHILDREN	FOUR CHILDREN	FIVE CHILDREN	SIX CHILDREN
$ 6,150.00		$ 999.00	$ 1,400.00	$ 1,605.00	$ 1,789.00	$ 1,968.00	$ 2,141.00
$ 6,200.00		$ 1,003.00	$ 1,405.00	$ 1,610.00	$ 1,796.00	$ 1,975.00	$ 2,149.00
$ 6,250.00		$ 1,007.00	$ 1,410.00	$ 1,616.00	$ 1,802.00	$ 1,982.00	$ 2,157.00
$ 6,300.00		$ 1,011.00	$ 1,416.00	$ 1,622.00	$ 1,809.00	$ 1,989.00	$ 2,164.00
$ 6,350.00		$ 1,015.00	$ 1,421.00	$ 1,628.00	$ 1,815.00	$ 1,996.00	$ 2,172.00
$ 6,400.00		$ 1,018.00	$ 1,426.00	$ 1,633.00	$ 1,821.00	$ 2,003.00	$ 2,180.00
$ 6,450.00		$ 1,023.00	$ 1,432.00	$ 1,639.00	$ 1,828.00	$ 2,011.00	$ 2,188.00
$ 6,500.00		$ 1,027.00	$ 1,437.00	$ 1,646.00	$ 1,835.00	$ 2,018.00	$ 2,196.00
$ 6,550.00		$ 1,031.00	$ 1,442.00	$ 1,652.00	$ 1,841.00	$ 2,026.00	$ 2,204.00
$ 6,600.00		$ 1,035.00	$ 1,448.00	$ 1,658.00	$ 1,848.00	$ 2,033.00	$ 2,212.00
$ 6,650.00		$ 1,039.00	$ 1,453.00	$ 1,664.00	$ 1,855.00	$ 2,040.00	$ 2,220.00
$ 6,700.00		$ 1,043.00	$ 1,459.00	$ 1,670.00	$ 1,862.00	$ 2,048.00	$ 2,228.00
$ 6,750.00		$ 1,047.00	$ 1,464.00	$ 1,676.00	$ 1,869.00	$ 2,055.00	$ 2,236.00
$ 6,800.00		$ 1,051.00	$ 1,470.00	$ 1,682.00	$ 1,875.00	$ 2,063.00	$ 2,244.00
$ 6,850.00		$ 1,055.00	$ 1,475.00	$ 1,688.00	$ 1,882.00	$ 2,070.00	$ 2,252.00
$ 6,900.00		$ 1,059.00	$ 1,480.00	$ 1,694.00	$ 1,889.00	$ 2,078.00	$ 2,260.00
$ 6,950.00		$ 1,063.00	$ 1,486.00	$ 1,700.00	$ 1,896.00	$ 2,085.00	$ 2,269.00
$ 7,000.00		$ 1,067.00	$ 1,491.00	$ 1,706.00	$ 1,902.00	$ 2,092.00	$ 2,277.00
$ 7,050.00		$ 1,071.00	$ 1,497.00	$ 1,712.00	$ 1,909.00	$ 2,100.00	$ 2,285.00
$ 7,100.00		$ 1,075.00	$ 1,502.00	$ 1,718.00	$ 1,916.00	$ 2,107.00	$ 2,293.00
$ 7,150.00		$ 1,079.00	$ 1,508.00	$ 1,724.00	$ 1,923.00	$ 2,115.00	$ 2,301.00
$ 7,200.00		$ 1,083.00	$ 1,513.00	$ 1,730.00	$ 1,929.00	$ 2,122.00	$ 2,309.00
$ 7,250.00		$ 1,087.00	$ 1,518.00	$ 1,736.00	$ 1,936.00	$ 2,130.00	$ 2,317.00
$ 7,300.00		$ 1,092.00	$ 1,524.00	$ 1,742.00	$ 1,943.00	$ 2,137.00	$ 2,325.00
$ 7,350.00		$ 1,096.00	$ 1,529.00	$ 1,748.00	$ 1,950.00	$ 2,144.00	$ 2,333.00
$ 7,400.00		$ 1,100.00	$ 1,535.00	$ 1,755.00	$ 1,956.00	$ 2,152.00	$ 2,341.00
$ 7,450.00		$ 1,104.00	$ 1,540.00	$ 1,761.00	$ 1,963.00	$ 2,159.00	$ 2,349.00
$ 7,500.00		$ 1,108.00	$ 1,546.00	$ 1,767.00	$ 1,970.00	$ 2,167.00	$ 2,357.00
$ 7,550.00		$ 1,112.00	$ 1,552.00	$ 1,773.00	$ 1,977.00	$ 2,175.00	$ 2,366.00
$ 7,600.00		$ 1,116.00	$ 1,556.00	$ 1,778.00	$ 1,983.00	$ 2,181.00	$ 2,373.00
$ 7,650.00		$ 1,117.00	$ 1,557.00	$ 1,779.00	$ 1,984.00	$ 2,182.00	$ 2,375.00
$ 7,700.00		$ 1,118.00	$ 1,559.00	$ 1,781.00	$ 1,986.00	$ 2,184.00	$ 2,376.00
$ 7,750.00		$ 1,119.00	$ 1,560.00	$ 1,782.00	$ 1,987.00	$ 2,186.00	$ 2,378.00
$ 7,800.00		$ 1,120.00	$ 1,562.00	$ 1,784.00	$ 1,989.00	$ 2,188.00	$ 2,380.00
$ 7,850.00		$ 1,122.00	$ 1,563.00	$ 1,785.00	$ 1,990.00	$ 2,189.00	$ 2,382.00
$ 7,900.00		$ 1,123.00	$ 1,565.00	$ 1,786.00	$ 1,992.00	$ 2,191.00	$ 2,384.00
$ 7,950.00		$ 1,124.00	$ 1,566.00	$ 1,788.00	$ 1,993.00	$ 2,193.00	$ 2,386.00
$ 8,000.00		$ 1,125.00	$ 1,567.00	$ 1,789.00	$ 1,995.00	$ 2,194.00	$ 2,387.00
$ 8,050.00		$ 1,127.00	$ 1,569.00	$ 1,790.00	$ 1,996.00	$ 2,196.00	$ 2,389.00
$ 8,100.00		$ 1,128.00	$ 1,570.00	$ 1,792.00	$ 1,998.00	$ 2,198.00	$ 2,391.00
$ 8,150.00		$ 1,129.00	$ 1,572.00	$ 1,793.00	$ 1,999.00	$ 2,199.00	$ 2,393.00
$ 8,200.00		$ 1,130.00	$ 1,573.00	$ 1,795.00	$ 2,001.00	$ 2,201.00	$ 2,395.00
$ 8,250.00		$ 1,131.00	$ 1,575.00	$ 1,796.00	$ 2,003.00	$ 2,203.00	$ 2,397.00
$ 8,300.00		$ 1,133.00	$ 1,576.00	$ 1,797.00	$ 2,004.00	$ 2,204.00	$ 2,398.00
$ 8,350.00		$ 1,134.00	$ 1,578.00	$ 1,799.00	$ 2,006.00	$ 2,206.00	$ 2,400.00
$ 8,400.00		$ 1,135.00	$ 1,579.00	$ 1,800.00	$ 2,007.00	$ 2,208.00	$ 2,402.00
$ 8,450.00		$ 1,136.00	$ 1,580.00	$ 1,802.00	$ 2,009.00	$ 2,210.00	$ 2,404.00
$ 8,500.00		$ 1,138.00	$ 1,582.00	$ 1,803.00	$ 2,010.00	$ 2,211.00	$ 2,406.00
$ 8,550.00		$ 1,139.00	$ 1,583.00	$ 1,804.00	$ 2,012.00	$ 2,213.00	$ 2,408.00
$ 8,600.00		$ 1,140.00	$ 1,585.00	$ 1,806.00	$ 2,013.00	$ 2,215.00	$ 2,410.00
$ 8,650.00		$ 1,141.00	$ 1,586.00	$ 1,807.00	$ 2,015.00	$ 2,216.00	$ 2,411.00
$ 8,700.00		$ 1,142.00	$ 1,588.00	$ 1,808.00	$ 2,016.00	$ 2,218.00	$ 2,413.00
$ 8,750.00		$ 1,144.00	$ 1,589.00	$ 1,810.00	$ 2,018.00	$ 2,220.00	$ 2,415.00
$ 8,800.00		$ 1,145.00	$ 1,591.00	$ 1,811.00	$ 2,019.00	$ 2,221.00	$ 2,417.00

Georgia
Schedule of Basic Child Support Obligations

COMBINED ADJUSTED GROSS INCOME		ONE CHILD	TWO CHILDREN	THREE CHILDREN	FOUR CHILDREN	FIVE CHILDREN	SIX CHILDREN
$ 8,850.00		$ 1,146.00	$ 1,592.00	$ 1,813.00	$ 2,021.00	$ 2,223.00	$ 2,419.00
$ 8,900.00		$ 1,147.00	$ 1,593.00	$ 1,814.00	$ 2,023.00	$ 2,225.00	$ 2,421.00
$ 8,950.00		$ 1,149.00	$ 1,595.00	$ 1,815.00	$ 2,024.00	$ 2,226.00	$ 2,422.00
$ 9,000.00		$ 1,150.00	$ 1,596.00	$ 1,817.00	$ 2,026.00	$ 2,228.00	$ 2,424.00
$ 9,050.00		$ 1,153.00	$ 1,601.00	$ 1,822.00	$ 2,032.00	$ 2,235.00	$ 2,431.00
$ 9,100.00		$ 1,159.00	$ 1,609.00	$ 1,831.00	$ 2,042.00	$ 2,246.00	$ 2,443.00
$ 9,150.00		$ 1,164.00	$ 1,617.00	$ 1,840.00	$ 2,052.00	$ 2,257.00	$ 2,455.00
$ 9,200.00		$ 1,170.00	$ 1,624.00	$ 1,849.00	$ 2,062.00	$ 2,268.00	$ 2,467.00
$ 9,250.00		$ 1,175.00	$ 1,632.00	$ 1,858.00	$ 2,071.00	$ 2,279.00	$ 2,479.00
$ 9,300.00		$ 1,181.00	$ 1,640.00	$ 1,867.00	$ 2,081.00	$ 2,290.00	$ 2,491.00
$ 9,350.00		$ 1,187.00	$ 1,648.00	$ 1,876.00	$ 2,091.00	$ 2,301.00	$ 2,503.00
$ 9,400.00		$ 1,192.00	$ 1,656.00	$ 1,885.00	$ 2,101.00	$ 2,311.00	$ 2,515.00
$ 9,450.00		$ 1,198.00	$ 1,663.00	$ 1,894.00	$ 2,111.00	$ 2,322.00	$ 2,527.00
$ 9,500.00		$ 1,203.00	$ 1,671.00	$ 1,902.00	$ 2,121.00	$ 2,333.00	$ 2,539.00
$ 9,550.00		$ 1,209.00	$ 1,679.00	$ 1,911.00	$ 2,131.00	$ 2,344.00	$ 2,551.00
$ 9,600.00		$ 1,214.00	$ 1,687.00	$ 1,920.00	$ 2,141.00	$ 2,355.00	$ 2,563.00
$ 9,650.00		$ 1,220.00	$ 1,694.00	$ 1,929.00	$ 2,151.00	$ 2,366.00	$ 2,574.00
$ 9,700.00		$ 1,226.00	$ 1,702.00	$ 1,938.00	$ 2,161.00	$ 2,377.00	$ 2,586.00
$ 9,750.00		$ 1,231.00	$ 1,710.00	$ 1,947.00	$ 2,171.00	$ 2,388.00	$ 2,598.00
$ 9,800.00		$ 1,237.00	$ 1,718.00	$ 1,956.00	$ 2,181.00	$ 2,399.00	$ 2,610.00
$ 9,850.00		$ 1,242.00	$ 1,725.00	$ 1,965.00	$ 2,191.00	$ 2,410.00	$ 2,622.00
$ 9,900.00		$ 1,248.00	$ 1,733.00	$ 1,974.00	$ 2,201.00	$ 2,421.00	$ 2,634.00
$ 9,950.00		$ 1,253.00	$ 1,741.00	$ 1,983.00	$ 2,211.00	$ 2,432.00	$ 2,646.00
$ 10,000.00		$ 1,259.00	$ 1,749.00	$ 1,992.00	$ 2,221.00	$ 2,443.00	$ 2,658.00
$ 10,050.00		$ 1,264.00	$ 1,757.00	$ 2,001.00	$ 2,231.00	$ 2,454.00	$ 2,670.00
$ 10,100.00		$ 1,270.00	$ 1,764.00	$ 2,010.00	$ 2,241.00	$ 2,465.00	$ 2,682.00
$ 10,150.00		$ 1,276.00	$ 1,772.00	$ 2,019.00	$ 2,251.00	$ 2,476.00	$ 2,694.00
$ 10,200.00		$ 1,281.00	$ 1,780.00	$ 2,028.00	$ 2,261.00	$ 2,487.00	$ 2,706.00
$ 10,250.00		$ 1,287.00	$ 1,788.00	$ 2,036.00	$ 2,271.00	$ 2,498.00	$ 2,718.00
$ 10,300.00		$ 1,292.00	$ 1,795.00	$ 2,045.00	$ 2,281.00	$ 2,509.00	$ 2,729.00
$ 10,350.00		$ 1,298.00	$ 1,803.00	$ 2,054.00	$ 2,291.00	$ 2,520.00	$ 2,741.00
$ 10,400.00		$ 1,303.00	$ 1,811.00	$ 2,063.00	$ 2,301.00	$ 2,531.00	$ 2,753.00
$ 10,450.00		$ 1,309.00	$ 1,819.00	$ 2,072.00	$ 2,311.00	$ 2,542.00	$ 2,765.00
$ 10,500.00		$ 1,313.00	$ 1,825.00	$ 2,079.00	$ 2,318.00	$ 2,550.00	$ 2,774.00
$ 10,550.00		$ 1,317.00	$ 1,830.00	$ 2,085.00	$ 2,325.00	$ 2,557.00	$ 2,782.00
$ 10,600.00		$ 1,321.00	$ 1,835.00	$ 2,091.00	$ 2,331.00	$ 2,564.00	$ 2,790.00
$ 10,650.00		$ 1,325.00	$ 1,841.00	$ 2,096.00	$ 2,338.00	$ 2,571.00	$ 2,798.00
$ 10,700.00		$ 1,329.00	$ 1,846.00	$ 2,102.00	$ 2,344.00	$ 2,578.00	$ 2,805.00
$ 10,750.00		$ 1,332.00	$ 1,851.00	$ 2,108.00	$ 2,351.00	$ 2,586.00	$ 2,813.00
$ 10,800.00		$ 1,336.00	$ 1,856.00	$ 2,114.00	$ 2,357.00	$ 2,593.00	$ 2,821.00
$ 10,850.00		$ 1,340.00	$ 1,862.00	$ 2,120.00	$ 2,364.00	$ 2,600.00	$ 2,829.00
$ 10,900.00		$ 1,344.00	$ 1,867.00	$ 2,126.00	$ 2,370.00	$ 2,607.00	$ 2,836.00
$ 10,950.00		$ 1,348.00	$ 1,872.00	$ 2,131.00	$ 2,377.00	$ 2,614.00	$ 2,844.00
$ 11,000.00		$ 1,351.00	$ 1,877.00	$ 2,137.00	$ 2,383.00	$ 2,621.00	$ 2,852.00
$ 11,050.00		$ 1,355.00	$ 1,883.00	$ 2,143.00	$ 2,390.00	$ 2,628.00	$ 2,860.00
$ 11,100.00		$ 1,359.00	$ 1,888.00	$ 2,149.00	$ 2,396.00	$ 2,636.00	$ 2,868.00
$ 11,150.00		$ 1,363.00	$ 1,893.00	$ 2,155.00	$ 2,403.00	$ 2,643.00	$ 2,875.00
$ 11,200.00		$ 1,367.00	$ 1,898.00	$ 2,161.00	$ 2,409.00	$ 2,650.00	$ 2,883.00
$ 11,250.00		$ 1,371.00	$ 1,904.00	$ 2,166.00	$ 2,415.00	$ 2,657.00	$ 2,891.00
$ 11,300.00		$ 1,374.00	$ 1,909.00	$ 2,172.00	$ 2,422.00	$ 2,664.00	$ 2,899.00
$ 11,350.00		$ 1,378.00	$ 1,914.00	$ 2,178.00	$ 2,428.00	$ 2,671.00	$ 2,906.00
$ 11,400.00		$ 1,382.00	$ 1,919.00	$ 2,184.00	$ 2,435.00	$ 2,678.00	$ 2,914.00
$ 11,450.00		$ 1,386.00	$ 1,925.00	$ 2,190.00	$ 2,441.00	$ 2,686.00	$ 2,922.00
$ 11,500.00		$ 1,390.00	$ 1,930.00	$ 2,195.00	$ 2,448.00	$ 2,693.00	$ 2,930.00

Georgia
Schedule of Basic Child Support Obligations

COMBINED ADJUSTED GROSS INCOME		ONE CHILD	TWO CHILDREN	THREE CHILDREN	FOUR CHILDREN	FIVE CHILDREN	SIX CHILDREN
$ 11,550.00		$ 1,394.00	$ 1,935.00	$ 2,201.00	$ 2,454.00	$ 2,700.00	$ 2,938.00
$ 11,600.00		$ 1,397.00	$ 1,940.00	$ 2,207.00	$ 2,461.00	$ 2,707.00	$ 2,945.00
$ 11,650.00		$ 1,401.00	$ 1,946.00	$ 2,213.00	$ 2,467.00	$ 2,714.00	$ 2,953.00
$ 11,700.00		$ 1,405.00	$ 1,951.00	$ 2,219.00	$ 2,474.00	$ 2,721.00	$ 2,961.00
$ 11,750.00		$ 1,409.00	$ 1,956.00	$ 2,225.00	$ 2,480.00	$ 2,728.00	$ 2,969.00
$ 11,800.00		$ 1,413.00	$ 1,961.00	$ 2,230.00	$ 2,487.00	$ 2,736.00	$ 2,976.00
$ 11,850.00		$ 1,417.00	$ 1,967.00	$ 2,236.00	$ 2,493.00	$ 2,743.00	$ 2,984.00
$ 11,900.00		$ 1,420.00	$ 1,972.00	$ 2,242.00	$ 2,500.00	$ 2,750.00	$ 2,992.00
$ 11,950.00		$ 1,424.00	$ 1,977.00	$ 2,248.00	$ 2,506.00	$ 2,757.00	$ 3,000.00
$ 12,000.00		$ 1,428.00	$ 1,982.00	$ 2,254.00	$ 2,513.00	$ 2,764.00	$ 3,007.00
$ 12,050.00		$ 1,432.00	$ 1,988.00	$ 2,260.00	$ 2,519.00	$ 2,771.00	$ 3,015.00
$ 12,100.00		$ 1,436.00	$ 1,993.00	$ 2,265.00	$ 2,526.00	$ 2,779.00	$ 3,023.00
$ 12,150.00		$ 1,439.00	$ 1,998.00	$ 2,271.00	$ 2,532.00	$ 2,786.00	$ 3,031.00
$ 12,200.00		$ 1,443.00	$ 2,003.00	$ 2,277.00	$ 2,539.00	$ 2,793.00	$ 3,039.00
$ 12,250.00		$ 1,447.00	$ 2,009.00	$ 2,283.00	$ 2,545.00	$ 2,800.00	$ 3,046.00
$ 12,300.00		$ 1,451.00	$ 2,014.00	$ 2,289.00	$ 2,552.00	$ 2,807.00	$ 3,054.00
$ 12,350.00		$ 1,455.00	$ 2,019.00	$ 2,295.00	$ 2,558.00	$ 2,814.00	$ 3,062.00
$ 12,400.00		$ 1,459.00	$ 2,024.00	$ 2,300.00	$ 2,565.00	$ 2,821.00	$ 3,070.00
$ 12,450.00		$ 1,462.00	$ 2,030.00	$ 2,306.00	$ 2,571.00	$ 2,829.00	$ 3,077.00
$ 12,500.00		$ 1,466.00	$ 2,035.00	$ 2,312.00	$ 2,578.00	$ 2,836.00	$ 3,085.00
$ 12,550.00		$ 1,470.00	$ 2,040.00	$ 2,318.00	$ 2,584.00	$ 2,843.00	$ 3,093.00
$ 12,600.00		$ 1,474.00	$ 2,045.00	$ 2,324.00	$ 2,591.00	$ 2,850.00	$ 3,101.00
$ 12,650.00		$ 1,477.00	$ 2,050.00	$ 2,329.00	$ 2,597.00	$ 2,857.00	$ 3,108.00
$ 12,700.00		$ 1,481.00	$ 2,055.00	$ 2,335.00	$ 2,603.00	$ 2,863.00	$ 3,115.00
$ 12,750.00		$ 1,484.00	$ 2,060.00	$ 2,340.00	$ 2,609.00	$ 2,870.00	$ 3,123.00
$ 12,800.00		$ 1,487.00	$ 2,064.00	$ 2,345.00	$ 2,615.00	$ 2,877.00	$ 3,130.00
$ 12,850.00		$ 1,491.00	$ 2,069.00	$ 2,351.00	$ 2,621.00	$ 2,883.00	$ 3,137.00
$ 12,900.00		$ 1,494.00	$ 2,074.00	$ 2,356.00	$ 2,627.00	$ 2,890.00	$ 3,144.00
$ 12,950.00		$ 1,497.00	$ 2,078.00	$ 2,361.00	$ 2,633.00	$ 2,896.00	$ 3,151.00
$ 13,000.00		$ 1,501.00	$ 2,083.00	$ 2,367.00	$ 2,639.00	$ 2,903.00	$ 3,158.00
$ 13,050.00		$ 1,504.00	$ 2,087.00	$ 2,372.00	$ 2,645.00	$ 2,909.00	$ 3,165.00
$ 13,100.00		$ 1,507.00	$ 2,092.00	$ 2,377.00	$ 2,651.00	$ 2,916.00	$ 3,172.00
$ 13,150.00		$ 1,510.00	$ 2,097.00	$ 2,383.00	$ 2,657.00	$ 2,922.00	$ 3,180.00
$ 13,200.00		$ 1,514.00	$ 2,101.00	$ 2,388.00	$ 2,663.00	$ 2,929.00	$ 3,187.00
$ 13,250.00		$ 1,517.00	$ 2,106.00	$ 2,393.00	$ 2,668.00	$ 2,935.00	$ 3,193.00
$ 13,300.00		$ 1,520.00	$ 2,110.00	$ 2,398.00	$ 2,674.00	$ 2,941.00	$ 3,200.00
$ 13,350.00		$ 1,523.00	$ 2,114.00	$ 2,403.00	$ 2,679.00	$ 2,947.00	$ 3,206.00
$ 13,400.00		$ 1,526.00	$ 2,118.00	$ 2,408.00	$ 2,685.00	$ 2,953.00	$ 3,213.00
$ 13,450.00		$ 1,529.00	$ 2,123.00	$ 2,413.00	$ 2,690.00	$ 2,959.00	$ 3,220.00
$ 13,500.00		$ 1,532.00	$ 2,127.00	$ 2,418.00	$ 2,696.00	$ 2,965.00	$ 3,226.00
$ 13,550.00		$ 1,535.00	$ 2,131.00	$ 2,423.00	$ 2,701.00	$ 2,971.00	$ 3,233.00
$ 13,600.00		$ 1,538.00	$ 2,136.00	$ 2,428.00	$ 2,707.00	$ 2,977.00	$ 3,239.00
$ 13,650.00		$ 1,541.00	$ 2,140.00	$ 2,432.00	$ 2,712.00	$ 2,983.00	$ 3,246.00
$ 13,700.00		$ 1,544.00	$ 2,144.00	$ 2,437.00	$ 2,718.00	$ 2,989.00	$ 3,253.00
$ 13,750.00		$ 1,547.00	$ 2,148.00	$ 2,442.00	$ 2,723.00	$ 2,996.00	$ 3,259.00
$ 13,800.00		$ 1,550.00	$ 2,153.00	$ 2,447.00	$ 2,729.00	$ 3,002.00	$ 3,266.00
$ 13,850.00		$ 1,553.00	$ 2,157.00	$ 2,452.00	$ 2,734.00	$ 3,008.00	$ 3,272.00
$ 13,900.00		$ 1,556.00	$ 2,161.00	$ 2,457.00	$ 2,740.00	$ 3,014.00	$ 3,279.00
$ 13,950.00		$ 1,559.00	$ 2,166.00	$ 2,462.00	$ 2,745.00	$ 3,020.00	$ 3,285.00
$ 14,000.00		$ 1,562.00	$ 2,170.00	$ 2,467.00	$ 2,751.00	$ 3,026.00	$ 3,292.00
$ 14,050.00		$ 1,565.00	$ 2,174.00	$ 2,472.00	$ 2,756.00	$ 3,032.00	$ 3,299.00
$ 14,100.00		$ 1,568.00	$ 2,178.00	$ 2,477.00	$ 2,762.00	$ 3,038.00	$ 3,305.00
$ 14,150.00		$ 1,571.00	$ 2,183.00	$ 2,482.00	$ 2,767.00	$ 3,044.00	$ 3,312.00
$ 14,200.00		$ 1,574.00	$ 2,187.00	$ 2,487.00	$ 2,773.00	$ 3,050.00	$ 3,318.00

Georgia
Schedule of Basic Child Support Obligations

COMBINED ADJUSTED GROSS INCOME		ONE CHILD	TWO CHILDREN	THREE CHILDREN	FOUR CHILDREN	FIVE CHILDREN	SIX CHILDREN
$ 14,250.00		$ 1,577.00	$ 2,191.00	$ 2,492.00	$ 2,778.00	$ 3,056.00	$ 3,325.00
$ 14,300.00		$ 1,581.00	$ 2,195.00	$ 2,497.00	$ 2,784.00	$ 3,062.00	$ 3,332.00
$ 14,350.00		$ 1,584.00	$ 2,200.00	$ 2,502.00	$ 2,789.00	$ 3,068.00	$ 3,338.00
$ 14,400.00		$ 1,587.00	$ 2,204.00	$ 2,506.00	$ 2,795.00	$ 3,074.00	$ 3,345.00
$ 14,450.00		$ 1,590.00	$ 2,208.00	$ 2,511.00	$ 2,800.00	$ 3,080.00	$ 3,351.00
$ 14,500.00		$ 1,593.00	$ 2,213.00	$ 2,516.00	$ 2,806.00	$ 3,086.00	$ 3,358.00
$ 14,550.00		$ 1,596.00	$ 2,217.00	$ 2,521.00	$ 2,811.00	$ 3,092.00	$ 3,365.00
$ 14,600.00		$ 1,599.00	$ 2,221.00	$ 2,526.00	$ 2,817.00	$ 3,098.00	$ 3,371.00
$ 14,650.00		$ 1,602.00	$ 2,225.00	$ 2,531.00	$ 2,822.00	$ 3,104.00	$ 3,378.00
$ 14,700.00		$ 1,605.00	$ 2,230.00	$ 2,536.00	$ 2,828.00	$ 3,111.00	$ 3,384.00
$ 14,750.00		$ 1,608.00	$ 2,234.00	$ 2,541.00	$ 2,833.00	$ 3,117.00	$ 3,391.00
$ 14,800.00		$ 1,611.00	$ 2,238.00	$ 2,546.00	$ 2,839.00	$ 3,123.00	$ 3,397.00
$ 14,850.00		$ 1,614.00	$ 2,243.00	$ 2,551.00	$ 2,844.00	$ 3,129.00	$ 3,404.00
$ 14,900.00		$ 1,617.00	$ 2,247.00	$ 2,556.00	$ 2,850.00	$ 3,135.00	$ 3,411.00
$ 14,950.00		$ 1,620.00	$ 2,251.00	$ 2,561.00	$ 2,855.00	$ 3,141.00	$ 3,417.00
$ 15,000.00		$ 1,623.00	$ 2,255.00	$ 2,566.00	$ 2,861.00	$ 3,147.00	$ 3,424.00
$ 15,050.00		$ 1,626.00	$ 2,260.00	$ 2,571.00	$ 2,866.00	$ 3,153.00	$ 3,430.00
$ 15,100.00		$ 1,629.00	$ 2,264.00	$ 2,576.00	$ 2,872.00	$ 3,159.00	$ 3,437.00
$ 15,150.00		$ 1,632.00	$ 2,268.00	$ 2,581.00	$ 2,877.00	$ 3,165.00	$ 3,444.00
$ 15,200.00		$ 1,635.00	$ 2,272.00	$ 2,585.00	$ 2,883.00	$ 3,171.00	$ 3,450.00
$ 15,250.00		$ 1,638.00	$ 2,277.00	$ 2,590.00	$ 2,888.00	$ 3,177.00	$ 3,457.00
$ 15,300.00		$ 1,641.00	$ 2,281.00	$ 2,595.00	$ 2,894.00	$ 3,183.00	$ 3,463.00
$ 15,350.00		$ 1,644.00	$ 2,285.00	$ 2,600.00	$ 2,899.00	$ 3,189.00	$ 3,470.00
$ 15,400.00		$ 1,647.00	$ 2,290.00	$ 2,605.00	$ 2,905.00	$ 3,195.00	$ 3,476.00
$ 15,450.00		$ 1,650.00	$ 2,294.00	$ 2,610.00	$ 2,910.00	$ 3,201.00	$ 3,483.00
$ 15,500.00		$ 1,653.00	$ 2,298.00	$ 2,615.00	$ 2,916.00	$ 3,207.00	$ 3,490.00
$ 15,550.00		$ 1,656.00	$ 2,302.00	$ 2,620.00	$ 2,921.00	$ 3,213.00	$ 3,496.00
$ 15,600.00		$ 1,659.00	$ 2,307.00	$ 2,625.00	$ 2,927.00	$ 3,219.00	$ 3,503.00
$ 15,650.00		$ 1,663.00	$ 2,311.00	$ 2,630.00	$ 2,932.00	$ 3,226.00	$ 3,509.00
$ 15,700.00		$ 1,666.00	$ 2,315.00	$ 2,635.00	$ 2,938.00	$ 3,232.00	$ 3,516.00
$ 15,750.00		$ 1,669.00	$ 2,320.00	$ 2,640.00	$ 2,943.00	$ 3,238.00	$ 3,523.00
$ 15,800.00		$ 1,672.00	$ 2,324.00	$ 2,645.00	$ 2,949.00	$ 3,244.00	$ 3,529.00
$ 15,850.00		$ 1,675.00	$ 2,328.00	$ 2,650.00	$ 2,954.00	$ 3,250.00	$ 3,536.00
$ 15,900.00		$ 1,678.00	$ 2,332.00	$ 2,655.00	$ 2,960.00	$ 3,256.00	$ 3,542.00
$ 15,950.00		$ 1,681.00	$ 2,337.00	$ 2,659.00	$ 2,965.00	$ 3,262.00	$ 3,549.00
$ 16,000.00		$ 1,684.00	$ 2,341.00	$ 2,664.00	$ 2,971.00	$ 3,268.00	$ 3,555.00
$ 16,050.00		$ 1,687.00	$ 2,345.00	$ 2,669.00	$ 2,976.00	$ 3,274.00	$ 3,562.00
$ 16,100.00		$ 1,690.00	$ 2,349.00	$ 2,674.00	$ 2,982.00	$ 3,280.00	$ 3,569.00
$ 16,150.00		$ 1,692.00	$ 2,353.00	$ 2,678.00	$ 2,986.00	$ 3,285.00	$ 3,574.00
$ 16,200.00		$ 1,695.00	$ 2,356.00	$ 2,682.00	$ 2,990.00	$ 3,289.00	$ 3,579.00
$ 16,250.00		$ 1,698.00	$ 2,360.00	$ 2,686.00	$ 2,994.00	$ 3,294.00	$ 3,584.00
$ 16,300.00		$ 1,700.00	$ 2,363.00	$ 2,689.00	$ 2,999.00	$ 3,299.00	$ 3,589.00
$ 16,350.00		$ 1,703.00	$ 2,367.00	$ 2,693.00	$ 3,003.00	$ 3,303.00	$ 3,594.00
$ 16,400.00		$ 1,706.00	$ 2,370.00	$ 2,697.00	$ 3,007.00	$ 3,308.00	$ 3,599.00
$ 16,450.00		$ 1,708.00	$ 2,374.00	$ 2,701.00	$ 3,011.00	$ 3,313.00	$ 3,604.00
$ 16,500.00		$ 1,711.00	$ 2,377.00	$ 2,705.00	$ 3,016.00	$ 3,317.00	$ 3,609.00
$ 16,550.00		$ 1,714.00	$ 2,381.00	$ 2,708.00	$ 3,020.00	$ 3,322.00	$ 3,614.00
$ 16,600.00		$ 1,716.00	$ 2,384.00	$ 2,712.00	$ 3,024.00	$ 3,327.00	$ 3,619.00
$ 16,650.00		$ 1,719.00	$ 2,388.00	$ 2,716.00	$ 3,028.00	$ 3,331.00	$ 3,624.00
$ 16,700.00		$ 1,722.00	$ 2,391.00	$ 2,720.00	$ 3,033.00	$ 3,336.00	$ 3,630.00
$ 16,750.00		$ 1,724.00	$ 2,395.00	$ 2,724.00	$ 3,037.00	$ 3,341.00	$ 3,635.00
$ 16,800.00		$ 1,727.00	$ 2,398.00	$ 2,728.00	$ 3,041.00	$ 3,345.00	$ 3,640.00
$ 16,850.00		$ 1,730.00	$ 2,402.00	$ 2,731.00	$ 3,045.00	$ 3,350.00	$ 3,645.00
$ 16,900.00		$ 1,732.00	$ 2,405.00	$ 2,735.00	$ 3,050.00	$ 3,355.00	$ 3,650.00

Georgia
Schedule of Basic Child Support Obligations

COMBINED ADJUSTED GROSS INCOME		ONE CHILD	TWO CHILDREN	THREE CHILDREN	FOUR CHILDREN	FIVE CHILDREN	SIX CHILDREN
$ 16,950.00		$ 1,735.00	$ 2,409.00	$ 2,739.00	$ 3,054.00	$ 3,359.00	$ 3,655.00
$ 17,000.00		$ 1,737.00	$ 2,412.00	$ 2,743.00	$ 3,058.00	$ 3,364.00	$ 3,660.00
$ 17,050.00		$ 1,740.00	$ 2,416.00	$ 2,747.00	$ 3,062.00	$ 3,369.00	$ 3,665.00
$ 17,100.00		$ 1,743.00	$ 2,419.00	$ 2,750.00	$ 3,067.00	$ 3,373.00	$ 3,670.00
$ 17,150.00		$ 1,745.00	$ 2,423.00	$ 2,754.00	$ 3,071.00	$ 3,378.00	$ 3,675.00
$ 17,200.00		$ 1,748.00	$ 2,426.00	$ 2,758.00	$ 3,075.00	$ 3,383.00	$ 3,680.00
$ 17,250.00		$ 1,751.00	$ 2,430.00	$ 2,762.00	$ 3,079.00	$ 3,387.00	$ 3,685.00
$ 17,300.00		$ 1,753.00	$ 2,433.00	$ 2,766.00	$ 3,084.00	$ 3,392.00	$ 3,691.00
$ 17,350.00		$ 1,756.00	$ 2,437.00	$ 2,769.00	$ 3,088.00	$ 3,397.00	$ 3,696.00
$ 17,400.00		$ 1,759.00	$ 2,440.00	$ 2,773.00	$ 3,092.00	$ 3,401.00	$ 3,701.00
$ 17,450.00		$ 1,761.00	$ 2,444.00	$ 2,777.00	$ 3,096.00	$ 3,406.00	$ 3,706.00
$ 17,500.00		$ 1,764.00	$ 2,447.00	$ 2,781.00	$ 3,101.00	$ 3,411.00	$ 3,711.00
$ 17,550.00		$ 1,767.00	$ 2,451.00	$ 2,785.00	$ 3,105.00	$ 3,415.00	$ 3,716.00
$ 17,600.00		$ 1,769.00	$ 2,454.00	$ 2,788.00	$ 3,109.00	$ 3,420.00	$ 3,721.00
$ 17,650.00		$ 1,772.00	$ 2,458.00	$ 2,792.00	$ 3,113.00	$ 3,425.00	$ 3,726.00
$ 17,700.00		$ 1,774.00	$ 2,461.00	$ 2,796.00	$ 3,118.00	$ 3,429.00	$ 3,731.00
$ 17,750.00		$ 1,777.00	$ 2,465.00	$ 2,800.00	$ 3,122.00	$ 3,434.00	$ 3,736.00
$ 17,800.00		$ 1,780.00	$ 2,468.00	$ 2,804.00	$ 3,126.00	$ 3,439.00	$ 3,741.00
$ 17,850.00		$ 1,782.00	$ 2,472.00	$ 2,808.00	$ 3,130.00	$ 3,443.00	$ 3,746.00
$ 17,900.00		$ 1,785.00	$ 2,475.00	$ 2,811.00	$ 3,135.00	$ 3,448.00	$ 3,752.00
$ 17,950.00		$ 1,788.00	$ 2,478.00	$ 2,815.00	$ 3,139.00	$ 3,453.00	$ 3,757.00
$ 18,000.00		$ 1,790.00	$ 2,482.00	$ 2,819.00	$ 3,143.00	$ 3,457.00	$ 3,762.00
$ 18,050.00		$ 1,793.00	$ 2,485.00	$ 2,823.00	$ 3,147.00	$ 3,462.00	$ 3,767.00
$ 18,100.00		$ 1,796.00	$ 2,489.00	$ 2,827.00	$ 3,152.00	$ 3,467.00	$ 3,772.00
$ 18,150.00		$ 1,798.00	$ 2,492.00	$ 2,830.00	$ 3,156.00	$ 3,471.00	$ 3,777.00
$ 18,200.00		$ 1,801.00	$ 2,496.00	$ 2,834.00	$ 3,160.00	$ 3,476.00	$ 3,782.00
$ 18,250.00		$ 1,804.00	$ 2,499.00	$ 2,838.00	$ 3,164.00	$ 3,481.00	$ 3,787.00
$ 18,300.00		$ 1,806.00	$ 2,503.00	$ 2,842.00	$ 3,169.00	$ 3,485.00	$ 3,792.00
$ 18,350.00		$ 1,809.00	$ 2,506.00	$ 2,846.00	$ 3,173.00	$ 3,490.00	$ 3,797.00
$ 18,400.00		$ 1,812.00	$ 2,510.00	$ 2,849.00	$ 3,177.00	$ 3,495.00	$ 3,802.00
$ 18,450.00		$ 1,814.00	$ 2,513.00	$ 2,853.00	$ 3,181.00	$ 3,499.00	$ 3,807.00
$ 18,500.00		$ 1,817.00	$ 2,517.00	$ 2,857.00	$ 3,186.00	$ 3,504.00	$ 3,813.00
$ 18,550.00		$ 1,819.00	$ 2,520.00	$ 2,861.00	$ 3,190.00	$ 3,509.00	$ 3,818.00
$ 18,600.00		$ 1,822.00	$ 2,524.00	$ 2,865.00	$ 3,194.00	$ 3,513.00	$ 3,823.00
$ 18,650.00		$ 1,825.00	$ 2,527.00	$ 2,868.00	$ 3,198.00	$ 3,518.00	$ 3,828.00
$ 18,700.00		$ 1,827.00	$ 2,531.00	$ 2,872.00	$ 3,203.00	$ 3,523.00	$ 3,833.00
$ 18,750.00		$ 1,830.00	$ 2,534.00	$ 2,876.00	$ 3,207.00	$ 3,528.00	$ 3,838.00
$ 18,800.00		$ 1,833.00	$ 2,538.00	$ 2,880.00	$ 3,211.00	$ 3,532.00	$ 3,843.00
$ 18,850.00		$ 1,835.00	$ 2,541.00	$ 2,884.00	$ 3,215.00	$ 3,537.00	$ 3,848.00
$ 18,900.00		$ 1,838.00	$ 2,545.00	$ 2,888.00	$ 3,220.00	$ 3,542.00	$ 3,853.00
$ 18,950.00		$ 1,841.00	$ 2,548.00	$ 2,891.00	$ 3,224.00	$ 3,546.00	$ 3,858.00
$ 19,000.00		$ 1,843.00	$ 2,552.00	$ 2,895.00	$ 3,228.00	$ 3,551.00	$ 3,863.00
$ 19,050.00		$ 1,846.00	$ 2,555.00	$ 2,899.00	$ 3,232.00	$ 3,556.00	$ 3,868.00
$ 19,100.00		$ 1,849.00	$ 2,559.00	$ 2,903.00	$ 3,237.00	$ 3,560.00	$ 3,874.00
$ 19,150.00		$ 1,851.00	$ 2,562.00	$ 2,907.00	$ 3,241.00	$ 3,565.00	$ 3,879.00
$ 19,200.00		$ 1,854.00	$ 2,566.00	$ 2,910.00	$ 3,245.00	$ 3,570.00	$ 3,884.00
$ 19,250.00		$ 1,856.00	$ 2,569.00	$ 2,914.00	$ 3,249.00	$ 3,574.00	$ 3,889.00
$ 19,300.00		$ 1,859.00	$ 2,573.00	$ 2,918.00	$ 3,254.00	$ 3,579.00	$ 3,894.00
$ 19,350.00		$ 1,862.00	$ 2,576.00	$ 2,922.00	$ 3,258.00	$ 3,584.00	$ 3,899.00
$ 19,400.00		$ 1,864.00	$ 2,580.00	$ 2,926.00	$ 3,262.00	$ 3,588.00	$ 3,904.00
$ 19,450.00		$ 1,867.00	$ 2,583.00	$ 2,929.00	$ 3,266.00	$ 3,593.00	$ 3,909.00
$ 19,500.00		$ 1,870.00	$ 2,587.00	$ 2,933.00	$ 3,271.00	$ 3,598.00	$ 3,914.00
$ 19,550.00		$ 1,872.00	$ 2,590.00	$ 2,937.00	$ 3,275.00	$ 3,602.00	$ 3,919.00
$ 19,600.00		$ 1,875.00	$ 2,594.00	$ 2,941.00	$ 3,279.00	$ 3,607.00	$ 3,924.00

Georgia
Schedule of Basic Child Support Obligations

COMBINED ADJUSTED GROSS INCOME		ONE CHILD	TWO CHILDREN	THREE CHILDREN	FOUR CHILDREN	FIVE CHILDREN	SIX CHILDREN
$ 19,650.00		$ 1,878.00	$ 2,597.00	$ 2,945.00	$ 3,283.00	$ 3,612.00	$ 3,929.00
$ 19,700.00		$ 1,880.00	$ 2,601.00	$ 2,948.00	$ 3,288.00	$ 3,616.00	$ 3,935.00
$ 19,750.00		$ 1,883.00	$ 2,604.00	$ 2,952.00	$ 3,292.00	$ 3,621.00	$ 3,940.00
$ 19,800.00		$ 1,886.00	$ 2,608.00	$ 2,956.00	$ 3,296.00	$ 3,626.00	$ 3,945.00
$ 19,850.00		$ 1,888.00	$ 2,611.00	$ 2,960.00	$ 3,300.00	$ 3,630.00	$ 3,950.00
$ 19,900.00		$ 1,891.00	$ 2,615.00	$ 2,964.00	$ 3,305.00	$ 3,635.00	$ 3,955.00
$ 19,950.00		$ 1,893.00	$ 2,618.00	$ 2,967.00	$ 3,309.00	$ 3,640.00	$ 3,960.00
$ 20,000.00		$ 1,896.00	$ 2,622.00	$ 2,971.00	$ 3,313.00	$ 3,644.00	$ 3,965.00
$ 20,050.00		$ 1,899.00	$ 2,625.00	$ 2,975.00	$ 3,317.00	$ 3,649.00	$ 3,970.00
$ 20,100.00		$ 1,901.00	$ 2,628.00	$ 2,979.00	$ 3,321.00	$ 3,654.00	$ 3,975.00
$ 20,150.00		$ 1,904.00	$ 2,632.00	$ 2,983.00	$ 3,326.00	$ 3,658.00	$ 3,980.00
$ 20,200.00		$ 1,907.00	$ 2,635.00	$ 2,987.00	$ 3,330.00	$ 3,663.00	$ 3,985.00
$ 20,250.00		$ 1,909.00	$ 2,639.00	$ 2,990.00	$ 3,334.00	$ 3,668.00	$ 3,990.00
$ 20,300.00		$ 1,912.00	$ 2,642.00	$ 2,994.00	$ 3,338.00	$ 3,672.00	$ 3,996.00
$ 20,350.00		$ 1,915.00	$ 2,646.00	$ 2,998.00	$ 3,343.00	$ 3,677.00	$ 4,001.00
$ 20,400.00		$ 1,917.00	$ 2,649.00	$ 3,002.00	$ 3,347.00	$ 3,682.00	$ 4,006.00
$ 20,450.00		$ 1,920.00	$ 2,653.00	$ 3,006.00	$ 3,351.00	$ 3,686.00	$ 4,011.00
$ 20,500.00		$ 1,923.00	$ 2,656.00	$ 3,009.00	$ 3,355.00	$ 3,691.00	$ 4,016.00
$ 20,550.00		$ 1,925.00	$ 2,660.00	$ 3,013.00	$ 3,360.00	$ 3,696.00	$ 4,021.00
$ 20,600.00		$ 1,928.00	$ 2,663.00	$ 3,017.00	$ 3,364.00	$ 3,700.00	$ 4,026.00
$ 20,650.00		$ 1,931.00	$ 2,667.00	$ 3,021.00	$ 3,368.00	$ 3,705.00	$ 4,031.00
$ 20,700.00		$ 1,933.00	$ 2,670.00	$ 3,025.00	$ 3,372.00	$ 3,710.00	$ 4,036.00
$ 20,750.00		$ 1,936.00	$ 2,674.00	$ 3,028.00	$ 3,377.00	$ 3,714.00	$ 4,041.00
$ 20,800.00		$ 1,938.00	$ 2,677.00	$ 3,032.00	$ 3,381.00	$ 3,719.00	$ 4,046.00
$ 20,850.00		$ 1,941.00	$ 2,681.00	$ 3,036.00	$ 3,385.00	$ 3,724.00	$ 4,051.00
$ 20,900.00		$ 1,944.00	$ 2,684.00	$ 3,040.00	$ 3,389.00	$ 3,728.00	$ 4,056.00
$ 20,950.00		$ 1,946.00	$ 2,688.00	$ 3,044.00	$ 3,394.00	$ 3,733.00	$ 4,062.00
$ 21,000.00		$ 1,949.00	$ 2,691.00	$ 3,047.00	$ 3,398.00	$ 3,738.00	$ 4,067.00
$ 21,050.00		$ 1,952.00	$ 2,695.00	$ 3,051.00	$ 3,402.00	$ 3,742.00	$ 4,072.00
$ 21,100.00		$ 1,954.00	$ 2,698.00	$ 3,055.00	$ 3,406.00	$ 3,747.00	$ 4,077.00
$ 21,150.00		$ 1,957.00	$ 2,702.00	$ 3,059.00	$ 3,411.00	$ 3,752.00	$ 4,082.00
$ 21,200.00		$ 1,960.00	$ 2,705.00	$ 3,063.00	$ 3,415.00	$ 3,756.00	$ 4,087.00
$ 21,250.00		$ 1,962.00	$ 2,709.00	$ 3,067.00	$ 3,419.00	$ 3,761.00	$ 4,092.00
$ 21,300.00		$ 1,965.00	$ 2,712.00	$ 3,070.00	$ 3,423.00	$ 3,766.00	$ 4,097.00
$ 21,350.00		$ 1,968.00	$ 2,716.00	$ 3,074.00	$ 3,428.00	$ 3,770.00	$ 4,102.00
$ 21,400.00		$ 1,970.00	$ 2,719.00	$ 3,078.00	$ 3,432.00	$ 3,775.00	$ 4,107.00
$ 21,450.00		$ 1,973.00	$ 2,723.00	$ 3,082.00	$ 3,436.00	$ 3,780.00	$ 4,112.00
$ 21,500.00		$ 1,975.00	$ 2,726.00	$ 3,086.00	$ 3,440.00	$ 3,784.00	$ 4,117.00
$ 21,550.00		$ 1,978.00	$ 2,730.00	$ 3,089.00	$ 3,445.00	$ 3,789.00	$ 4,123.00
$ 21,600.00		$ 1,981.00	$ 2,733.00	$ 3,093.00	$ 3,449.00	$ 3,794.00	$ 4,128.00
$ 21,650.00		$ 1,983.00	$ 2,737.00	$ 3,097.00	$ 3,453.00	$ 3,798.00	$ 4,133.00
$ 21,700.00		$ 1,986.00	$ 2,740.00	$ 3,101.00	$ 3,457.00	$ 3,803.00	$ 4,138.00
$ 21,750.00		$ 1,989.00	$ 2,744.00	$ 3,105.00	$ 3,462.00	$ 3,808.00	$ 4,143.00
$ 21,800.00		$ 1,991.00	$ 2,747.00	$ 3,108.00	$ 3,466.00	$ 3,812.00	$ 4,148.00
$ 21,850.00		$ 1,994.00	$ 2,751.00	$ 3,112.00	$ 3,470.00	$ 3,817.00	$ 4,153.00
$ 21,900.00		$ 1,997.00	$ 2,754.00	$ 3,116.00	$ 3,474.00	$ 3,822.00	$ 4,158.00
$ 21,950.00		$ 1,999.00	$ 2,758.00	$ 3,120.00	$ 3,479.00	$ 3,827.00	$ 4,163.00
$ 22,000.00		$ 2,002.00	$ 2,761.00	$ 3,124.00	$ 3,483.00	$ 3,831.00	$ 4,168.00
$ 22,050.00		$ 2,005.00	$ 2,765.00	$ 3,127.00	$ 3,487.00	$ 3,836.00	$ 4,173.00
$ 22,100.00		$ 2,007.00	$ 2,768.00	$ 3,131.00	$ 3,491.00	$ 3,841.00	$ 4,178.00
$ 22,150.00		$ 2,010.00	$ 2,772.00	$ 3,135.00	$ 3,496.00	$ 3,845.00	$ 4,184.00
$ 22,200.00		$ 2,012.00	$ 2,775.00	$ 3,139.00	$ 3,500.00	$ 3,850.00	$ 4,189.00
$ 22,250.00		$ 2,015.00	$ 2,779.00	$ 3,143.00	$ 3,504.00	$ 3,855.00	$ 4,194.00
$ 22,300.00		$ 2,018.00	$ 2,782.00	$ 3,147.00	$ 3,508.00	$ 3,859.00	$ 4,199.00

Georgia
Schedule of Basic Child Support Obligations

COMBINED ADJUSTED GROSS INCOME		ONE CHILD	TWO CHILDREN	THREE CHILDREN	FOUR CHILDREN	FIVE CHILDREN	SIX CHILDREN
$ 22,350.00		$ 2,020.00	$ 2,785.00	$ 3,150.00	$ 3,513.00	$ 3,864.00	$ 4,204.00
$ 22,400.00		$ 2,022.00	$ 2,788.00	$ 3,153.00	$ 3,515.00	$ 3,867.00	$ 4,207.00
$ 22,450.00		$ 2,024.00	$ 2,790.00	$ 3,155.00	$ 3,517.00	$ 3,869.00	$ 4,210.00
$ 22,500.00		$ 2,025.00	$ 2,792.00	$ 3,157.00	$ 3,520.00	$ 3,872.00	$ 4,212.00
$ 22,550.00		$ 2,027.00	$ 2,793.00	$ 3,158.00	$ 3,522.00	$ 3,874.00	$ 4,215.00
$ 22,600.00		$ 2,028.00	$ 2,795.00	$ 3,160.00	$ 3,524.00	$ 3,876.00	$ 4,217.00
$ 22,650.00		$ 2,029.00	$ 2,797.00	$ 3,162.00	$ 3,526.00	$ 3,878.00	$ 4,220.00
$ 22,700.00		$ 2,031.00	$ 2,799.00	$ 3,164.00	$ 3,528.00	$ 3,881.00	$ 4,222.00
$ 22,750.00		$ 2,032.00	$ 2,801.00	$ 3,166.00	$ 3,530.00	$ 3,883.00	$ 4,225.00
$ 22,800.00		$ 2,034.00	$ 2,803.00	$ 3,168.00	$ 3,532.00	$ 3,885.00	$ 4,227.00
$ 22,850.00		$ 2,035.00	$ 2,804.00	$ 3,169.00	$ 3,534.00	$ 3,888.00	$ 4,230.00
$ 22,900.00		$ 2,036.00	$ 2,806.00	$ 3,171.00	$ 3,536.00	$ 3,890.00	$ 4,232.00
$ 22,950.00		$ 2,038.00	$ 2,808.00	$ 3,173.00	$ 3,538.00	$ 3,892.00	$ 4,235.00
$ 23,000.00		$ 2,039.00	$ 2,810.00	$ 3,175.00	$ 3,540.00	$ 3,894.00	$ 4,237.00
$ 23,050.00		$ 2,041.00	$ 2,812.00	$ 3,177.00	$ 3,542.00	$ 3,897.00	$ 4,240.00
$ 23,100.00		$ 2,042.00	$ 2,814.00	$ 3,179.00	$ 3,544.00	$ 3,899.00	$ 4,242.00
$ 23,150.00		$ 2,044.00	$ 2,816.00	$ 3,181.00	$ 3,546.00	$ 3,901.00	$ 4,245.00
$ 23,200.00		$ 2,045.00	$ 2,817.00	$ 3,182.00	$ 3,548.00	$ 3,904.00	$ 4,247.00
$ 23,250.00		$ 2,046.00	$ 2,819.00	$ 3,184.00	$ 3,550.00	$ 3,906.00	$ 4,250.00
$ 23,300.00		$ 2,048.00	$ 2,821.00	$ 3,186.00	$ 3,552.00	$ 3,908.00	$ 4,252.00
$ 23,350.00		$ 2,049.00	$ 2,823.00	$ 3,188.00	$ 3,555.00	$ 3,910.00	$ 4,254.00
$ 23,400.00		$ 2,051.00	$ 2,825.00	$ 3,190.00	$ 3,557.00	$ 3,913.00	$ 4,257.00
$ 23,450.00		$ 2,052.00	$ 2,827.00	$ 3,192.00	$ 3,559.00	$ 3,915.00	$ 4,259.00
$ 23,500.00		$ 2,053.00	$ 2,828.00	$ 3,193.00	$ 3,561.00	$ 3,917.00	$ 4,262.00
$ 23,550.00		$ 2,055.00	$ 2,830.00	$ 3,195.00	$ 3,563.00	$ 3,919.00	$ 4,264.00
$ 23,600.00		$ 2,056.00	$ 2,832.00	$ 3,197.00	$ 3,565.00	$ 3,922.00	$ 4,267.00
$ 23,650.00		$ 2,058.00	$ 2,834.00	$ 3,199.00	$ 3,567.00	$ 3,924.00	$ 4,269.00
$ 23,700.00		$ 2,059.00	$ 2,836.00	$ 3,201.00	$ 3,569.00	$ 3,926.00	$ 4,272.00
$ 23,750.00		$ 2,061.00	$ 2,838.00	$ 3,203.00	$ 3,571.00	$ 3,929.00	$ 4,274.00
$ 23,800.00		$ 2,062.00	$ 2,840.00	$ 3,204.00	$ 3,573.00	$ 3,931.00	$ 4,277.00
$ 23,850.00		$ 2,063.00	$ 2,841.00	$ 3,206.00	$ 3,575.00	$ 3,933.00	$ 4,279.00
$ 23,900.00		$ 2,065.00	$ 2,843.00	$ 3,208.00	$ 3,577.00	$ 3,935.00	$ 4,282.00
$ 23,950.00		$ 2,066.00	$ 2,845.00	$ 3,210.00	$ 3,579.00	$ 3,938.00	$ 4,284.00
$ 24,000.00		$ 2,068.00	$ 2,847.00	$ 3,212.00	$ 3,581.00	$ 3,940.00	$ 4,287.00
$ 24,050.00		$ 2,069.00	$ 2,849.00	$ 3,214.00	$ 3,583.00	$ 3,942.00	$ 4,289.00
$ 24,100.00		$ 2,070.00	$ 2,851.00	$ 3,216.00	$ 3,585.00	$ 3,945.00	$ 4,292.00
$ 24,150.00		$ 2,072.00	$ 2,852.00	$ 3,217.00	$ 3,587.00	$ 3,947.00	$ 4,294.00
$ 24,200.00		$ 2,073.00	$ 2,854.00	$ 3,219.00	$ 3,589.00	$ 3,949.00	$ 4,297.00
$ 24,250.00		$ 2,075.00	$ 2,856.00	$ 3,221.00	$ 3,592.00	$ 3,951.00	$ 4,299.00
$ 24,300.00		$ 2,076.00	$ 2,858.00	$ 3,223.00	$ 3,594.00	$ 3,954.00	$ 4,302.00
$ 24,350.00		$ 2,077.00	$ 2,860.00	$ 3,225.00	$ 3,596.00	$ 3,956.00	$ 4,304.00
$ 24,400.00		$ 2,079.00	$ 2,862.00	$ 3,227.00	$ 3,598.00	$ 3,958.00	$ 4,307.00
$ 24,450.00		$ 2,080.00	$ 2,864.00	$ 3,228.00	$ 3,600.00	$ 3,961.00	$ 4,309.00
$ 24,500.00		$ 2,082.00	$ 2,865.00	$ 3,230.00	$ 3,602.00	$ 3,963.00	$ 4,312.00
$ 24,550.00		$ 2,083.00	$ 2,867.00	$ 3,232.00	$ 3,604.00	$ 3,965.00	$ 4,314.00
$ 24,600.00		$ 2,085.00	$ 2,869.00	$ 3,234.00	$ 3,606.00	$ 3,967.00	$ 4,317.00
$ 24,650.00		$ 2,086.00	$ 2,871.00	$ 3,236.00	$ 3,608.00	$ 3,970.00	$ 4,319.00
$ 24,700.00		$ 2,087.00	$ 2,873.00	$ 3,238.00	$ 3,610.00	$ 3,972.00	$ 4,322.00
$ 24,750.00		$ 2,089.00	$ 2,875.00	$ 3,240.00	$ 3,612.00	$ 3,974.00	$ 4,324.00
$ 24,800.00		$ 2,090.00	$ 2,876.00	$ 3,241.00	$ 3,614.00	$ 3,977.00	$ 4,326.00
$ 24,850.00		$ 2,092.00	$ 2,878.00	$ 3,243.00	$ 3,616.00	$ 3,979.00	$ 4,329.00
$ 24,900.00		$ 2,093.00	$ 2,880.00	$ 3,245.00	$ 3,618.00	$ 3,981.00	$ 4,331.00
$ 24,950.00		$ 2,094.00	$ 2,882.00	$ 3,247.00	$ 3,620.00	$ 3,983.00	$ 4,334.00
$ 25,000.00		$ 2,096.00	$ 2,884.00	$ 3,249.00	$ 3,622.00	$ 3,986.00	$ 4,336.00

Georgia
Schedule of Basic Child Support Obligations

COMBINED ADJUSTED GROSS INCOME		ONE CHILD	TWO CHILDREN	THREE CHILDREN	FOUR CHILDREN	FIVE CHILDREN	SIX CHILDREN
$ 25,050.00		$ 2,097.00	$ 2,886.00	$ 3,251.00	$ 3,624.00	$ 3,988.00	$ 4,339.00
$ 25,100.00		$ 2,099.00	$ 2,887.00	$ 3,252.00	$ 3,626.00	$ 3,990.00	$ 4,341.00
$ 25,150.00		$ 2,100.00	$ 2,889.00	$ 3,254.00	$ 3,629.00	$ 3,993.00	$ 4,344.00
$ 25,200.00		$ 2,102.00	$ 2,891.00	$ 3,256.00	$ 3,631.00	$ 3,995.00	$ 4,346.00
$ 25,250.00		$ 2,103.00	$ 2,893.00	$ 3,258.00	$ 3,633.00	$ 3,997.00	$ 4,349.00
$ 25,300.00		$ 2,104.00	$ 2,895.00	$ 3,260.00	$ 3,635.00	$ 3,999.00	$ 4,351.00
$ 25,350.00		$ 2,106.00	$ 2,897.00	$ 3,262.00	$ 3,637.00	$ 4,002.00	$ 4,354.00
$ 25,400.00		$ 2,107.00	$ 2,899.00	$ 3,264.00	$ 3,639.00	$ 4,004.00	$ 4,356.00
$ 25,450.00		$ 2,109.00	$ 2,900.00	$ 3,265.00	$ 3,641.00	$ 4,006.00	$ 4,359.00
$ 25,500.00		$ 2,110.00	$ 2,902.00	$ 3,267.00	$ 3,643.00	$ 4,009.00	$ 4,361.00
$ 25,550.00		$ 2,111.00	$ 2,904.00	$ 3,269.00	$ 3,645.00	$ 4,011.00	$ 4,364.00
$ 25,600.00		$ 2,113.00	$ 2,906.00	$ 3,271.00	$ 3,647.00	$ 4,013.00	$ 4,366.00
$ 25,650.00		$ 2,114.00	$ 2,908.00	$ 3,273.00	$ 3,649.00	$ 4,015.00	$ 4,369.00
$ 25,700.00		$ 2,116.00	$ 2,910.00	$ 3,275.00	$ 3,651.00	$ 4,018.00	$ 4,371.00
$ 25,750.00		$ 2,117.00	$ 2,911.00	$ 3,276.00	$ 3,653.00	$ 4,020.00	$ 4,374.00
$ 25,800.00		$ 2,119.00	$ 2,913.00	$ 3,278.00	$ 3,655.00	$ 4,022.00	$ 4,376.00
$ 25,850.00		$ 2,120.00	$ 2,915.00	$ 3,280.00	$ 3,657.00	$ 4,024.00	$ 4,379.00
$ 25,900.00		$ 2,121.00	$ 2,917.00	$ 3,282.00	$ 3,659.00	$ 4,027.00	$ 4,381.00
$ 25,950.00		$ 2,123.00	$ 2,919.00	$ 3,284.00	$ 3,661.00	$ 4,029.00	$ 4,384.00
$ 26,000.00		$ 2,124.00	$ 2,921.00	$ 3,286.00	$ 3,663.00	$ 4,031.00	$ 4,386.00
$ 26,050.00		$ 2,126.00	$ 2,923.00	$ 3,287.00	$ 3,666.00	$ 4,034.00	$ 4,389.00
$ 26,100.00		$ 2,127.00	$ 2,924.00	$ 3,289.00	$ 3,668.00	$ 4,036.00	$ 4,391.00
$ 26,150.00		$ 2,128.00	$ 2,926.00	$ 3,291.00	$ 3,670.00	$ 4,038.00	$ 4,394.00
$ 26,200.00		$ 2,130.00	$ 2,928.00	$ 3,293.00	$ 3,672.00	$ 4,040.00	$ 4,396.00
$ 26,250.00		$ 2,131.00	$ 2,930.00	$ 3,295.00	$ 3,674.00	$ 4,043.00	$ 4,399.00
$ 26,300.00		$ 2,133.00	$ 2,932.00	$ 3,297.00	$ 3,676.00	$ 4,045.00	$ 4,401.00
$ 26,350.00		$ 2,134.00	$ 2,934.00	$ 3,299.00	$ 3,678.00	$ 4,047.00	$ 4,403.00
$ 26,400.00		$ 2,136.00	$ 2,935.00	$ 3,300.00	$ 3,680.00	$ 4,050.00	$ 4,406.00
$ 26,450.00		$ 2,137.00	$ 2,937.00	$ 3,302.00	$ 3,682.00	$ 4,052.00	$ 4,408.00
$ 26,500.00		$ 2,138.00	$ 2,939.00	$ 3,304.00	$ 3,684.00	$ 4,054.00	$ 4,411.00
$ 26,550.00		$ 2,140.00	$ 2,941.00	$ 3,306.00	$ 3,686.00	$ 4,056.00	$ 4,413.00
$ 26,600.00		$ 2,141.00	$ 2,943.00	$ 3,308.00	$ 3,688.00	$ 4,059.00	$ 4,416.00
$ 26,650.00		$ 2,143.00	$ 2,945.00	$ 3,310.00	$ 3,690.00	$ 4,061.00	$ 4,418.00
$ 26,700.00		$ 2,144.00	$ 2,947.00	$ 3,311.00	$ 3,692.00	$ 4,063.00	$ 4,421.00
$ 26,750.00		$ 2,145.00	$ 2,948.00	$ 3,313.00	$ 3,694.00	$ 4,066.00	$ 4,423.00
$ 26,800.00		$ 2,147.00	$ 2,950.00	$ 3,315.00	$ 3,696.00	$ 4,068.00	$ 4,426.00
$ 26,850.00		$ 2,148.00	$ 2,952.00	$ 3,317.00	$ 3,698.00	$ 4,070.00	$ 4,428.00
$ 26,900.00		$ 2,150.00	$ 2,954.00	$ 3,319.00	$ 3,701.00	$ 4,072.00	$ 4,431.00
$ 26,950.00		$ 2,151.00	$ 2,956.00	$ 3,321.00	$ 3,703.00	$ 4,075.00	$ 4,433.00
$ 27,000.00		$ 2,153.00	$ 2,958.00	$ 3,323.00	$ 3,705.00	$ 4,077.00	$ 4,436.00
$ 27,050.00		$ 2,154.00	$ 2,959.00	$ 3,324.00	$ 3,707.00	$ 4,079.00	$ 4,438.00
$ 27,100.00		$ 2,155.00	$ 2,961.00	$ 3,326.00	$ 3,709.00	$ 4,082.00	$ 4,441.00
$ 27,150.00		$ 2,157.00	$ 2,963.00	$ 3,328.00	$ 3,711.00	$ 4,084.00	$ 4,443.00
$ 27,200.00		$ 2,158.00	$ 2,965.00	$ 3,330.00	$ 3,713.00	$ 4,086.00	$ 4,446.00
$ 27,250.00		$ 2,160.00	$ 2,967.00	$ 3,332.00	$ 3,715.00	$ 4,088.00	$ 4,448.00
$ 27,300.00		$ 2,161.00	$ 2,969.00	$ 3,334.00	$ 3,717.00	$ 4,091.00	$ 4,451.00
$ 27,350.00		$ 2,162.00	$ 2,970.00	$ 3,335.00	$ 3,719.00	$ 4,093.00	$ 4,453.00
$ 27,400.00		$ 2,164.00	$ 2,972.00	$ 3,337.00	$ 3,721.00	$ 4,095.00	$ 4,456.00
$ 27,450.00		$ 2,165.00	$ 2,974.00	$ 3,339.00	$ 3,723.00	$ 4,098.00	$ 4,458.00
$ 27,500.00		$ 2,167.00	$ 2,976.00	$ 3,341.00	$ 3,725.00	$ 4,100.00	$ 4,461.00
$ 27,550.00		$ 2,168.00	$ 2,978.00	$ 3,343.00	$ 3,727.00	$ 4,102.00	$ 4,463.00
$ 27,600.00		$ 2,170.00	$ 2,980.00	$ 3,345.00	$ 3,729.00	$ 4,104.00	$ 4,466.00
$ 27,650.00		$ 2,171.00	$ 2,982.00	$ 3,347.00	$ 3,731.00	$ 4,107.00	$ 4,468.00
$ 27,700.00		$ 2,172.00	$ 2,983.00	$ 3,348.00	$ 3,733.00	$ 4,109.00	$ 4,471.00

Georgia
Schedule of Basic Child Support Obligations

COMBINED ADJUSTED GROSS INCOME		ONE CHILD	TWO CHILDREN	THREE CHILDREN	FOUR CHILDREN	FIVE CHILDREN	SIX CHILDREN
$ 27,750.00		$ 2,174.00	$ 2,985.00	$ 3,350.00	$ 3,735.00	$ 4,111.00	$ 4,473.00
$ 27,800.00		$ 2,175.00	$ 2,987.00	$ 3,352.00	$ 3,738.00	$ 4,114.00	$ 4,475.00
$ 27,850.00		$ 2,177.00	$ 2,989.00	$ 3,354.00	$ 3,740.00	$ 4,116.00	$ 4,478.00
$ 27,900.00		$ 2,178.00	$ 2,991.00	$ 3,356.00	$ 3,742.00	$ 4,118.00	$ 4,480.00
$ 27,950.00		$ 2,179.00	$ 2,993.00	$ 3,357.00	$ 3,744.00	$ 4,120.00	$ 4,483.00
$ 28,000.00		$ 2,181.00	$ 2,994.00	$ 3,359.00	$ 3,746.00	$ 4,122.00	$ 4,485.00
$ 28,050.00		$ 2,182.00	$ 2,996.00	$ 3,361.00	$ 3,748.00	$ 4,125.00	$ 4,488.00
$ 28,100.00		$ 2,184.00	$ 2,998.00	$ 3,363.00	$ 3,750.00	$ 4,127.00	$ 4,490.00
$ 28,150.00		$ 2,185.00	$ 3,000.00	$ 3,365.00	$ 3,752.00	$ 4,129.00	$ 4,492.00
$ 28,200.00		$ 2,186.00	$ 3,001.00	$ 3,366.00	$ 3,754.00	$ 4,131.00	$ 4,495.00
$ 28,250.00		$ 2,188.00	$ 3,003.00	$ 3,368.00	$ 3,756.00	$ 4,133.00	$ 4,497.00
$ 28,300.00		$ 2,189.00	$ 3,005.00	$ 3,370.00	$ 3,758.00	$ 4,136.00	$ 4,500.00
$ 28,350.00		$ 2,190.00	$ 3,007.00	$ 3,372.00	$ 3,759.00	$ 4,138.00	$ 4,502.00
$ 28,400.00		$ 2,192.00	$ 3,009.00	$ 3,374.00	$ 3,761.00	$ 4,140.00	$ 4,504.00
$ 28,450.00		$ 2,193.00	$ 3,010.00	$ 3,375.00	$ 3,763.00	$ 4,142.00	$ 4,507.00
$ 28,500.00		$ 2,194.00	$ 3,012.00	$ 3,377.00	$ 3,765.00	$ 4,145.00	$ 4,509.00
$ 28,550.00		$ 2,196.00	$ 3,014.00	$ 3,379.00	$ 3,767.00	$ 4,147.00	$ 4,512.00
$ 28,600.00		$ 2,197.00	$ 3,016.00	$ 3,381.00	$ 3,769.00	$ 4,149.00	$ 4,514.00
$ 28,650.00		$ 2,199.00	$ 3,017.00	$ 3,382.00	$ 3,771.00	$ 4,151.00	$ 4,516.00
$ 28,700.00		$ 2,200.00	$ 3,019.00	$ 3,384.00	$ 3,773.00	$ 4,153.00	$ 4,519.00
$ 28,750.00		$ 2,201.00	$ 3,021.00	$ 3,386.00	$ 3,775.00	$ 4,156.00	$ 4,521.00
$ 28,800.00		$ 2,203.00	$ 3,023.00	$ 3,388.00	$ 3,777.00	$ 4,158.00	$ 4,524.00
$ 28,850.00		$ 2,204.00	$ 3,025.00	$ 3,390.00	$ 3,779.00	$ 4,160.00	$ 4,526.00
$ 28,900.00		$ 2,205.00	$ 3,026.00	$ 3,391.00	$ 3,781.00	$ 4,162.00	$ 4,528.00
$ 28,950.00		$ 2,207.00	$ 3,028.00	$ 3,393.00	$ 3,783.00	$ 4,164.00	$ 4,531.00
$ 29,000.00		$ 2,208.00	$ 3,030.00	$ 3,395.00	$ 3,785.00	$ 4,167.00	$ 4,533.00
$ 29,050.00		$ 2,210.00	$ 3,032.00	$ 3,397.00	$ 3,787.00	$ 4,169.00	$ 4,536.00
$ 29,100.00		$ 2,211.00	$ 3,034.00	$ 3,398.00	$ 3,789.00	$ 4,171.00	$ 4,538.00
$ 29,150.00		$ 2,212.00	$ 3,035.00	$ 3,400.00	$ 3,791.00	$ 4,173.00	$ 4,540.00
$ 29,200.00		$ 2,214.00	$ 3,037.00	$ 3,402.00	$ 3,793.00	$ 4,175.00	$ 4,543.00
$ 29,250.00		$ 2,215.00	$ 3,039.00	$ 3,404.00	$ 3,795.00	$ 4,178.00	$ 4,545.00
$ 29,300.00		$ 2,216.00	$ 3,041.00	$ 3,406.00	$ 3,797.00	$ 4,180.00	$ 4,548.00
$ 29,350.00		$ 2,218.00	$ 3,042.00	$ 3,407.00	$ 3,799.00	$ 4,182.00	$ 4,550.00
$ 29,400.00		$ 2,219.00	$ 3,044.00	$ 3,409.00	$ 3,801.00	$ 4,184.00	$ 4,552.00
$ 29,450.00		$ 2,220.00	$ 3,046.00	$ 3,411.00	$ 3,803.00	$ 4,186.00	$ 4,555.00
$ 29,500.00		$ 2,222.00	$ 3,048.00	$ 3,413.00	$ 3,805.00	$ 4,189.00	$ 4,557.00
$ 29,550.00		$ 2,223.00	$ 3,050.00	$ 3,415.00	$ 3,807.00	$ 4,191.00	$ 4,560.00
$ 29,600.00		$ 2,225.00	$ 3,051.00	$ 3,416.00	$ 3,809.00	$ 4,193.00	$ 4,562.00
$ 29,650.00		$ 2,226.00	$ 3,053.00	$ 3,418.00	$ 3,811.00	$ 4,195.00	$ 4,564.00
$ 29,700.00		$ 2,227.00	$ 3,055.00	$ 3,420.00	$ 3,813.00	$ 4,197.00	$ 4,567.00
$ 29,750.00		$ 2,229.00	$ 3,057.00	$ 3,422.00	$ 3,815.00	$ 4,200.00	$ 4,569.00
$ 29,800.00		$ 2,230.00	$ 3,058.00	$ 3,423.00	$ 3,817.00	$ 4,202.00	$ 4,572.00
$ 29,850.00		$ 2,231.00	$ 3,060.00	$ 3,425.00	$ 3,819.00	$ 4,204.00	$ 4,574.00
$ 29,900.00		$ 2,233.00	$ 3,062.00	$ 3,427.00	$ 3,821.00	$ 4,206.00	$ 4,576.00
$ 29,950.00		$ 2,234.00	$ 3,064.00	$ 3,429.00	$ 3,823.00	$ 4,208.00	$ 4,579.00
$ 30,000.00		$ 2,236.00	$ 3,066.00	$ 3,431.00	$ 3,825.00	$ 4,211.00	$ 4,581.00

CHILD SUPPORT WORKSHEET

| IN THE | COURT OF | COUNTY |

STATE OF GEORGIA

_____ Plaintiff,

vs.

_____ Defendant,

Civil Action Case No. _____

IV-D Case No. _____

☐ Initial Action

☐ Modification

Date of Initial Child Support Order: _____

| Mother: | | Father: | |

Children for Whom Support is Being Determined in This Case

	Name	Birth Date		Name	Birth Date
☐			☐		
☐			☐		
☐			☐		
☐			☐		
☐			☐		
☐			☐		

Total Number of Children: _____

Submitted by: _____

Noncustodial Parent
☐ **Mother**
☐ **Father**

Nonparent Custodian ☐

		Mother	Father	Total
1.	**Monthly Gross Income** (from **Schedule A**, Line 23)	$ -	$ -	$ -
2.	**Monthly Adjusted Income** > If either parent pays self-employment tax or pays child support under a pre-existing order or is entitled to a credit for other qualified children living in the home, complete **Schedule B** and enter amount from **Schedule B**, Line 9 or Line 14 here. >Otherwise, enter amount from Line 1 here.	$ -	$ -	$ -
3.	**Pro Rata Shares of Combined Income** on Line 2 above (Divide each parent's income by the combined income to find %)	%	%	%
4.	**Basic Child Support Obligation** (from Table)			$ -
5.	Pro rata shares of Basic Child Support Obligation (Multiply Line 4 by percentages on Line 3)	$ -	$ -	
6.	**Adjustment for Work Related Child Care and Health Insurance Expenses** > Complete **Schedule D** and enter amount from **Schedule D**, Line 5 here. > If none, skip **Schedule D** and enter zero here.	$ -	$ -	
7.	Add Lines 5 & 6 and enter results here.	$ -	$ -	
8.	**Adjustment for Additional Expenses Paid.** Insert amounts PAID by each parent for child care & children's insurance from **Schedule D,** Line 3, Columns (a) and (b).	$ -	$ -	
9.	**Subtotal** > If Line 8 is zero, carry down amount from Line 7. >Otherwise, subtract Line 8 from Line 7.	$ -	$ -	

The amount on Line 9 is the Presumptive Child Support Amount.

CHILD SUPPORT WORKSHEET

		Mother	Father	Total
10.	**Deviations from Presumptive Child Support Amount** > Enter amount from *Schedule E*, Line 14 here.	$ -	$ -	
11.	**Subtotal** < If Line 10 is zero, then enter amount on Line 9 here. < If Line 10 is positive (+), then add Line 10 to Line 9 and enter result here. < If Line 10 is negative (-), then subtract Line 10 from Line 9 and enter result here.	$ -	$ -	
12.	**Social Security Payments** > If children receive Title II benefits as dependents on a parent's account, enter the monthly amount in that parent's column here. > If none, enter zero.	$ -	$ -	
13.	>If the amount on Line 12 is equal to or greater than Line 11, the child support responsibility is met and no further obligation is owed. Enter zero here. < Otherwise, subtract Line 12 from Line 11 and enter result here.	$ -	$ -	

The amount on Line 13 is the Final Child Support Amount.
Uninsured Health Expenses

14.	**Uninsured Health Expenses** <Carry down the percentage from Line 3 or enter the percentage otherwise ordered by the Court.	%	%	

Schedules

		Attached	Not Applicable
A	Gross Income	☐	
B	Adjusted Income	☐	☐
C	Schedule C is not in use and is intentionally left blank		
D	Additional Expenses	☐	☐
E	Deviations from Presumptive Amount	☐	☐

Names of Parties: _____ vs. _____

Submitted by: _____ Today's Date: _____

Case #: _____

CHILD SUPPORT SCHEDULE A
GROSS INCOME

	(a) Mother	(b) Father	(c) Combined
TANF (Temporary Assistance for Needy Families)			
>If a parent receives TANF, please check the box and enter any amounts for Gross Income below that apply.	☐	☐	
Gross Income (convert all amounts to monthly average)			
1. Salary and Wages (Do not include TANF or imputed income here. Enter Imputed Income on Line 22 below.)	$ -	$ -	
2. Commissions, Fees, Tips	$ -	$ -	
3. Income From Self-Employment	$ -	$ -	
4. Bonuses	$ -	$ -	
5. Overtime Payments	$ -	$ -	
6. Severance Pay	$ -	$ -	
7. Recurring Income from Pensions or Retirement Plans	$ -	$ -	
8. Interest Income	$ -	$ -	
9. Income from Dividends	$ -	$ -	
10. Trust Income	$ -	$ -	
11. Income from Annuities	$ -	$ -	
12. Capital Gains	$ -	$ -	
13. Social Security Disability or Retirement Benefits (*Do not include SSI or payments for children*)	$ -	$ -	
14. Worker's Compensation Benefits	$ -	$ -	
15. Unemployment Benefits	$ -	$ -	
16. Judgments from Personal Injury or Other Civil Cases	$ -	$ -	
17. Gifts (cash or other gifts that can be converted to cash)	$ -	$ -	
18. Prizes / Lottery Winnings	$ -	$ -	
19. Alimony & maintenance from persons not in this case	$ -	$ -	
20. Assets which are used for support of family	$ -	$ -	
21. Fringe Benefits (if significantly reduce living expenses)	$ -	$ -	
22. Any Other Income including Imputed Income. (*Do **not** include means-tested public assistance, such as TANF or food stamps.*)	$ -	$ -	
23. **TOTAL GROSS MONTHLY INCOME** Enter this amount on Line 1 of the *Child Support Worksheet*.	$ -	$ -	$ -

Names of Parties: _____ vs. _____

Submitted by: _____   Today's Date: _____

Case #: _____

CHILD SUPPORT SCHEDULE B
ADJUSTED INCOME

		(a) Mother	(b) Father
1.	**Total Gross Monthly Income** (*Schedule A*, Line 23)	$ -	$ -
	Self Employment Tax Adjustment		
2.	Monthly Self-Employment Income on which parent pays Self-Employment Taxes for FICA & Medicare	$ -	$ -
3.	For FICA, multiply Line 2 above by .062 (For maximum amount of self-employment income subject to Social Security tax, see IRS Publication 533 for the current taxable year).	$ -	$ -
4.	For Medicare tax, multiply Line 2 above by 0.0145 and enter results here.	$ -	$ -
5.	Add Lines 3 & 4 and enter results here.	$ -	$ -
6.	Subtract Line 5 from Line 1 and enter results here.	$ -	$ -
	Adjustment for Pre-Existing Child Support Orders Being Paid for Other Children		

For each pre-existing order, list the required information and the amount actually paid monthly. (Do not include arrears payments.)

	Court Name	Court Case #	Names and Birthdates of Children	Initial Date of Order	Pre-existing Child Support Amount Paid by Mother	Pre-existing Child Support Amount Paid by Father
7(a)					$ -	$ -
7(b)					$ -	$ -
7(c)					$ -	$ -
7(d)					$ -	$ -
8.	Total Adjustment for Pre-Existing Child Support Orders (Add all Pre-Existing Child Support amounts identified in Line 7)				$ -	$ -
9.	Subtract Line 8 from Line 6. If a discretionary adjustment is being claimed for other qualified children living in the home, complete Page 2. Otherwise, enter this amount on Line 2 of the **Child Support Worksheet**.				$ -	$ -

CHILD SUPPORT SCHEDULE B
ADJUSTED INCOME

Discretionary Adjustment to Income for Children Living in Parent's Home
<The Court has the discretion to consider an Adjustment to Income for qualified children under this section for the purpose of reducing the parent's gross income if failure to consider an adjustment would cause substantial hardship to the parent.
< If the Court considers an Adjustment to Income under this section, then the Court must also consider whether this Adjustment to Income is in the best interest of the child(ren) in this action
Adjustment may be considered only for children who meet ALL FIVE of the following requirements:

A. The parent is legally responsible for the qualified child (Step children do no qualify);

B. The qualified child lives in the parent's home;

C. The parent is actually supporting the qualified child;

D. The qualified child is not subject to a preexisting child support order; and

E. The qualified child is not currently before the court to set, modify or enforce child support.

Adjustment for other QUALIFIED children pursuant to the five factors listed above			
	Name(s)	Birth Date	Mark X if Mother is Claiming Credit	Mark X if Father is Claiming Credit
10.			☐	☐
			☐	☐
			☐	☐
			☐	☐
			☐	☐
			☐	☐
	Total number of QUALIFIED children for whom adjustment is being claimed	☐	-	-
11.	Bring down amount from Line 6 above (Gross Income less Self-Employment tax only) for the parent(s) seeking adjustment.		$ -	$ -
12.	Using the Basic Child Support Obligation Table, enter the Basic Child Support Obligation for the number of children on Line 10 and the income amount on Line 11 for only the parent seeking the adjustment.		$ -	$ -
13.	Enter 75% of the amount on Line 12 for the parent seeking the adjustment.		$ -	$ -
14.	If this adjustment is allowed, subtract Line 13 from Line 9 and enter this amount on Line 2 of the *Child Support Worksheet*.		$ -	$ -

Names of Parties: _____ vs. _____

Submitted by: _____   Today's Date: _____

Case #: _____

Child Support Schedule C
Is not in use and is intentionally left blank

Schedule C is not in use and is intentionally left blank

CHILD SUPPORT SCHEDULE D
ADDITIONAL EXPENSES

		(a) Mother	(b)Father	(c) Nonparent Custodian	(d) Combined
1.	Child Care Expenses Necessary for Parent's Employment, Education or Vocational Training. Enter monthly average amount paid by each Parent (or Nonparent Custodian) for child care for the children for whom support is being determined from all Supplemental Tables (Line 7 for Mother, Line 13 for Father, and Line 19 for Nonparent Custodian)	$ -	$ -	$ -	$ -
2.	Health Insurance Premiums Paid for the Children > Enter monthly amount paid or will be paid by each parent, or amount paid by Nonparent Custodian, for health insurance premium. >If the children's portion of the premium is not known, divide the total health insurance premium by the number of persons covered, then multiply that by the number of covered children for whom support is being determined and enter that amount.	$ -	$ -	$ -	$ -
3.	Total Monthly Additional Expenses (Line 1 + Line 2)	$ -	$ -	$ -	$ -
4.	Pro Rata Share of Parents' Income (from Child Support Worksheet Line 3)	%	%		%
5.	Pro Rata Share of Additional Expenses. (Multiply total amount in Column (d) of Line 3 by percentages in Line 4 above.) Enter result on Line 6 of Child Support Worksheet.	$ -	$ -		$ -

Supplemental Table 1. Use these tables to calculate amounts for line 1 Schedule D. For additional children use Supplemental Table 2.

		Child 1	Child 2	Child 3	
1.	Children's Names →				

Child Care Paid by Mother					**Totals**
2.	Total yearly amount paid for child care during school	$ -	$ -	$ -	$ -
3.	Total yearly amount paid for child care during summer break	$ -	$ -	$ -	$ -
4.	Total yearly amount paid for child care during other school breaks	$ -	$ -	$ -	$ -
5.	Total yearly amount of other child care (e.g. pre-school age child or child with disability)	$ -	$ -	$ -	$ -
6.	Total Yearly Amounts	$ -	$ -	$ -	$ -
7.	Monthly Average (Divide Line 6 by 12)	$ -	$ -	$ -	$ -

Child Care Paid by Father					**Totals**
8.	Total yearly amount paid for child care during school	$ -	$ -	$ -	$ -
9.	Total yearly amount paid for child care during summer break	$ -	$ -	$ -	$ -
10.	Total yearly amount paid for child care during other school breaks	$ -	$ -	$ -	$ -
11.	Total yearly amount of other child care (e.g. pre-school age child or child with disability)	$ -	$ -	$ -	$ -
12.	Total Yearly Amounts	$ -	$ -	$ -	$ -
13.	Monthly Average (Divide Line 12 by 12)	$ -	$ -	$ -	$ -

Child Care Paid by Nonparent Custodian					**Totals**
14.	Total yearly amount paid for child care during school	$ -	$ -	$ -	$ -
15.	Total yearly amount paid for child care during summer break	$ -	$ -	$ -	$ -
16.	Total yearly amount paid for child care during other school breaks	$ -	$ -	$ -	$ -
17.	Total yearly amount of other child care (e.g. pre-school age child or child with disability)	$ -	$ -	$ -	$ -
18.	Total Yearly Amounts	$ -	$ -	$ -	$ -
19.	Monthly Average (Divide Line 18 by 12)	$ -	$ -	$ -	$ -

Names of Parties: _____ vs. _____

Submitted by: _____   Today's Date: _____

Case #: _____

CHILD SUPPORT SCHEDULE D
ADDITIONAL EXPENSES

		Child 4	Child 5	Child 6	
Supplemental Table 2. Use these tables to calculate amounts for line 1 Schedule D. For additional children use Supplemental Table 3.					
1.	Children's Names →				
Child Care Paid by Mother					**Totals**
2.	Total yearly amount paid for child care during school	$ -	$ -	$ -	$ -
3.	Total yearly amount paid for child care during summer break	$ -	$ -	$ -	$ -
4.	Total yearly amount paid for child care during other school breaks	$ -	$ -	$ -	$ -
5.	Total yearly amount of other child care (e.g. pre-school age child or child with disability)	$ -	$ -	$ -	$ -
6.	Total Yearly Amounts	$ -	$ -	$ -	$ -
7.	Monthly Average (Divide Line 6 by 12)	$ -	$ -	$ -	$ -
Child Care Paid by Father					**Totals**
8.	Total yearly amount paid for child care during school	$ -	$ -	$ -	$ -
9.	Total yearly amount paid for child care during summer break	$ -	$ -	$ -	$ -
10.	Total yearly amount paid for child care during other school breaks	$ -	$ -	$ -	$ -
11.	Total yearly amount of other child care (e.g. pre-school age child or child with disability)	$ -	$ -	$ -	$ -
12.	Total Yearly Amounts	$ -	$ -	$ -	$ -
13.	Monthly Average (Divide Line 12 by 12)	$ -	$ -	$ -	$ -
Child Care Paid by Nonparent Custodian					**Totals**
14.	Total yearly amount paid for child care during school	$ -	$ -	$ -	$ -
15.	Total yearly amount paid for child care during summer break	$ -	$ -	$ -	$ -
16.	Total yearly amount paid for child care during other school breaks	$ -	$ -	$ -	$ -
17.	Total yearly amount of other child care (e.g. pre-school age child or child with disability)	$ -	$ -	$ -	$ -
18.	Total Yearly Amounts	$ -	$ -	$ -	$ -
19.	Monthly Average (Divide Line 18 by 12)	$ -	$ -	$ -	$ -

Names of Parties: _____ vs. _____

Submitted by: _____   Today's Date: _____

Case #: _____

CHILD SUPPORT SCHEDULE D
ADDITIONAL EXPENSES

		Child 7	Child 8	Child 9	
Supplemental Table 3. Use these tables to calculate amounts for line 1 Schedule D. For additional children use Supplemental Table 4.					
1.	Children's Names →				
Child Care Paid by Mother					**Totals**
2.	Total yearly amount paid for child care during school	$ -	$ -	$ -	$ -
3.	Total yearly amount paid for child care during summer break	$ -	$ -	$ -	$ -
4.	Total yearly amount paid for child care during other school breaks	$ -	$ -	$ -	$ -
5.	Total yearly amount of other child care (e.g. pre-school age child or child with disability)	$ -	$ -	$ -	$ -
6.	Total Yearly Amounts	$ -	$ -	$ -	$ -
7.	Monthly Average (Divide Line 6 by 12)	$ -	$ -	$ -	$ -
Child Care Paid by Father					**Totals**
8.	Total yearly amount paid for child care during school	$ -	$ -	$ -	$ -
9.	Total yearly amount paid for child care during summer break	$ -	$ -	$ -	$ -
10.	Total yearly amount paid for child care during other school breaks	$ -	$ -	$ -	$ -
11.	Total yearly amount of other child care (e.g. pre-school age child or child with disability)	$ -	$ -	$ -	$ -
12.	Total Yearly Amounts	$ -	$ -	$ -	$ -
13.	Monthly Average (Divide Line 12 by 12)	$ -	$ -	$ -	$ -
Child Care Paid by Nonparent Custodian					**Totals**
14.	Total yearly amount paid for child care during school	$ -	$ -	$ -	$ -
15.	Total yearly amount paid for child care during summer break	$ -	$ -	$ -	$ -
16.	Total yearly amount paid for child care during other school breaks	$ -	$ -	$ -	$ -
17.	Total yearly amount of other child care (e.g. pre-school age child or child with disability)	$ -	$ -	$ -	$ -
18.	Total Yearly Amounts	$ -	$ -	$ -	$ -
19.	Monthly Average (Divide Line 18 by 12)	$ -	$ -	$ -	$ -

Names of Parties: _____ vs. _____

Submitted by: _____   Today's Date: _____

Case #: _____

CHILD SUPPORT SCHEDULE D
ADDITIONAL EXPENSES

		Child 10	Child 11	Child 12	
	Supplemental Table 4. Use these tables to calculate amounts for line 1 Schedule D.				
1.	Children's Names →				

Child Care Paid by Mother — Totals

		Child 10	Child 11	Child 12	Totals
2.	Total yearly amount paid for child care during school	$ -	$ -	$ -	$ -
3.	Total yearly amount paid for child care during summer break	$ -	$ -	$ -	$ -
4.	Total yearly amount paid for child care during other school breaks	$ -	$ -	$ -	$ -
5.	Total yearly amount of other child care (e.g. pre-school age child or child with disability)	$ -	$ -	$ -	$ -
6.	Total Yearly Amounts	$ -	$ -	S -	$ -
7.	Monthly Average (Divide Line 6 by 12)	$ -	$ -	S -	$ -

Child Care Paid by Father — Totals

		Child 10	Child 11	Child 12	Totals
8.	Total yearly amount paid for child care during school	$ -	$ -	S -	$ -
9.	Total yearly amount paid for child care during summer break	$ -	$ -	S -	$ -
10.	Total yearly amount paid for child care during other school breaks	$ -	$ -	S -	$ -
11.	Total yearly amount of other child care (e.g. pre-school age child or child with disability)	$ -	$ -	S -	$ -
12.	Total Yearly Amounts	$ -	$ -	S -	$ -
13.	Monthly Average (Divide Line 12 by 12)	$ -	$ -	S -	$ -

Child Care Paid by Nonparent Custodian — Totals

		Child 10	Child 11	Child 12	Totals
14.	Total yearly amount paid for child care during school	$ -	$ -	S -	$ -
15.	Total yearly amount paid for child care during summer break	$ -	$ -	S -	$ -
16.	Total yearly amount paid for child care during other school breaks	$ -	$ -	S -	$ -
17.	Total yearly amount of other child care (e.g. pre-school age child or child with disability)	$ -	$ -	S -	$ -
18.	Total Yearly Amounts	$ -	$ -	S -	$ -
19.	Monthly Average (Divide Line 18 by 12)	$ -	$ -	S -	$ -

Names of Parties: _____ vs. _____

Submitted by: _____ Today's Date: _____

Case #: _____

CHILD SUPPORT SCHEDULE E
Deviation (Special Circumstances)

Special Circumstances	(a) Mother	(b) Father	(c) Nonparent Custodian	(d) Combined
A. For each section completed, provide monthly amounts or other information as required.				
Low Income Deviation with Self Support Reserve **Complete this section if Noncustodial Parent's Gross Income is at or below $1,850/month.** **Otherwise skip this entire section and begin at Line 2(a) of Schedule E.**				
1(a). >If Gross Income of Noncustodial Parent is at or below $1,850/month, enter that parent's Adjusted Income from **Child Support Worksheet**, Line 2 here. >If Gross Income of Custodial Parent is at or below $1,850/month, enter that parent's Adjusted Income from **Child Support Worksheet**, Line 2 here.	$ -	$ -		
1(b). Self Support Reserve – enter $900 here for each parent.	$ -	$ -		
1(c). Income available for support. Subtract Line 1(b) from Line 1(a), and enter result here.	$ -	$ -		
1(d). Parent's Share of Presumptive Child Support Award (**Child Support Worksheet** Line 9)	$ -	$ -		
1(e). Lesser of Line 1(c) and Line 1(d) in NONCUSTODIAL Parent's column only.	$ -	$ -		
1(f). Minimum amount of child support when applying Low Income Deviation – enter $75 here for Noncustodial Parent only.	$ -	$ -		
1(g). If Line 1(e) is greater than Line 1(f), enter amount from Line 1(e) in NONCUSTODIAL Parent's column. If Line 1(f) is greater than Line 1(e), enter amount from Line 1(f) in NONCUSTODIAL Parent's column.	$ -	$ -		
1(h). >If CUSTODIAL Parent is considered a low income person (at or below $1,850 gross income per month) AND Line 1(c) for CUSTODIAL Parent is less than Line 1(d) for CUSTODIAL Parent, the NONCUSTODIAL Parent is not allowed a deviation for self-support reserve. In this case, enter line 1(d) for NONCUSTODIAL Parent in NONCUSTODIAL Parent's column. >Otherwise, if Line 1(c) for CUSTODIAL Parent is greater than or equal to Line 1(d) for CUSTODIAL Parent, enter Line 1(g) for NONCUSTODIAL Parent in NONCUSTODIAL Parent's column.	$ -	$ -		
1(i). Subtract Line 1(h) from Line 1(d) for the NONCUSTODIAL Parent. This is the amount of deviation.	$ -	$ -		
High Income and Other Amounts				
2(a). High Income - Combined Adjusted Income greater than $30,000/month from Line 2 on **Child Support Worksheet**.				$ -
2(b). Deviation Based on High Income	$ -	$ -		$ -
3. Other Health Related Insurance (dental, vision)	$ -	$ -		$ -
4. Life Insurance	$ -	$ -		$ -
5. Child and Dependent Care Tax Credit	$ -	$ -		$ -
6. Visitation Related Travel Expenses	$ -	$ -		$ -
7. Alimony PAID	$ -	$ -		$ -
8. Mortgage (if Noncustodial Parent is providing cost of home where child resides)	$ -	$ -		$ -
9. Permanency Plan or Foster Care Plan	$ -	$ -		$ -
10. Other - Non-specific Deviations	$ -	$ -		$ -
11. Enter on this line the deviation, indicated by a positive(+) for increase or negative(-) for decrease. This is the recommended deviation based on the amounts entered above.	$ -	$ -		$ -

CHILD SUPPORT SCHEDULE E
Deviation (Special Circumstances)

			(a) Mother	(b) Father	(c) Nonparent Custodian	(d) Combined
		Extraordinary and Special Expenses - Complete Supplemental Tables				
12(a).		Extraordinary Educational Expenses >Add all Total amounts from Line 9(a) of each Supplemental Table and enter amount in Mother's column. >Add all Total amounts from Line 9(b) of each Supplemental Table and enter amount in Father's column. >Add all Total amounts from Line 9(c) of each Supplemental Table and enter amount in Nonparent's column.	$ -	$ -	$ -	$ -
12(b).		Extraordinary Medical Expenses >Add all Total amounts from Line 14(a) of each Supplemental Table and enter amount in Mother's column. >Add all Total amounts from Line 14(b) of each Supplemental Table and enter amount in Father's column. >Add all Total amounts from Line 14(c) of each Supplemental Table and enter amount in Nonparent's column.	$ -	$ -	$ -	$ -
12(c).		Allowable Special Expenses >Enter amount from Line 28 of Supplemental Table 1 in Mother's column. >Enter amount from Line 29 of Supplemental Table 1 in Father's column. >Enter amount from Line 30 of Supplemental Table 1 in Nonparent's column.	$ -	$ -	$ -	$ -
12(d).		Total Extraordinary and Allowable Special Expenses (Add lines 12(a), 12(b) and 12(c) and enter results here.)	$ -	$ -	$ -	$ -
12(e).		Parent's Pro Rata Share of Income (from *Child Support Worksheet* Line 3)	%	%		%
12(f).		Multiply Line 12(d) Combined amount by percentages for each Parent on Line 12(e) and enter results here for each Parent, and enter the total result under column (d) Combined.	$ -	$ -		$ -
12(g).		Subtract Line 12(d) from Line 12(f). This is the deviation amount for each Parent for Extraordinary Expenses.	$ -	$ -		
		Parenting Time Deviation **(Complete only if Parenting Time Deviation is being considered for Noncustodial Parent)**				
13.		>Enter amount of Parenting Time Adjustment deviation here. (Deviation is deducted from the Noncustodial Parent's Basic Child Support Obligation on *Child Support Worksheet* Line 5.) > If no Parenting Time Adjustment deviation applies, then enter zero here.	$ -	$ -		
		Total Allowable Deviation				
14.		Total Allowable Deviations - Add or subtract the allowable deviations on Line 1(j), 11 and 12(g), together, if any apply. Enter the total here and on *Child Support Worksheet* Line 10. (The total can be a negative number.)	$ -	$ -		

B. Would the presumptive amount be unjust or inappropriate? Explain

C. Would deviation serve the best interests of the children for whom support is being determined? Explain

D. Would deviation seriously impair the ability of the CUSTODIAL Parent or NONPARENT Custodian to maintain minimally adequate housing, food and clothing for the children being supported by the order and to provide other basic necessities? Explain

CHILD SUPPORT SCHEDULE E
Deviation (Special Circumstances)

	Supplemental Table 1. Use these tables to calculate amount for Line 12 Schedule E. For additional children use Supplemental Table 2		Child 1	Child 2	Child 3	
1.	Children's Names					
Extraordinary Educational Expenses		**Paid by**				**Totals**
2.	Total yearly amount paid for Tuition, Room & Board, Fees and Books	Mother	$.	$.	$.	$.
3.	Total yearly amount paid for Other Extraordinary Educational Expenses	Mother	$.	$.	$.	$.
4.	Total yearly amount paid for Tuition, Room & Board, Fees and Books	Father	$.	$.	$.	$.
5.	Total yearly amount paid for Other Extraordinary Educational Expenses	Father	$.	$.	$.	$.
6.	Total yearly amount paid for Tuition, Room & Board, Fees and Books	Nonparent Custodian	$.	$.	$.	$.
7.	Total yearly amount paid for Other Extraordinary Educational Expenses	Nonparent Custodian	$.	$.	$.	$.
8.	Total Yearly Amounts		$.	$.	$.	$.
9.	Monthly Average (Divide Line 8 by 12)		$.	$.	$.	$.
9(a)	Mother's monthly Extraordinary Educational Expenses	Mother	$.	$.	$.	$.
9(b)	Father's monthly Extraordinary Educational Expenses	Father	$.	$.	$.	$.
9(c)	Nonparent's monthly Extraordinary Educational Expenses	Nonparent Custodian	$.	$.	$.	$.
Extraordinary Medical Expenses		**Paid by**				**Totals**
10.	Total yearly amount paid for extraordinary medical expenses	Mother	$.	$.	$.	$.
11.	Total yearly amount paid for extraordinary medical expenses	Father	$.	$.	$.	$.
12.	Total yearly amount paid for extraordinary medical expenses	Nonparent Custodian	$.	$.	$.	$.
13.	Total Yearly Amounts		$.	$.	$.	$.
14.	Monthly Average (Divide Line 13 by 12)		$.	$.	$.	$.
14a)	Mother's monthly Extraordinary Medical Expenses	Mother	$.	$.	$.	$.
14(b)	Father's monthly Extraordinary Medical Expenses	Father	$.	$.	$.	$.
14(c)	Nonparent's monthly Extraordinary Medical Expenses	Nonparent Custodian	$.	$.	$.	$.
Special Expenses for Child Rearing (including, but not limited to summer camp, music or art lessons, travel, band, clubs, athletics, etc.)		**Paid by**				**Totals**
15.	Total yearly amount paid for:	Mother	$.	$.	$.	$.
16.	Total yearly amount paid for:	Father	$.	$.	$.	$. .
17.	Total yearly amount paid for:	Nonparent Custodian	$.	$.	$.	$.
18.	Total Yearly Amounts (Add Lines 15, 16 & 17)		$.	$.	$.	$.
19.	Monthly Average (Divide Line 18 by 12)		$.	$.	$.	$.
7 Percent Test to Calculate Allowable Expenses		**Paid by**				**Totals**
20.	Total Yearly amount paid for Special Expenses for Child Rearing >Add all Total amounts from Line 15 of each Supplemental Table and enter here.	Mother				$.
21.	Total Yearly amount paid for Special Expenses for Child Rearing >Add all Total amounts from Line 16 of each Supplemental Table and enter here.	Father				$.
22.	Total Yearly amount paid for Special Expenses for Child Rearing >Add all Total amounts from Line 17 of each Supplemental Table and enter here.	Nonparent Custodian				$.
23.	Total Yearly Amounts (Add Lines 20, 21 & 22)					$.
24.	Monthly Average (Divide Line 23 by 12)					$.
25.	Basic Child Support Obligation (from Line 4 of Child Support Worksheet)					$.
26.	Special Expenses Limitation (Multiply Line 25 x 7% (.07))					$.
27.	If Line 24 is greater than Line 26, then subtract Line 26 from Line 24, enter difference here. If Line 24 is less than Line 26, then enter zero here.					$.
28.	Mother's Monthly Allowable Special Expenses for Child Rearing >Divide Line 20 by Line 23 to obtain Mother's Pro-rata share of the Special Expenses. >Multiply Mother's Pro-rata percentage by the amount on Line 27 and enter amount here.					$.
29.	Father's Monthly Allowable Special Expenses for Child Rearing >Divide Line 21 by Line 23 to obtain Father's Pro-rata share of the Special Expenses. >Multiply Father's Pro-rata percentage by the amount on Line 27 and enter amount here.					$.
30.	Nonparent's Monthly Allowable Special Expenses for Child Rearing >Divide Line 22 by Line 23 to obtain Nonparent's Pro-rata share of the Special Expenses. >Multiply Nonparent's Pro-rata percentage by the amount on Line 27 and enter amount here.					$.

Names of Parties: _____ vs. _____

Submitted by: _____   Today's Date: _____

Case #: _____

CHILD SUPPORT SCHEDULE E
ADDITIONAL CIRCUMSTANCES

Supplemental Table 2. Use these tables to calculate amount for Line 12 Schedule E. For additional children use Supplemental Table

			Child 4	Child 5	Child 6	Totals
1.	Children's Names →					
Extraordinary Educational Expenses		**Paid by**				**Totals**
2.	Total yearly amount paid for Tuition, Room & Board, Fees and Books	Mother	$ -	$ -	$ -	$ -
3.	Total yearly amount paid for Other Extraordinary Educational Expenses	Mother	$ -	$ -	$ -	$ -
4.	Total yearly amount paid for Tuition, Room & Board, Fees and Books	Father	$ -	$ -	$ -	$ -
5.	Total yearly amount paid for Other Extraordinary Educational Expenses	Father	$ -	$ -	$ -	$ -
6.	Total yearly amount paid for Tuition, Room & Board, Fees and Books	Nonparent Custodian	$ -	$ -	$ -	$ -
7.	Total yearly amount paid for Other Extraordinary Educational Expenses	Nonparent Custodian	$ -	$ -	$ -	$ -
8.	Total Yearly Amounts		$ -	$ -	$ -	$ -
9.	Monthly Average (Divide Line 8 by 12)		$ -	$ -	$ -	$ -
9(a)	Mother's monthly Extraordinary Educational Expenses	Mother	$ -	$ -	$ -	$ -
9(b)	Father's monthly Extraordinary Educational Expenses	Father	$ -	$ -	$ -	$ -
9(c)	Nonparent's monthly Extraordinary Educational Expenses	Nonparent Custodian	$ -	$ -	$ -	$ -
Extraordinary Medical Expenses		**Paid by**				**Totals**
10.	Total yearly amount paid for extraordinary medical expenses	Mother	$ -	$ -	$ -	$ -
11.	Total yearly amount paid for extraordinary medical expenses	Father	$ -	$ -	$ -	$ -
12.	Total yearly amount paid for extraordinary medical expenses	Nonparent Custodian	$ -	$ -	$ -	$ -
13.	Total Yearly Amounts		$ -	$ -	$ -	$ -
14.	Monthly Average (Divide Line 13 by 12)		$ -	$ -	$ -	$ -
14(a).	Mother's monthly Extraordinary Medical Expenses	Mother	$ -	$ -	$ -	$ -
14(b).	Father's monthly Extraordinary Medical Expenses	Father	$ -	$ -	$ -	$ -
14(c).	Nonparent's monthly Extraordinary Medical Expenses	Nonparent Custodian	$ -	$ -	$ -	$ -
Special Expenses for Child Rearing (including, but not limited to summer camp, music or art lessons, travel, band, clubs, athletics, etc.)		**Paid by**				**Totals**
15.	Total yearly amount paid for:	Mother	$ -	$ -	$ -	$ -
16.	Total yearly amount paid for:	Father	$ -	$ -	$ -	$ -
17.	Total yearly amount paid for:	Nonparent Custodian	$ -	$ -	$ -	$ -
18.	Total Yearly Amounts (Add Lines 15, 16 & 17)		$ -	$ -	$ -	$ -
19.	Monthly Average (Divide Line 18 by 12)		$ -	$ -	$ -	$ -

Names of Parties: _____ vs. _____

Submitted by: _____   Today's Date: _____

Case #: _____

CHILD SUPPORT SCHEDULE E
ADDITIONAL CIRCUMSTANCES

Supplemental Table 3. Use these tables to calculate amount for Line 12 Schedule E. For additional children use Supplemental Table

		Paid by	Child 7	Child 8	Child 9	Totals
1.	Children's Names →					
Extraordinary Educational Expenses		**Paid by**				**Totals**
2.	Total yearly amount paid for Tuition, Room & Board, Fees and Books	Mother	$ -	$ -	$ -	$ -
3.	Total yearly amount paid for Other Extraordinary Educational Expenses	Mother	$ -	$ -	$ -	$ -
4.	Total yearly amount paid for Tuition, Room & Board, Fees and Books	Father	$ -	$ -	$ -	$ -
5.	Total yearly amount paid for Other Extraordinary Educational Expenses	Father	$ -	$ -	$ -	$ -
6.	Total yearly amount paid for Tuition, Room & Board, Fees and Books	Nonparent Custodian	$ -	$ -	$ -	$ -
7.	Total yearly amount paid for Other Extraordinary Educational Expenses	Nonparent Custodian	$ -	$ -	$ -	$ -
8.	Total Yearly Amounts		$ -	$ -	$ -	$ -
9.	Monthly Average (Divide Line 8 by 12)		$ -	$ -	$ -	$ -
9(a).	Mother's monthly Extraordinary Educational Expenses	Mother	$ -	$ -	$ -	$ -
9(b).	Father's monthly Extraordinary Educational Expenses	Father	$ -	$ -	$ -	$ -
9(c).	Nonparent's monthly Extraordinary Educational Expenses	Nonparent Custodian	$ -	$ -	$ -	$ -
Extraordinary Medical Expenses		**Paid by**				**Totals**
10.	Total yearly amount paid for extraordinary medical expenses	Mother	$ -	$ -	$ -	$ -
11.	Total yearly amount paid for extraordinary medical expenses	Father	$ -	$ -	$ -	$ -
12.	Total yearly amount paid for extraordinary medical expenses	Nonparent Custodian	$ -	$ -	$ -	$ -
13.	Total Yearly Amounts		$ -	$ -	$ -	$ -
14.	Monthly Average (Divide Line 13 by 12)		$ -	$ -	$ -	$ -
14a)	Mother's monthly Extraordinary Medical Expenses	Mother	$ -	$ -	$ -	$ -
14(b)	Father's monthly Extraordinary Medical Expenses	Father	$ -	$ -	$ -	$ -
14(c).	Nonparent's monthly Extraordinary Medical Expenses	Nonparent Custodian	$ -	$ -	$ -	$ -
Special Expenses for Child Rearing (including, but not limited to summer camp, music or art lessons, travel, band, clubs, athletics, etc.)		**Paid by**				**Totals**
15.	Total yearly amount paid for:	Mother	$ -	$ -	$ -	$ -
16.	Total yearly amount paid for:	Father	$ -	$ -	$ -	$ -
17.	Total yearly amount paid for:	Nonparent Custodian	$ -	$ -	$ -	$ -
18.	Total Yearly Amounts (Add Lines 15, 16 & 17)		$ -	$ -	$ -	$ -
19.	Monthly Average (Divide Line 18 by 12)		$ -	$ -	$ -	$ -

Names of Parties: vs.

Submitted by _____   Today's Date: _____

Case #: _____

CHILD SUPPORT SCHEDULE E
ADDITIONAL CIRCUMSTANCES

Supplemental Table 4 Use these tables to calculate amount for Line 12 Schedule E.			Child 10	Child 11	Child 12	
1.	Children's Names →					
Extraordinary Educational Expenses		Paid by				Totals
2.	Total yearly amount paid for Tuition, Room & Board, Fees and Books	Mother	$ -	$ -	$ -	$ -
3.	Total yearly amount paid for Other Extraordinary Educational Expenses	Mother	$ -	$ -	$ -	$ -
4.	Total yearly amount paid for Tuition, Room & Board, Fees and Books	Father	$ -	$ -	$ -	$ -
5.	Total yearly amount paid for Other Extraordinary Educational Expenses	Father	$ -	$ -	$ -	$ -
6.	Total yearly amount paid for Tuition, Room & Board, Fees and Books	Nonparent Custodian	$ -	$ -	$ -	$ -
7.	Total yearly amount paid for Other Extraordinary Educational Expenses	Nonparent Custodian	$ -	$ -	$ -	$ -
8.	Total Yearly Amounts		$ -	$ -	$ -	$ -
9.	Monthly Average (Divide Line 8 by 12)		$ -	$ -	$ -	$ -
9(a)	Mother's monthly Extraordinary Educational Expenses	Mother	$ -	$ -	$ -	$ -
9(b)	Father's monthly Extraordinary Educational Expenses	Father	$ -	$ -	$ -	$ -
9(c)	Nonparent's monthly Extraordinary Educational Expenses	Nonparent Custodian	$ -	$ -	$ -	$ -
Extraordinary Medical Expenses		Paid by				Totals
10.	Total yearly amount paid for extraordinary medical expenses	Mother	$ -	$ -	$ -	$ -
11.	Total yearly amount paid for extraordinary medical expenses	Father	$ -	$ -	$ -	$ -
12.	Total yearly amount paid for extraordinary medical expenses	Nonparent Custodian	$ -	$ -	$ -	$ -
13.	Total Yearly Amounts		$ -	$ -	$ -	$ -
14.	Monthly Average (Divide Line 13 by 12)		$ -	$ -	$ -	$ -
14a)	Mother's monthly Extraordinary Medical Expenses	Mother	$ -	$ -	$ -	$ -
14(b)	Father's monthly Extraordinary Medical Expenses	Father	$ -	$ -	$ -	$ -
14(c)	Nonparent's monthly Extraordinary Medical Expenses	Nonparent Custodian	$ -	$ -	$ -	$ -
Special Expenses for Child Rearing (including, but not limited to summer camp, music or art lessons, travel, band, clubs, athletics, etc.)		Paid by				Totals
15.	Total yearly amount paid for:	Mother	$ -	$ -	$ -	$ -
16.	Total yearly amount paid for:	Father	$ -	$ -	$ -	$ -
17.	Total yearly amount paid for:	Nonparent Custodian	$ -	$ -	$ -	$ -
18.	Total Yearly Amounts (Add Lines 15, 16 & 17)		$ -	$ -	$ -	$ -
19.	Monthly Average (Divide Line 18 by 12)		$ -	$ -	$ -	$ -

Names of Parties: _____ vs. _____

Submitted by: _____ Today's Date: _____

Case #: _____

IN THE SUPERIOR COURT OF _____ COUNTY
STATE OF GEORGIA

_____

_____

_____

PLAINTIFF

v.

_____

_____

_____

DEFENDANT

CIVIL ACTION
NUMBER _____

COST DEPOSIT _____

SUMMONS

TO THE ABOVE NAMED DEFENDANT:

You are hereby summoned and required to file with the Clerk of said court and serve upon the Plaintiff's attorney, whose name and address is:

an answer to the complaint which is herewith served upon you, within 30 days after service of this summons upon you, exclusive of the day of service. If you fail to do so, judgment by default will be taken against you for the relief demanded in the complaint.

This _____ day of _____, _____

Clerk of Superior Court

By _____
                                        Clerk

To Defendant upon whom this petition is served:

This copy of complaint and summons was served upon you _____, _____.

_____
Deputy Sheriff,   County, Georgia

This page intentionally blank.

_____COURT OF _____ COUNTY GEORGIA

	)	CASE NUMBER _____
_____	)	
Plaintiff	)	
	)	
v.)		Attorney or Plaintiff's Name & Address
	)	
_____	)	_____
Defendant	)	

_____

_____   Defendant Address

_____

_____

_____

❏

Designate Party to be served by placing a
check in box above

SHERIFF'S ENTRY OF SERVICE

I have this day served the defendant ....personally with a copy
of the within action and summons.

I have this day served the defendant ....by leaving
a copy of the action and summons at his or her most notorious place of abode in this County.

Delivered same into hands of .... described as follows
age, about .... years; weight, about .... pounds; height, about ....feet and ....inches,
domiciled at the residence of defendant, at .... a.m./p.m.

Served the (defendant, Garnishee) .... a corporation
by leaving a copy of the within action and summons with ....
in charge of the office and place of doing business of said Corporation in this County, at ....a.m./p.m.

I have this day served the above affidavit and summons on the defendant(s) by posting a copy of the same to
the door of the premises designated in said affidavit, and on the same day of such posting by depositing a
true copy of same in the United States Mail, First Class, in an envelope properly addressed to the defendant(s)
at the address shown in said summons, with adequate postage affixed thereon containing notice to the
defendant(s) to answer said summons at the place in the summons.

Diligent search made and defendant ....
not to be found in the jurisdiction of this Court.

The defendant is required to answer no later than .... , ... ,
at the place stated in the summons.

This _____ day of _____, _____

SHERIFF DOCKET _____ Page_____   _____

This page intentionally blank.

IN THE SUPERIOR COURT OF _____ COUNTY

STATE OF GEORGIA

_____	)	
Plaintiff	)	CIVIL ACTION
v.	)	FILE #: _____
_____	)	
Defendant	)	

RULE NISI

The within and foregoing Petition of the Plaintiff [or Defendant] having been read and considered, the matter is set down for a hearing on the issues raised therein before this Court on the ____ day of _____, _____, at _____ o'clock ____. m., or as soon thereafter as the parties may be heard, and the Defendant [or Plaintiff] ordered and directed to appear at said hearing and to show cause why the prayers of the Plaintiff [or Defendant] should not be granted.

_____

Judge/Clerk _____ Superior Court

Submitted by:

_____

Pro Se

Address and phone number:

_____

_____

_____

_____

This page intentionally blank.

CERTIFICATE OF SERVICE

I HEREBY CERTIFY THAT I HAVE SERVED THIS _____

_____,

UPON _____, BY

□ HAND DELIVERY

□ DEPOSITING SAME IN THE UNITED STATES MAIL
IN A PROPERLY ADDRESSED ENVELOPE WITH
ADEQUATE POSTAGE THEREON.

This _____, _____

_____

Plaintiff [or Defendant]

Address:

_____

_____

_____

_____

This page intentionally blank.

DISCLOSURE STATEMENT
CLERK OF SUPERIOR COURT

_____)
Plaintiff)
v.)   CASE NUMBER_____
)   Assigned by Clerk
_____)
Defendant)

TYPE OF ACTION

1. ____Divorce without Agreement Attached

2. ____Divorce with Agreement Attached

3. ____Domestic Relations

4. ____Damages arising out of Contract

5. ____Damages arising out of Tort

6. ____Condemnation

7. ____Equity

8. ____Zoning—County Ordinance violations (i.e., injunctive relief-zoning)

9. ____Zoning Appeals (denovo)

10. ____Appeal, including denovo appeal—excluding Zoning

11. ____URESA

12. ____Name Change

13. ____Other

14. ____Recusal

____Adoption

PREVIOUS RELATED CASES

Does this case involve substantially the same parties, or substantially the same subject matter, or substantially the same factual issues, as any other case filed in this court? (Whether pending simultaneously or not.)

_____NO

_____YES—If yes, please fill out the following:

1. Case #_____

2. Parties _____ vs. _____

3. Assigned Judge_____

4. Is this case still pending? _____Yes   _____No

5. Brief description of similarities:

_____

_____

_____
Attorney or Party Filing Suit

This page intentionally blank.

Domestic Relations Case Filing Information Form

Superior Court   County _____   **Date Filed** _____
MM-DD-YYYY

Docket # _____

Plaintiff(s)   **Defendant(s)**

_____   _____
Last   First   Middle I. Suffix Prefix   Maiden   Last   First   Middle I. Suffix Prefix   Maiden

_____   _____
Last   First   Middle I. Suffix Prefix   Maiden   Last   First   Middle I. Suffix Prefix   Maiden

Plaintiff/Petitioner's Attorney   ☐ **Pro Se**

                                                             Bar # _____
_____
Last   First   Middle I.   Suffix

Check Case Type (one or more)

☐ Divorce (includes annulment)

☐ Separate Maintenance

☐ Adoption

☐ Paternity (includes legitimation)

☐ Interstate Support Enforcement Action

☐ Domestication of Foreign Custody Decree

☐ Family Violence Act Petition

MODIFICATION

☐ Modification - Custody and/or Visitation

☐ Modification - Child Support and Alimony

☐ Modification - Child Support

☐ Modification - Alimony

CONTEMPT

☐ Contempt - Custody and/or Visitation

☐ Contempt - Child Support and Alimony

☐ Contempt - Child Support

☐ Contempt - Alimony

☐ Other Domestic Contempt

☐ Other Domestic Relations Specify _____
_____
_____

FAMILY VIOLENCE

Additional Information - Ex Parte Relief

Did the initial pleading include a request for relief

1. From alleged family violence?   ☐ Yes   ☐ No

2. Was ex parte relief requested?   ☐ Yes   ☐ No

3. Was ex parte relief granted?   ☐ Yes   ☐ No

This page intentionally blank.

Domestic Relations Case Final Disposition Information Form

Superior Court   **County** _____   **Date Disposed** _____
MM-DD-YYYY

Docket # _____

Reporting Party _____   _____
Last   First   Middle I. Suffix Prefix   Maiden   Title

Name of Plaintiff/Petitioner(s)   **Name of Defendant/Respondent(s)**

_____   _____
Last   First   Middle I. Suffix Prefix   Maiden   Last   First   Middle I. Suffix Prefix   Maiden

Plaintiff/Petitioner's Attorney ☐ **Pro Se**   **Defendant/Respondent's Attorney** ☐ **Pro Se**

_____   _____
Last   First   Middle I.   Suffix   Last   First   Middle I.   Suffix

Bar # _____   **Bar #** _____

Type of Disposition (Check all that apply)

1. ☐ Dismissed Without Final Order

   A. ☐ Voluntary (by parties)

   B. ☐ Involuntary (by court)

2. ☐ Pre-Trial Settlement

3. ☐ Judgment on the Pleadings

4. ☐ Summary Judgment

5. ☐ Trial

   A. ☐ Bench Trial

   B. ☐ Jury Trial

      1. ☐ Dismissal after jury selected

      2. ☐ Settlement during trial

      3. ☐ Judgment on Verdict

      4. ☐ Directed Verdict or JNOV

ADR

1. Was mediation utilized? ☐ Yes ☐ No

2. If yes, was it (check if applicable)
   ☐ court annexed?
   ☐ court mandated?

Relief Granted (Check all that apply)

1. ☐ Ex Parte Relief

2. ☐ Temporary Relief

3. ☐ Final Relief

   a. ☐ Divorce/Annulment/Separate Maintenance

   b. ☐ Child Custody

   c. ☐ Visitation

   d. ☐ Child Support

   e. ☐ Legitimation/Paternity

   f. ☐ Alimony

   g. ☐ Contempt

   h. ☐ Equitable Division

   i. ☐ Restraining Order

      ☐ Person   ☐ Property

   j. ☐ Adoption

   k. ☐ Other (Specify) _____

      _____

4. ☐ Dismissed prior to granting of relief.

This page intentionally blank.

IN THE SUPERIOR COURT OF _____ **COUNTY**
STATE OF GEORGIA

_____

Plaintiff   CIVIL ACTION

v.   FILE #: _____

_____

Defendant

PETITION FOR DIVORCE

Comes now, Plaintiff in the above-styled action and files this Petition for Divorce against Defendant and respectfully shows the Court the following:

1.

Plaintiff _____ has been a resident of the State of Georgia, and county of _____ for more than six months immediately preceding the filing of this action.

2.

❏ Defendant _____ is a resident of the State of Georgia, and has consented to the jurisdiction of this Court and has acknowledged service of process and jurisdiction and venue of this Court are correct.

[or]

❏ Defendant _____ may be served at Defendant's residence address of _____, and is subject to the jurisdiction and venue of this Court.

3.

Plaintiff and Defendant were married on or about _____, _____, and lived together as Husband and Wife until on or about _____, _____, when they separated, and they have remained in a bona fide state of separation since that date.

4.

❏ There are no children as issue of this marriage.

❏ The child(ren) as issue of this marriage, are:

Name   Age   Date of Birth

The Petitioner is employed with _____, and earns approximately $_____ per year. The Respondent is employed with _____ _____and earns approximately $_____ per year.

5.

❏ There is no undivided marital property as evidenced by the settlement agreement between the parties hereto, and the plaintiff prays the agreement be made the order of the court.

❏ The Plaintiff seeks the following: [choose which items are appropriate]

  ❏ Temporary and permanent child support;

  ❏ Temporary and permanent alimony;

  ❏ An equitable division of the assets and liabilities of the parties;

  ❏ Costs incurred in bringing this action.

6.

Plaintiff brings this divorce on the grounds that the marriage is irretrievably broken, as defined by Georgia law.

7.

The Wife desires the restoration of her maiden name, to wit: _____.

WHEREFORE, the Plaintiff prays:

(a) That a date be set for a hearing on the claims of the parties, and that process issue if required;

(b) That Plaintiff be granted a total divorce, that is a divorce *a vinculo matrimonii*;

(c) That the Plaintiff be given relief as sought, or that any agreement between the parties hereto be made a part of any final decree issued by the Court;

(d) That Plaintiff and Defendant receive such other relief as the Court deems just and equitable.

This _____, _____.

_____

Plaintiff, *Pro Se*

Name and address

_____

_____

_____

_____

STATE OF GEORGIA

COUNTY OF _____

VERIFICATION

PERSONALLY appeared before the undersigned attesting officer authorized by law to administer oaths, _____, who, being first duly sworn, on oath depose and says that the facts alleged in the above and foregoing Complaint for Divorce are true and correct.

Sworn to and subscribed before me
this _____, _____

_____
Notary Public

This page intentionally blank.

IN THE SUPERIOR COURT OF _____ COUNTY
STATE OF GEORGIA

_____	)	
Plaintiff	)	
	)	CIVIL ACTION
	)	
v.	)	FILE #:
	)	
_____	)	
Defendant	)	

PETITION FOR DIVORCE

Comes now, Plaintiff in the above-styled action and files this Complaint for Divorce against Defendant and respectfully shows the Court the following:

1.

Plaintiff _____ has been a resident of the State of Georgia for more than six months immediately preceding the filing of this action. Subject matter jurisdiction and venue are therefore properly before this Court.

2.

Defendant _____ is a resident of the State of Georgia, and has consented to the jurisdiction of this Court and has acknowledged service of process. In the event of a detriment of service, the Defendant may be served at the residence address of_____GA, _____ County, GA.

Personal jurisdiction is therefore properly before this Court.

Plaintiff and Defendant were married on or about _____, and lived together as Husband and Wife until on or about _____ when they separated, and they have remained in a *bona fide* state of separation since that date.

4.

❏ There are no children as issue of this marriage and none are anticipated

or

❏ The children of the parties and their ages are :

5.

The Plaintiff prays that the agreement attached hereto be made the order of the Court and shows that the Agreement provides for an equitable distribution of the interests of the parties.

6.

Plaintiff brings this divorce on the grounds that the marriage is irretrievably broken, as defined by Georgia law, but reserves the right to amend and to include additional grounds.

WHEREFORE, the Plaintiff prays:

(a)   That unless an acknowledgment of service and consent to jurisdiction is incorporated with this filing, that process issue;

(b)   That Plaintiff be granted a total divorce, that is a divorce *a vinculo matrimonii;*

(c)   That any agreement between the parties hereto be made a part of any final decree issued by the Court;

(d)   That Plaintiff and Defendant receive such other relief as the Court deems just and equitable.

This _____ day of _____, 200__ .

_____
Plaintiff

IN THE SUPERIOR COURT OF _____ **COUNTY**
STATE OF GEORGIA

_____ ,   )
              Plaintiff   )
)
)
              v.   )   **CIVIL ACTION**
)   **FILE NO.:** _____
_____ ,   )
              Defendant   )

DOMESTIC RELATIONS FINANCIAL AFFIDAVIT

1. <u>AFFIANT'S NAME</u> (person filling out Affidavit): _____

    Affiant's Age: _____   Affiant's Social Security Number: _____

    Spouse's Name: _____   Spouse's Age: _____

    Date of Marriage: _____   Date of Separation: _____

    Name and birthdates of children of this marriage:

    Name of child   Sex (m/f)   Date of Birth   Resides with:

    _____   _____   _____   _____

    _____   _____   _____   _____

    _____   _____   _____   _____

    Name and birthdates of children of prior relationship residing with Affiant:

    Name of child   Sex (m/f)   Date of Birth   Resides with:

    _____   _____   _____   _____

    _____   _____   _____   _____

2. <u>SUMMARY OF AFFIANT'S INCOME AND NEEDS</u>

    a)   Gross monthly income (before taxes) – include all sources of income, including, but not necessarily limited to wages, automobile allowance, employer contribution to retirement/stock, etc. $_____

    b)   Net monthly income (after taxes) – from item 4(a): $_____

    c)   Total monthly expenses – from item 6: $_____

    d)   Amount of spousal/child support needed by Affiant: $_____

    e)   Amount of child support indicated by Child Support Guidelines (chart below): $_____

Number of Children	1	2	3	4	5 or more
Percentage Range of Non-Custodial Parent's Gross Income	17%-23%	23%-28%	25%-32%	29%-35%	31%-37%

3.   AFFIANT'S GROSS MONTHLY INCOME

All income must be entered based on monthly average, regardless of date of receipt. If you do not receive income from one or more of the sources listed below, write "$0" or "n/a" in the blank.

a)   Salary/wages: $_____

b)   Bonuses, commissions, allowances, overtime, tips and
     similar payments (based on past 12 month average or
     time of employment if less than one year): $_____

c)   Business income from sources such as self-employment,
     partnership, close corporations, and/or independent
     contracts (gross receipts minus ordinary and necessary
     expenses required to produce income): $_____

d)   Disability/unemployment/worker's compensation: $_____

e)   Pension, retirements or annuity payments: $_____

f)   Social Security Benefits: $_____

g)   Other public benefits (specify source): $_____

h)   Spousal or child support from prior marriage: $_____

i)   Interest and dividends: $_____

j)   Rental income (gross receipts minus ordinary and
     necessary expenses required to produce income): $_____

k)   Income from royalties, trusts or estates: $_____

l)   Other income of a recurring nature (specify source): $_____

➤   **Affiant's gross monthly income:** $_____

4.   AFFIANT'S NET MONTHLY INCOME:

a)   Net monthly income from employment (after tax deductions): $_____

b)   Affiant's pay period (i.e., weekly, monthly, etc.):   _____

5.   ASSETS:

If you claim or agree that all or part of an asset is non-marital, indicate the non-marital portion under the appropriate spouse column. The total value of each asset must be listed in the "Value" column. "Value" means what you feel the item would be worth if it were offered for sale.

Description	Value	Separate Asset of Husband	Separate Asset of Wife
Cash	$	$	$
Stocks/Bonds/CDs	$	$	$
Retirement/IRA	$	$	$
Real Estate: home/other	$	$	$
Automobiles	$	$	$
Money owed to you	$	$	$
Jewelry	$	$	$
Furniture/furnishings	$	$	$
Collectibles	$	$	$
Life Insurance (Cash Value)	$	$	$
Other Assets	$	$	$
TOTAL ASSETS	$	$	$

6. AVERAGE MONTHLY EXPENSES:

Household

a)	Mortgage/rent payments:	$_____
b)	Property taxes:	$_____
c)	Insurance/renter's insurance:	$_____
d)	Electricity:	$_____
e)	Water & Sewer:	$_____
f)	Garbage:	$_____
g)	Telephone/cell phone:	$_____
h)	Gas (natural or propane):	$_____
i)	Repairs and maintenance:	$_____
j)	Lawn care/shrubs/plants:	$_____
k)	Pest/termite control:	$_____
l)	Cable TV/Satellite:	$_____
m)	Miscellaneous household and grocery items:	$_____
n)	Meals outside the home:	$_____
o)	Security/Alarm:	$_____
p)	Homeowner's fees:	$_____
q)	Housekeeper:	$_____
r)	Internet service:	$_____

Automobile

a)	Gasoline and oil:	$_____
b)	Repairs and maintenance:	$_____
c)	Auto tags and license:	$_____
d)	Insurance:	$_____

Children's Expenses

a)	Babysitters/day care:	$_____
b)	School tuition/supplies/expenses:	$_____
c)	Lunch money/allowance:	$_____
d)	Clothing/diapers:	$_____
e)	Medical/dental/prescription (uncovered):	$_____
f)	Grooming/hygiene:	$_____
g)	Gifts for other people (Christmas, birthdays, etc.):	$_____
h)	Entertainment/activities and supplies (sports, trips, etc.):	$_____
i)	Counseling (uncovered):	$_____
j)	Summer camps (averaged over 12 months):	$_____

Affiant's Other Expenses

a)	Health insurance (on Affiant only):	$_____
b)	Health insurance for dependents:	$_____
c)	Life insurance:	$_____
d)	Other insurance (e.g., disability, etc.):	$_____
e)	Club/health club/gym dues:	$_____
f)	Dry cleaning and laundry:	$_____
g)	Clothing for Affiant:	$_____
h)	Medical/dental/optical/prescriptions (uncovered):	$_____
i)	Counseling (uncovered):	$_____
j)	Gifts for other people (Christmas, birthdays, etc.):	$_____

k)   Entertainment/hobbies/sports: $_____
l)   Vacations (averaged over 12 months): $_____
m)   Publications: $_____
n)   Religious/charitable contributions: $_____
o)   Personal hygiene/haircuts: $_____
p)   Retirement/savings contributions: $_____
q)   Professional services (e.g., CPA): $_____
r)   Pet expenses (e.g., vet, food, etc.): $_____
s)   Rental expenses (e.g. storage, deposit boxes, etc.): $_____
t)   Expenses for other dependents (e.g., Affiant's parents): $_____
u)   Alimony paid to former spouse: $_____
v)   Child support paid for children from previous relationship: $_____
w)   Other (attach sheet itemizing these expenses): $_____

➤   **Total Household/Automobile/Children/Affiant Expenses:** $_____

7.   <u>PAYMENTS TO CREDITORS:</u>

Creditor Name (e.g., bank, auto financing company, etc.)	Balance Due	Monthly Payment
	$	$
	$	$
	$	$
	$	$
	$	$

➤   **Total Monthly Payments to Creditors:** $_____

➤   **TOTAL MONTHLY EXPENSES:** $_____

This the _____ day _____, 200____.

_____
(Sign your name here) PRO SE
Affiant's name *(print or type)*:

_____
Affiant's address: _____

_____
Affiant's phone number: (   )_____

Sworn to and subscribed before me, this
_____ day of _____, 200___.

_____
NOTARY PUBLIC
My commission expires _____.

IN THE SUPERIOR COURT OF
_____ COUNTY
STATE OF GEORGIA

_____   )
                         Plaintiff   )
)   CIVIL ACTION
                              v.   )
)   FILE #:
_____   )
                        Defendant   )

AGREEMENT

This Agreement is made and entered into by and between Plaintiff and Defendant.

WITNESSETH:

WHEREAS, the parties hereto are Husband and Wife, having gotten married _____, _____; and

WHEREAS, the parties hereto have lived in a bona fide state of separation since on or about _____, _____; and

WHEREAS, without agreeing in any sense to a divorce, said parties hereto desire to settle between themselves certain issues, including alimony, and the division of property between them;

NOW THEREFORE, the said parties hereto, for and in consideration of the promises and recitals herein contained, do mutually agree and promise as follows:

1. CHILD CUSTODY & VISITATION

❏   There are no minor children as issue of this marriage and there is no issue of child custody or visitation.

❏   The   ❏ Plaintiff   ❏ Defendant shall have temporary and permanent custody and control of the minor child(ren) being issue of this marriage, and shall be denominated as the "Custodial Parent." The other party shall be denominated as the "Noncustodial Parent," and shall have the right of reasonable and liberal visitation with said child at times and places to be agreed upon by the parties, unless more specific visitation provisions are set forth in this Agreement.

❏ The Plaintiff and Defendant shall share "Joint Custody" of the minor child, however, the ❏ Plaintiff ❏ Defendant shall have temporary and permanent primary legal and physical custody and control of the minor child being issue of this marriage, and shall be denominated the "Primary Custodial Parent." The other party shall The Defendant shall be denominated as the "Secondary Custodial Parent," and shall have the right of reasonable and liberal visitation with said child at times and places to be agreed upon by the parties, unless more specific visitation provisions are set forth in this Agreement.

SPECIFIC VISITATION PROVISIONS: The parties agree to the following provisions for visitation by the Noncustodial Parent:

Standard Visitation Language

The visitation of the Noncustodial Parent shall be at such place of his or her choice, and such visitation shall be reasonable and liberal, but in the event that the parties are unable to agree to such visitation the agreed upon schedule shall be as follows:

(a) During the first and third weekends of each month from Friday at 6:00 p.m. until Sunday at 6:00 p.m. provided that the Noncustodial Parent shall give the Custodial Parent at least 24 hours advance notice, written or oral, of any intention to exercise this right;

(b) For any four (4) weeks during summer vacation so long as the Noncustodial Parent does not interfere with or interrupt any of the child's school and further provided that the Noncustodial Parent shall give the Custodial Parent at least (14) days advance notice, written or oral, of each summer visitation;

(c) During even-number years, the Thanksgiving holiday, from 6:00 p.m. on the Wednesday before Thanksgiving to 6:00 p.m. on the Sunday following Thanksgiving, and the New Years holiday from December 27, at 6:00 p.m. to January 1, at 6:00 p.m., provided that the Noncustodial Parent shall give the Custodial Parent at least fourteen (14) days advance notice of each intended visitation;

(d) During odd-numbered years, the Christmas holiday from December 23, at 6:00 p.m. to December 27, at 6:00 p.m; the spring vacation specified by the child's school district, from the first day at 6:00 p.m. to the 7th day at 6:00 p.m. (the Custodial Parent shall give the Noncustodial Parent thirty (30) days notice as to the specified dates of the spring vacation); and the children's birthdays, from 6:00 p.m. of the day preceding until 6:00 p.m. of birthday; all provided that the Noncustodial Parent shall give the Custodial Parent fourteen (14) days advance notice of each intended visitation; and,

(e) The Noncustodial Parent shall be responsible for transportation and promptness in each visitation. For each visitation, the Noncustodial Parent shall receive the children at the residence of the Custodial Parent, and after such visitation, shall return the child to the residence of the Custodial Parent.

Visitation in the Event of Geographical Separation Notwithstanding the aforementioned, should the parties be domiciled more than one hundred miles apart, and the minor child be above the age of three years, the following minimum visitation shall apply:

(a)   The Noncustodial Parent shall be entitled to four days regular visitation per month. In no event shall the monthly four days be cumulative, nor shall the four days of regular visitation in any one month exceed ninety-six consecutive hours.

(b)   In addition, the Noncustodial Parent shall be entitled to six weeks of visitation to take place during the Summer, or contemporaneously with the child's vacation, that may be exercised during any calendar year. The purpose of this visitation is to allow the Noncustodial Parent extended time with the minor child. This vacation visitation shall not exceed forty-two consecutive days per visit, and shall be in lieu of the regular visitation for the months in which vacation visitation is exercised. In the event that vacation visitation bridges two months, it shall be in lieu of the regular visitation for both months.

(c)   The Noncustodial Parent shall be responsible for the expenses of transporting the minor child to the residence of the Noncustodial Parent and the Custodial Parent shall be responsible for the expenses of returning the child to the residence of the Custodial Parent.

(d)   In the event that either parent moves more than 500 miles from the present marital residence in then the primary residence of the children shall be with the nonmoving parent who shall become the Custodial parent if he or she is not already so designated and the parent who has moved more than 500 miles or to another city in another state will have the same visitation rights with the child as are previously defined.

2. ACCESS AND DECISIONS

The parties agree that the Noncustodial Parent shall be entitled to equal access to all teachers, schools, counselors, psychologists, physicians, and dentists of said child and agree further that the Custodial Parent shall provide the Noncustodial Parent with copies of the child's report cards, and progress reports as received. Although the Noncustodial Parent shall have a voice in all major decisions concerning said child's education and upbringing, the Custodial Parent shall have the ultimate right and responsibility to decide substantial issues including but not limited to where said child will live and what schools will be attended. In the event of any disagreement regarding same, the Custodial Parent's decisions shall prevail.

3. COMMUNICATIONS WITH CHILDREN

The parties mutually agree that is of great importance that the children of the parties be taught and encouraged to love and respect both of their parents. The parties therefore covenant that neither will make derogatory remarks about the other in the presence of the children; that each will notify the other of any illness of the children; that each shall cooperate and work together to encourage and assist the child in attaining the highest possible educational levels and achievements; and, that the parties will work with one another towards helping the child overcome any problems which may arise the child's life.

4. CHILD SUPPORT

❑   There is no issue of child support.

❑   The Noncustodial Parent shall pay to the Custodial Parent the sum of $_____ per _____ from the date of Agreement until the minor child has attained the age of 18, dies, marries or becomes self-supporting, unless the child is still enrolled full-time in secondary school, however, support under this paragraph shall not continue past the child's twentieth birthday. The parties testify that this sum represents _____% of the Noncustodial Parent's gross income, and falls within the parameters required by the Uniform Superior Court guidelines for child support.

❑   The parent receiving support shall have the right to submit an income deduction order at his or her sole election.

❑   The parties further agree to the following provisions regarding child support:

5. ALIMONY

❑   Both parties waive any claim for alimony against the other including any claim for retirement benefits to which either may be entitled.

❑   The ❑ Plaintiff ❑ Defendant shall pay to the other party the sum of $_____ dollars a week/month/year, for a period of _____ consecutive weeks/months/years, or unless said recipient of alimony remarries or dies, at which time the alimony obligation shall cease.

❑   The parties further agree to the following provisions regarding alimony:

6. DIVISION OF PROPERTY

All of the property which the parties presently own jointly or severally, whether real, personal, or mixed, and of whatever kind or nature and wheresoever situated, and all property in which either has any interest, shall be divided as follows:

(a) Real Property:

❑ The parties own no real property.

❑ The parties own a parcel of real property in _____ County, Georgia, being _____. The parties agree that the _____ shall be the sole owner, free and clear of any claim of the _____ of the property and shall be fully responsible therefor. Within forty-eight hours of an order being entered, the _____ will execute a Quit Claim Deed in favor of the _____.

❑ The parties own a parcel of real property in _____ County, Georgia, being _____. The parties agree that said property shall be sold and the proceeds shall be divided equally between parties.

(b) Personal Property: Each party shall have possession of and title to all those personal items presently in their respective possession, and shall be responsible for any indebtedness associated with same.

(c) Household Goods: All furniture and household goods have been previously divided between the parties, and each shall retain and have title to such furniture and household goods as are in their respective possessions and shall be responsible for any indebtedness associated with same.

(d) Cash: All cash presently in the possession of either party shall be and remain their separate property, free and clear of any claim whatsoever on the part of the other party.

(e) Bank Accounts and Investments: All bank accounts and investments have been previously divided between the parties, and each shall retain and have title to bank accounts and investments as are in their respective possessions. All other joint accounts whether saving or checking have been closed, and the funds therein apportioned between the parties.

(f) Automobiles, Boats, Etc.: The Plaintiff shall be the sole owner, free and clear of any claim of the Defendant of the _____, VIN # _____, and shall be fully responsible therefor. The Defendant shall be the sole owner, free and clear of any claim of the Plaintiff, of the _____, VIN # _____. Each party shall retain title to such other vehicles as are in their own names, and shall be fully responsible therefor.

All of the other property which the parties presently own jointly or severally, whether real, personal, or mixed, and of whatever kind or nature and wheresoever situated, and all property in which either has any interest has been previously divided and the property belonging to each is in his or her possession and control.

7. INSURANCE

❏ The parties agree to provide for their own health insurance, and neither shall have any responsibility for any insurance with respect to the other. Any disposition of any other life insurance policies currently in force shall be at the sole discretion of the individual owner of said policy. The parties shall each be responsible for their own medical and dental insurance. Any coverage currently in force and offered through an employer shall be maintained pursuant to COBRA by the Defendant and in favor of the Plaintiff.

❏ The Noncustodial Parent shall keep the minor child insured under such medical, dental, and hospitalization plans as may be available through the employer. Any necessary medical, dental, or related health care expenses not covered by such insurance shall be borne equally by the parties. Any such medical bills submitted to one party by the other, and which have been paid by the other party, shall be reimbursed within thirty days of receipt.

8. SEPARATE RIGHTS

From and after the date of this Agreement, the parties hereto shall have the right to live separate, undisturbed, and apart from each other.

9. DEBTS

The parties agree to each be responsible for their own obligations and have previously apportioned all joint obligations. Each party's assumption of debt and indemnification is an integral part of the support agreement in that if said assumption and indemnification had not taken place, the amount of spousal support would have been different in order to provide the support necessary to ensure that the daily needs of the Wife [and Children] are satisfied. Therefore, the assumption of debt and indemnification in this agreement shall not be considered dischargeable in any bankruptcy proceeding by either party as against the other.

The Wife shall specifically be responsible for the following obligations:

Name	Account Number	Amount

The Husband shall specifically be responsible for the following obligations:

Name	Account Number	Amount

10. TAXES

The parties agree to file ❏ separate ❏ joint income tax returns for _____ and to be individually responsible for their own tax liabilities thereafter. The parties shall equally share any jointly accrued tax liability from the years prior to _____.

The ❏ Plaintiff ❏ Defendant shall be responsible for any accrued tax liability for the period of _____, _____, to _____, _____.

The Custodial Parent shall be entitled to claim the child(ren) of the parties for federal and state income tax purposes, however, in the event of any agreement to the contrary, the Noncustodial Parent shall only be entitled to claim the child(ren) with a written consent from the Custodial Parent in compliance with Federal guidelines, and only if the Noncustodial Parent is current on all other obligations created under this Agreement.

11. KNOWLEDGE OF CONTENTS

Each party expressly acknowledges that he or she has read this Agreement in its entirety prior to the execution thereof, understands the provisions thereof, executes this Agreement as his or her voluntary act, and that there are no agreements or promises between the parties except as herein set forth. Both parties consent to this Agreement being made a part of the Final Judgment and Decree of the Court in the divorce action to be filed in the Superior Court of this County, if said divorce is granted by the Court.

12. MODIFICATION

Any modification or waiver of any of the provisions of this Agreement shall be effective only if made in writing and executed by both parties with the same formality as this Agreement. The failure of either party to insist upon strict compliance with any of the provisions of this Agreement shall not be construed as a waiver of any subsequent default of the same or similar nature.

13. FULL SETTLEMENT

This Agreement shall constitute a full and final settlement of all claims of every nature between the parties hereto.

14. AGREEMENT TO TRY

The parties agree that the divorce action filed in conjunction with this Agreement may be tried at any time after thirty-one (31) days from the date of service of the Complaint for Divorce.

15. EFFECTIVE DATE

This Agreement shall become effective on the date of the execution hereof by the parties hereto.

16. ENFORCEMENT

Each of the parties hereto shall strictly obey and abide by each and every term and provision of this Agreement. Upon this Agreement's being incorporated in any Order of any Court, and in the event then of any breach of this Agreement, the offending party shall be subject to attachment for contempt and garnishment of any alimony or child support award.

17. WAIVER OF DISCOVERY

Each party acknowledges their right to discovery as provided by the Georgia Civil Practice Act and desires not to proceed with discovery.

18. ATTORNEYS

The parties agree that each shall be responsible for their own incurred attorney's fees and neither shall have any responsibility with respect to fees incurred by the other. Each party has either had this Agreement carefully explained to them by counsel, or has explicitly chosen not to avail themselves of that right despite opportunity and encouragement to so do.

IN WITNESS WHEREOF, the parties hereto have hereunto set their hands and seals, and affirmed the contents and veracity of the statements contained herein this _____, _____.

_____   _____

PLAINTIFF   DEFENDANT

Sworn to and subscribed before me this   Sworn to and subscribed before me this

____ day of _____, _____.   ____ day of _____, _____.

_____   _____

Notary Public   Notary Public

This page intentionally blank.

IN THE SUPERIOR COURT OF _____ COUNTY

STATE OF GEORGIA

_____	)	
Plaintiff	)	CIVIL ACTION
	)	
v.	)	
	)	FILE #: _____
_____	)	
Defendant	)	

AFFIDAVIT REGARDING CUSTODY

Pursuant to the requirements of the O.C.G.A. § 19-9-49, the Petitioner gives the following information under oath:

1.

The minor child(ren) of the parties is/are

Name	Age	Birth Date	Living with	Address
_____	____	_____	_____	_____
_____	____	_____	_____	_____
_____	____	_____	_____	_____
_____	____	_____	_____	_____
_____	____	_____	_____	_____

2.

The forenamed minor children have, for the past five years, resided with the parties at the following addresses:

1. _____.

2. _____.

3.

Petitioner has not participated as a party, witness, or in any other capacity in any other litigation concerning the custody of the named children in this or any other state, unless indicated below:

4.

Petitioner has no information of any custody proceeding concerning the children in a Court of this or any other state, unless indicated below:

5.

Petitioner knows of no other person not a party to this proceeding who has physical custody of the children or claims to have custody or visitation rights with respect to the children, unless indicated below:

_____
Plaintiff

Sworn to and subscribed before me this
_____ day of _____, _____.

_____
Notary Public

IN THE SUPERIOR COURT OF _____ COUNTY

STATE OF GEORGIA

_____	)	
	)	
Plaintiff	)	CIVIL ACTION
	)	
v.	)	FILE #: _____
	)	
	)	
_____	)	
Defendant	)	

ANSWER AND COUNTERCLAIM

COMES NOW Defendant in the above styled action and files this, Answer and Counterclaim to the Plaintiff's Complaint, as follows:

1.

Defendant admits the allegations contained in Plaintiff's Complaint.

COUNTERCLAIM

COMES NOW Defendant herein and files her Counterclaim, showing to the Court the following:

1.

Plaintiff is subject to the jurisdiction of this Court.

2.

The marriage of the parties is irretrievably broken and Defendant is entitled to a total divorce from Plaintiff.

3.

Defendant files this counterclaim for the limited purpose of securing the restoration of her former name, to wit: _____.

WHEREFORE, Defendant prays:

(a) That Defendant be awarded a total divorce from Plaintiff, that is to say, a divorce *a vinculo matrimonii*;

(b) That Defendant be restored to her maiden name, to wit:

_____; and,

(c) That Plaintiff have such other and further relief as to the Court may seem meet and proper.

_____

Pro Se Defendant

Address

_____

_____

_____

_____

IN THE SUPERIOR COURT OF _____ COUNTY
STATE OF GEORGIA

_____	)
Plaintiff	)
	)
	)
v.	) NO._____
	)
_____	)
Defendant	)

FINAL JUDGMENT AND DECREE

Upon consideration of this case, upon evidence submitted as provided by law, it is the judgment of the Court that a total divorce be granted, that is to say, a divorce *a vinculo matrimonii*, between the parties to the above-stated case upon legal principles.

It is considered, ordered, and decreed by the Court that the marriage contract heretofore entered into between the parties to this case, from and after this date, be and is set aside and dissolved as fully and effectually as if no such contract had ever been made or entered into.

Petitioner and respondent, formerly husband and wife, in the future shall be held and considered as separate and distinct persons altogether unconnected by any nuptial union or civil contract, whatsoever, and both shall have the right to remarry.

The settlement agreement between the parties, dated _____, is incorporated herein.

The costs of these proceedings are taxed against the _____.

Decree entered this _____ day of _____, _____

_____
Judge, Superior Court

This page intentionally blank.

IN THE SUPERIOR COURT OF _____ COUNTY
STATE OF GEORGIA

_____   )
                  Petitioner/Plaintiff   )   Civil Action File Number
)
)   _____
v.   )
)
)
_____   )
                  Respondent/Defendant   )

FINAL JUDGMENT AND DECREE OF DIVORCE

Upon consideration of this case, upon evidence submitted as provided by law, it is the judgment of this court that a total divorce be granted, that is to say, a divorce *a vinculo matrimonii*, between the parties to the above-stated case upon legal principles.

It is considered, ordered and decreed by the court that the marriage contract heretofore entered into between the parties to this case, from and after this date, be and is set aside and dissolved as fully and effectually as if no such contract had ever been made or entered into.

Petitioner and respondent in the future shall be held and considered as separate and distinct persons altogether unconnected by any nuptial union or civil contract whatsoever and both shall have the right to remarry.

1.

The court restores to (Plaintiff/Defendant) his/her prior maiden name, to wit:
_____.

2.

The settlement agreement entered into between the parties and filed with the court on _____ is hereby incorporated into and made a part of this Final Judgment and Decree of Divorce.

3.

In determining child support, the court finds as follows:
The gross income of the father is $_____ monthly.
The gross income of the mother is $_____ monthly.
In this case, child support is being determined for _____ children.

The applicable percentage of gross income to be considered is:

# of children	Percentage range of gross income
1	17 % to 23 %
2	23 % to 28 %
3	25 % to 32 %
4	29 % to 35 %
5	31 % to 37 %

Thus,_____ % of_____ (gross income of obligor) equals $_____per month.

The court has considered the existence of special circumstances and has found the following special circumstances marked with an "X" to be present in this case:

_____ 1. Ages of the children.

_____ 2. A child's extraordinary medical costs or needs in addition to accident and sickness insurance, provided that all such costs or needs shall be considered if no insurance is available.

_____ 3. Educational costs.

_____ 4. Day care costs.

_____ 5. Shared physical custody arrangements, including extended visitation.

_____ 6. A party's other support obligations to another household.

_____ 7. Income that should be imputed to a party because of suppression of income.

_____ 8. In-kind income for the self-employed, such as reimbursed meals or a company car.

_____ 9. Other support a party is providing or will be providing, such as payment of mortgage.

_____ 10. A party's own extraordinary needs, such as medical expenses.

_____ 11. Extreme economic circumstances, including but not limited to:

(A) Unusually high debt structure or

(B) Unusually high income of either party or both parties, which shall be construed as individual gross income of over $75,000 per annum.

_____ 12. Historical spending in the family for children which varies significantly from the percentage table.

_____ 13. Consideration of the economic cost of living factors of the community of each party, as determined by the trier of fact.

_____ 14. In-kind contribution of either parent.

_____ 15. The income of the custodial parent.

_____ 16. The cost of accident and sickness insurance coverage for dependent children included in this Order.

_____ 17. Extraordinary travel expenses to exercise visitation or shared physical custody.

_____ 18. Any other factor which the trier of fact deems to be required by the ends of justice, as described below:

4.

A. Having found that no special circumstances exist, or that special circumstances numbered _____ exist, the final award of child support which Plaintiff/Defendant shall pay to Plaintiff/Defendant for support of the child or children is $_____ per week/month, beginning on the ___ day of_____ 20____ and payable thereafter on the _____ and day of each week/month. Plaintiff/Defendant shall continue to pay child support for the benefit of each child of the parties until each such child becomes 18 years of age, dies, marries, or otherwise becomes emancipated, except that if the child becomes 18 years of age while enrolled in and attending secondary school on a full-time basis, then such support shall/shall not continue until the child completes secondary school, provided that such support shall not be required after the child attains 20 years of age.

B. Plaintiff____/Defendant____ is ordered to provide accident and sickness insurance for the child or children so long as he or she is obligated by this Order to provide child support for each such child or children.

5.

In accordance with O.C.G.A. § 19-6-32(a.1),
_____ Alimony and Support Unit and Income Deduction Orders are entered contemporaneously with the entry of this Final Judgment and Decree requiring the immediate withholding of child support from the wages of the parent required by this Order to furnish support; or
_____ No Income Deduction Order(s) accompany this Final Judgment and Decree as:
_____ The parent required to furnish support is self-employed; or
_____ An Order or Consent Order for income deduction of child support is already in place; or
_____ "[B]oth parties...have reached ... (a) written agreement...which provides for an alternative arrangement." O.C.G.A. § 19-6-32(a.1)(B) (Supp. 1994).

6.

WHENEVER IN VIOLATION OF THE TERMS OF THIS ORDER THERE SHALL HAVE BEEN A FAILURE TO MAKE THE SUPPORT PAYMENTS DUE HEREUNDER SO THAT THE AMOUNT UNPAID IS EQUAL TO OR GREATER THAN THE AMOUNT PAYABLE FOR ONE (1) MONTH, THE PAYMENTS REQUIRED TO BE MADE MAY BE COLLECTED BY THE PROCESS OF CONTINUING GARNISHMENT FOR SUPPORT. O.C.G.A. § 19-6-30(a) (Supp. 1994).

7.

_____ The parties have both completed any court ordered mediation and/or parenting class as required, or
_____ Until such time as mandatory parenting classes have been completed, any party failing to complete the class shall not be entitled to seek enforcement of any visitation provided through this order.

SO ORDERED, this the _____ day of _____ 20_____.

_____

JUDGE, SUPERIOR COURT

Prepared by:

_____
_____
_____

Name, address, phone

IN THE SUPERIOR COURT OF _____ COUNTY

STATE OF GEORGIA

_____   )
                              Plaintiff   )   CIVIL ACTION
)
    v.   )   FILE #: _____
_____   )
                              Defendant   )
)
)

REQUEST FOR PRODUCTION OF DOCUMENTS

To:

GREETINGS:

    You are requested to produce, pursuant to O.C.G.A. § 9-11-34 (c), the documents and records set forth below for inspection and copying by the [Plaintiff] [Defendant] at

_____

_____, on or before the 30th day after service of this request, where adequate facilities are available for copying. Alternately, you may provide copies of documents requested on or before the expiration of the aforesaid thirty days.

This _____, _____

                `

                              _____
                              [Plaintiff] [Defendant]
                              Address

                              _____
                              _____
                              _____
                              Phone_____

I HEREBY CERTIFY THAT I HAVE SERVED THIS REQUEST FOR PRODUCTION TO ALL OTHER PARTIES, (AND/OR WHERE APPROPRIATE, THEIR ATTORNEY(S)) BY EITHER HAND DELIVERY OR DEPOSITING SAME IN THE UNITED STATES MAIL IN A PROPERLY ADDRESSED ENVELOPE WITH ADEQUATE POSTAGE THEREON.

This _____, _____

_____
[Plaintiff] [Defendant]

Address

_____
_____
_____

Phone_____

IN THE SUPERIOR COURT OF _____ **COUNTY**
STATE OF GEORGIA

_____)
                    Plaintiff) CIVIL ACTION
)
     v.   ) FILE #:_____
)
_____)
                   Defendant)

AFFIDAVIT OF PUBLICATION AND DILIGENT SEARCH

Comes now the Plaintiff who states on oath that diligent search has been made and that the Defendant cannot be found. The Plaintiff has made the following effort to find the Defendant:

_____
_____
_____
_____

However, the Defendant cannot be located and the Plaintiff asks this Court to enter an Order for Publication in the within and foregoing action.

This _____, _____

                                        _____
                                        Affiant Signature

Sworn to and subscribed before me   Name _____
this _____, _____.   Address _____

                                        _____
_____   Telephone _____
Notary Public

This page intentionally blank.

STATE OF GEORGIA   **ORDER OF PUBLICATION**
COUNTY OF _____

  It appearing to the satisfaction of the court by Affidavit, that _____,
a defendant on whom service is to be made in Case Number _____, _____
resides out of the State, or has departed from the State, or cannot after due diligence, be found within the State, or
conceals (him) (her) self to avoid service of the Summons, and it further appearing, either by Affidavit or by verified
Complaint on file, that a claim exists against the defendant in respect to whom service is to be made, and that (he) (she)
is a necessary or proper party to the action,
  IT IS HEREBY CONSIDERED, ORDERED AND DECREED THAT:
  (1) Service be perfected by publication to be made in the paper in which sheriff's advertisements are printed four
times within the ensuing sixty (60) days, publications to be at least (7) days apart.
  (2) The party obtaining the Order for Publication deposit or pay, at the time of filing to cost of publication.
  (3) Said notice shall contain (a) the name of the parties - plaintiff and defendant (b) a caption setting forth the
court (c) the character of the action (d) the date the action was filed (e) the date of the Order for Service By Publication
(f) notice directed and addressed to the party to be served commanding him to file with _____,
the Clerk and serve upon the plaintiff's attorney, an Answer in writing within sixty (60) days from the date of this Order for
Publication (g) teste in the name of the Judge, and (h) the signature of _____, the Clerk of
_____ Superior Court.
  (4) Where the residence or abiding place of said absent or nonresident party is known, the party obtaining the
Order shall advise _____, the Clerk, who shall, within fifteen (15) days after filing the Order
for service by Publication, enclose, direct, stamp and mail a copy of this order for Service By Publication and Complaint
(if any) to said Party at his last known address, if any and make entry of his actions.
  (5) The copy of the notice to be mailed shall be a duplicate of the one published in the newspaper, but need not
necessarily be a copy of the newspaper itself.
  SO ORDERED this _____ day of _____, _____

                     _____
                JUDGE,   SUPERIOR COURT

STATE OF GEORGIA   **RETURN OF SERVICE**
COUNTY OF

  I hereby certify that I have published a Notice in the manner and form prescribed in the foregoing Order, and
that I have enclosed, directed, stamped and mailed a copy of the said Notice together with a copy of the Order for Service
by Publication and Complaint (if any), to _____
_____
  This the _____ day of _____, _____.

                     _____
                DEPUTY CLERK
                Clerk of Superior Court

STATE OF GEORGIA   **ORDER PERFECTING SERVICE**
COUNTY OF

  It appearing to the Court that service upon _____
has been perfected by publication of notice on the _____ day of _____, _____,
and on _____ days of _____ 200_____ in the _____,
and by enclosing, directing, stamping, and mailing a copy of the notice together with a copy of the Order for Publication
and the Complaint (if any) to said defendant at (his) (her) last known address, and by entry on said case of the actions
by the clerk.
  IT IS HEREBY ORDERED that said service by publication be, and is approved.

                     _____
                JUDGE,   SUPERIOR COURT

PUBLICATION DATES OK: This the_____ day of _____, _____.

                     _____
                DEPUTY CLERK
                Clerk of Superior Court

This page intentionally blank.

IN THE SUPERIOR COURT OF _____ COUNTY
STATE OF GEORGIA

_____)   CIVIL ACTION
           PLAINTIFF   )   #_____

                  v.   )

_____)
          DEFENDANT   )

TO:

NOTICE OF PUBLICATION

By **ORDER** of the Court for service by publication dated _____,
You are hereby notified that _____, the above-named
Plaintiff filed suit against you for:

_____.

You are required to file with the Clerk of the Superior Court, and to serve upon the plaintiff's
attorney whose name and address is: _____

_____

_____

_____ an
Answer in writing within sixty (60) days of _____.

Witness the Honorable _____, Judge of the
_____ Superior Court.

This the _____ day of _____, _____.

#_____
by:

_____
Deputy Clerk of Superior Court

This page intentionally blank.

IN THE SUPERIOR COURT OF _____ COUNTY

STATE OF GEORGIA

_____)
)
              Plaintiff   )   CIVIL ACTION
)
)
      v.   )   FILE #:_____
)
)
_____)
)
              Defendant   )
)

AFFIDAVIT OF INDIGENCE

Pursuant to OCGA § 9-15-2, the undersigned swears under oath that because of indigence the undersigned is unable to pay the costs associated with filing of pleadings in this case and prays to be relieved from said costs.

This _____ day of _____, _____

_____

Affiant

Sworn to and subscribed before me   Name _____

this _____, _____.   Address _____

_____

Telephone _____

_____

Notary Public

This page intentionally blank.

IN THE SUPERIOR COURT OF _____ COUNTY
STATE OF GEORGIA

_____   )
)
                          Plaintiff)
)
) CIVIL ACTION
)
v.   )
) FILE #:_____
_____   )
)
                          Defendant)
)

ACKNOWLEDGMENT OF SERVICE AND CONSENT TO JURISDICTION

Comes now _____, Defendant in the above-styled action, who hereby acknowledges service of the above and foregoing Petition for Divorce, consents to the jurisdiction of this Court, and waives notice of further hearings on the within and foregoing matter.

This _____ day of _____, _____

_____
Defendant

Sworn and subscribed before me
this _____ day of _____, _____.

_____
Notary Public

This page intentionally blank.

STATE OF GEORGIA
Report of Divorce, Annulment or Dissolution of Marriage
Type or print all information

1. Civil Action Number	2. Date Decree Granted (mo., day, year)	3. County Decree Granted
4. Wife's Name (first, middle, last)	**5. Maiden (Birth) Last Name**	**6. Date of Birth (mo., day, year)**
7. County of Residence	**8. Number of This Marriage (1st, 2nd, etc.)**	
9. Husband's Name (first, middle, last, generation)	**10. Date of Birth (mo., day, year)**	**11. County of Residence**
12. Number of This Marriage (1st, 2nd, etc.)	**13. Date of This Marriage (mo., day, year)**	
14. Specify Grounds For Divorce (19-5-3, OCGA)	**15. Number of Children Less Than 18 Affected by This Decree**	

This above Report may be reproduced by use of a computer. However, the finished Report must be a close reproduction of the original, and prior review and approval must be obtained from the State Registrar before use. (31-10-7, O.C.G.A.)

31-10-22. Record of divorce, dissolutions, and annulments.

(a) A record of each divorce, dissolution of marriage, or annulment granted by any court of competent jurisdiction in this state shall be filed by the clerk of the court with the department and shall be registered if it has been completed and filed in accordance with this Code section. The record shall be prepared by the petitioner or the petitioner's legal representative on a form prescribed and furnished by the state registrar and shall be presented to the clerk of the court with the petition. **In all cases, the completed record shall be a prerequisite to the granting of the final decree.**

(b) The clerk of the superior court shall complete and forward to the department on or before the tenth day of each calendar month the records of each divorce, dissolution of marriage, or annulment decree granted during the preceding calendar month.

This page intentionally blank.

SUPERIOR COURT

_____ COUNTY, GEORGIA

_____	)	
Plaintiff	)	
v.	)	NO. _____
	)	
	)	
_____	)	
Defendant	)	

TEMPORARY ORDER

Upon consideration of this case, upon evidence submitted as provided by law, it is the temporary order of the Court that, during the pendency of this action:

IT IS ADJUDGED THAT:

❑   1.   The parties shall share parenting responsibilities; however, physical custody of the minor child(ren) of the parties shall be awarded to the party designated below:

<u>Name of Child</u>   <u>Birthdate</u>   <u>Custody Awarded To:</u>

Each party shall have the right to visit any child not in his or her physical custody at reasonable times and places after reasonable notice to the custodial party.

❑   2.   The ❑ Husband   ❑ Wife shall pay temporary child support to the other party in the sum of $ _____ per _____, beginning _____, _____.

❑   3.   The ❑ Husband   ❑ Wife shall provide health insurance coverage for the minor child(ren) whenever such insurance is reasonably available.

❑   4.   The ❑ Husband   ❑ Wife shall pay temporary alimony to the other party in the sum of $ _____ per _____, beginning

❏ 5. The ❏ Husband ❏ Wife shall pay the other party's attorney's fees, set at $ _____ (to be paid to _____), and court costs, taxed at $ _____, both of which shall be paid within _____ days of the date of this order.

❏ 6. Other provisions:

ORDERED this _____ day of _____, _____.

_____
Judge, Superior Court
_____ County, Georgia

IN THE SUPERIOR COURT OF _____ COUNTY
STATE OF GEORGIA

_____)
)
                        Plaintiff) CIVIL ACTION
)
)
        v.   ) FILE #:_____
)
)
_____)
)
                        Defendant)

INCOME DEDUCTION ORDER

This Court, having entered an order on _____ {date} identifying an obligation of support on behalf of the Plaintiff/Defendant {cross out whichever does not apply} in favor of the Plaintiff/Defendant {cross out whichever does not apply}, and the Court having been provided the within and foregoing Income Deduction Order at the request of the Plaintiff/Defendant {cross out whichever does not apply} and it having been determined that an Income Deduction Order was applicable thereto, in accord with OCGA § 19-6-32, *et seq.*,

IT IS THEREFORE ORDERED AND ADJUDGED

1. INCOME DEDUCTION

That the Plaintiff's/Defendant's {cross out whichever does not apply} employer, future employer, or any other person, private entity, federal or state government, or any unit of local government providing or administering income due the Plaintiff/Defendant {cross out whichever does not apply} as wage shall deduct from all monies due and payable to the Plaintiff/Defendant {cross out whichever does not apply} current support in the amount of $_____ {amount} to be deducted in approximate equal amounts each and every pay period during the month.

2. PLACE OF PAYMENT

The employer shall make the amounts deducted payable to, and forward them within two business days after each payment date to _____ *{name of receiving spouse}*.

3. CONSUMER CREDIT PROTECTION ACT

The maximum amount to be deducted shall not exceed the amounts allowed under 303(b) of the Consumer Credit Protection Act, 15 U.S.C. § 1673(b) as amended.

4. EFFECTIVE DATE

This income deduction order shall be effective immediately.

5. DURATION

This income deduction order supersedes any income deduction order which may have been previously entered in this case. This income deduction order will remain in full force and effect until modified, suspended, or terminated by further Order of this Court. This Order and all further papers required to be served pursuant to OCGA § 19-6-33 shall be served upon the employer by regular first class mail.

DECREE ENTERED, this _____ day of _____, _____.

_____
JUDGE, _____*{county}* Superior Court

Submitted by:

_____

IN THE SUPERIOR COURT OF _____ COUNTY

STATE OF GEORGIA

_____	)
Plaintiff	) CIVIL ACTION
	)
	)
v.	) FILE #:_____
	)
_____	)
Defendant	)
	)

NOTICE TO PAYOR

To: Human Resources Department

_____

_____

{Employer of paying spouse}

Pursuant to OCGA § 19-6-33 the Payor is hereby notified:

1)   That the payor is hereby required to deduct $_____ *{amount}* of Plaintiff's/Defendant's *{cross out whichever does not apply}* gross income and that amount is to be paid to _____ _____ *{name and address of receiving spouse}*. The amount actually deducted plus all administrative charges shall not be in excess of the amount allowed under Section 303(b) of the Federal Consumer Credit Protection Act, 15 U.S.C. § 1673(b);

2)   That the payor is to implement the income deduction order no later than the first pay period that occurs after 14 days following the date the notice was mailed;

3)   That the payor is to forward to within two business days after each payment date to _____ *{name and address of receiving spouse}* the amount deducted from _____ _____'s *{paying spouse}* income and a statement as to whether that amount totally or partially satisfies the periodic amount specified in the income deduction order;

4)   That if a payor willfully fails to deduct the proper amount from _____'s *{paying spouse}* income, the payor is liable for the amount the payor should have deducted, plus costs, interest, and reasonable attorney fees;

5)   That the payor may collect up to $25.00 against _____'s *{paying spouse}* income to reimburse the payor for administrative costs for the first income deduction order and up to $3.00 for each deduction thereafter;

6)   That the income deduction order and the notice to payor are binding on the payor until further notice by obligee or the court or until the payor no longer provides income to the obligor;

7)   That when the payor no longer provides income to _____ *{paying spouse}* the payor shall notify _____ *{receiving spouse}* and shall also provide _____'s *{paying spouse}* last known address and the name and address of _____'s *{paying spouse}* new payor, if known, and that, if the payor willfully violates this provision, the payor is subject to a civil penalty not to exceed $250.00 for the first violation or $500.00 for any subsequent violation. Penalties shall be paid to _____ *{receiving spouse}*;

8)   That no payor may discharge an obligor by reason of the fact that income has been subject to an income deduction order under Code Section 19-6-32 and that violation of this provision subjects the payor to a civil penalty not to exceed $250.00 for the first violation or $500.00 for a subsequent violation. Penalties will be paid to _____ _____ *{receiving spouse}*. If no support is owing the penalty shall be paid to the obligor;

9)   That the income deduction order has priority over all other legal processes under state law pertaining to the same income and that payment as required by the income deduction order is a complete defense by the payor against any claims of the obligor or his creditors as to the sum paid;

10)   That if the payor received income deduction orders requiring that the income of two or more obligors be deducted and sent to the same depository he may combine the amounts paid to the depository in a single payment as long as he identifies that portion of the payment attributable to each obligor; and,

11)   If payor receives income deduction orders against the same obligor he shall contact the court for further instructions. Upon being contacted the court shall allocate amounts available for income deduction giving priority to current child support obligations up to the limits imposed under Section 303(b) of the Federal Consumer Credit Protection Act, 15 U.S.C. § 1673(b).

DECREE ENTERED this _____ day of _____, _____.

_____
JUDGE, _____ {county} Superior Court

Submitted by:

_____

This page intentionally blank.

THE SUPERIOR COURT FOR THE COUNTY OF _____

STATE OF GEORGIA

_____,)   :
          Petitioner,   )   Civil Action File
)
v.   )   No. _____
)
_____,)
          Respondent.   )

PETITION FOR TEMPORARY PROTECTIVE ORDER

The Petitioner, pursuant to the Family Violence Act at O.C.G.A. §§ 19-13-1 et seq., files this Petition for a Family Violence Protective Order and in support shows the Court the following:

1.   The Petitioner is a resident of _____ County, Georgia and is over 18 years of age.

2.   The Respondent is a resident of_____ County, and may be served at_____, _____ Georgia. Jurisdiction and venue are proper with this Court.

OR

2a.   Respondent is a resident of the State of _____. Under O.C.G.A. § 19-13-2(b) jurisdiction and venue are proper with this Court because the abuse occurred in the State of Georgia in _____ county and/or the Petitioner lives in _____ County. Respondent is subject to the jurisdiction of this court   and   may   be   served   at   _____

_____.

3.   Respondent's Social Security number is _____, sex is ___, and is employed by_____ at _____ and works from ____ to ____ on (days)_____. Respondent's date of birth is _____, color of hair _____, color of eyes _____, height _____, weight _____. Respondent's race is _____. Respondent drives a _____, license _____ and has a _____ driver's license, number _____. Respondent has distinguishing marks (tattoos, scars, etc.) _____.

4.   Petitioner and Respondent are:

      ____   1.   Present or past spouses.

Civil Action File Number _____

_____ 2. Parents of the same child/ren.

_____ 3. Parent and child/ren.

_____ 4. Persons who used to live in the same household.

_____ 5. Persons currently living in the same household.

_____ 6. Foster parent and foster child.

_____ 7. Stepparent and stepchild.

5. Petitioner and Respondent have _____ child/ren under the age of 18. Their names, birth dates, sex, and ages are_____

_____

_____.

These child/ren have resided only with Petitioner and Respondent for the past five (5) years. (If the child/ren have resided with persons other than solely with the parties give names of these persons, their address, and dates the child/ren resided with them)_____

_____

_____

_____

_____

_____.

6. The parties are not married and the Respondent (has OR has not) legitimated the child/ren of the parties.

7. Petitioner (does OR does not) have knowledge concerning custody or claims of custody concerning these child/ren. Specify court and type of case (if applicable) _____.

8. Petitioner has the following minor child/ren living with Petitioner and wishes them to be protected from the Respondent by a Protective Order (Other than those named in paragraph 5)—(Names and ages):_____

_____

Civil Action File Number _____

9.   On or about _____, _____ the Respondent committed the following acts of family violence against the Petitioner and/or his or her child/ren:_____

_____

_____

_____

_____

_____

_____

_____

_____

_____

_____

_____

_____

_____

_____

_____

_____

_____

_____

_____

_____

_____

_____.

Petitioner is in reasonable fear for Petitioner's own safety and/or the safety of Petitioner's child/ren

10.   At other times the Respondent has committed other such acts, including, but not limited to (approximate dates and what happened): _____

_____

_____

_____

_____

_____

_____

_____

_____.

Civil Action File Number _____

11. There is a substantial likelihood that the Respondent will commit such acts of violence against the Petitioner and her child/ren in the immediate future if relief is not granted as provided pursuant to O.C.G.A. § 19-13-4.

12. Respondent has a criminal record and has committed the following: (Approximate dates and crimes) _____

    _____.

13. Petitioner fears that if Respondent learns of Petitioner's current address that Respondent will hurt Petitioner or Petitioner's immediate family. Petitioner requests that Respondent not be informed of Petitioner's current residence and states in support that Respondent_____

    _____.

14. Petitioner is dependent upon the family residence for shelter for the Petitioner and the minor child/ren and asks that Petitioner be granted the temporary use and possession of said residence, located at _____ together with all personal property contained therein with the exception of Respondent's personal clothing.

15. Petitioner and the minor child/ren are substantially/solely dependent upon the Respondent for support and requests that Petitioner be awarded temporary support and child support.

16. The minor child/ren are currently in the custody and control of the Petitioner/Respondent and Petitioner requests that Petitioner be awarded temporary legal and physical custody.

17. Respondent is in possession of the following assets/property of the Petitioner

    _____

    which petitioner asks to be returned.

THEREFORE, Petitioner asks:

(a) That the Court set a hearing no later than thirty (30) days from the filing of the Petition and direct Respondent to appear before this Court and show any reasons why the demands of the Petitioner should not be granted;

(b) That the Respondent be served a copy of this Petition and Temporary Protective Order as required by law;

Civil Action File Number _____

(c)   That this Court direct law enforcement to enforce this Order;

(d)   That this Court direct Respondent to stop abusing, harassing and intimidating Petitioner and/or Petitioner's child/ren;

(e)   That this Court restrain and enjoin Respondent from having any direct or indirect contact with the Petitioner and/or Petitioner's child/ren;

(f)   That this Court order that Respondent be enjoined from approaching within _____ yards of Petitioner;

(g)   That this Court make findings of fact and conclusions of law concerning the issues in this case;

(h)   That Petitioner have such other and further relief as the Court may deem just and proper; and,

(i)   That this Court issue a Temporary Protective Order to:

_____ award Petitioner temporary sole legal and physical custody of the minor child/ren;

_____ order Respondent to vacate the family residence at _____

_____ instantly and grant Petitioner exclusive temporary use and possession of the family residence and all personal property of the parties located at the family residence and Petitioner's current residence with the exception of Respondent's personal clothing; that the Sheriff's Office of _____ County assist Petitioner in returning to the family residence and in ensuring that the Respondent vacates said residence and that all keys, garage door openers, and other security devices to the family residence are secured and given to the Petitioner;

_____ order Respondent to stay away from Petitioner's and /or Petitioner's minor child/ren's place of residence, work and/or school;

_____ order Respondent's visitation with the minor child/ren be limited to _____

_____;

_____ order Respondent to pay to Petitioner child support for the minor child/ren;

_____ order Respondent to pay support for Petitioner;

Civil Action File Number _____

___ award the Petitioner costs and attorney fees for having to bring this action;

___ order that Petitioner's current address be kept confidential;

___ enjoin and restrain Respondent not to sell, dispose or encumber, trade, contract to sell, or otherwise dispose or remove from the jurisdiction of this Court any of the property of Petitioner or of the parties except in the ordinary course of business;

___ grant Petitioner the use of the following automobile: Make_____, Model _____, Year____, and the Sheriff's Office of _____ County ensure that all keys to said vehicle be immediately returned to Petitioner;

___ enjoin and restrain Respondent from disconnecting the home utilities, changing and/or canceling auto, health or life insurance for Respondent, Petitioner, and/or the Petitioner's minor child/ren, and/or interfering with Petitioner's or the Petitioner's minor child/ren's mail; and,

___ permit Petitioner to remove the following property from the residence for the exclusive use by Petitioner and/or the minor child/ren _____

_____

_____

and the Sheriff's Office of _____ County be ordered to assist the Petitioner during this removal;

___ order Respondent to return _____

_____ to Petitioner immediately.

___ order Respondent to undergo an evaluation for drug/alcohol abuse and to follow the recommended treatment;

___ make a referral, where appropriate, to the Adult Protective Services or _____ for appropriate assistance and referrals;

___ order Respondent to undergo a batterer's intervention program and to follow the recommended treatment;

Civil Action File Number _____

___ That: _____

_____.

Respectfully submitted,

_____

Address _____   Petitioner

_____

Phone_____

Civil Action File Number _____

VERIFICATION

Personally appeared _____, who being duly sworn states that he or she is the Petitioner in the above styled case and that the facts set forth in the foregoing Petition for Temporary Protective Order are true and correct.

_____

Petitioner

Sworn and subscribed before

me this _____ day of _____, _____.

_____

NOTARY PUBLIC

My commission expires:

Civil Action File Number _____

IN THE SUPERIOR COURT OF _____ COUNTY
STATE OF GEORGIA

_____

Petitioner

v.

_____

Respondent

* Civil Action File No:

* _____

* Prior/Pending Case Nos:

* _____

PETITION FOR RELIEF UNDER THE FAMILY VIOLENCE ACT

Comes now the Petitioner and submits this Petition for Relief under the Family Violence Act, as follows:

1.   **The Petitioner:** (In the event Petitioner is staying at a confidential location, list an alternate address and alternate phone number(s) through which Petitioner can still receive mail and messages which will not affect Petitioner's safety.)

Name:
Mailing Address:
City, State, Zip:
All Phone Numbers:

2.   **Respondent:**

Name:
Home Address:
City, State, Zip:
Phone Numbers:
You Must Complete Document Labeled " Respondent's Identifying Fact Sheet" **Listing Additional Information Concerning This Respondent.**

3.   This Court has jurisdiction over this matter because:

(a)   [ ]   the Respondent is a resident of this county

(b)   [ ]   the Respondent is a resident of the State of _____, and the Respondent has committed an act of family violence within the State of Georgia or has committed an act of family violence outside of the State of Georgia having an effect inside the State of Georgia, and

(1)   [ ]   the Petitioner is a resident of _____ County, Georgia.
(2)   [ ]   the Petitioner is a resident of the State of Georgia and the act of family violence committed by the Respondent occurred in _____ County.

4.   This action is brought under the provisions of the Family Violence Act (OCGA § 19-13-1, *et seq.*) The parties are related to each other as follows:

Check One	Relationship	Date Relationship Began	Date Relationship Ended
	Present Spouse [ ] Ceremonial [ ] Common Law		Not Applicable
	Former Spouse		
	Persons living in the same household		Not Applicable
	Persons formerly living in the same household		
	Parents of the Same Children	Not Applicable	Not Applicable
	Parent and Child	Not Applicable	Not Applicable
	Stepparent and Stepchild	Not Applicable	Not Applicable
	Foster Parent and Foster Child	Not Applicable	Not Applicable

5. The Minor Children of the parties or children residing with the parties are as follows:

Name of Child	Date of Birth	Resides with:	Related to:
		[ ] Both [ ] Petitioner [ ] Respondent	[ ] Both [ ] Petitioner [ ] Respondent
		[ ] Both [ ] Petitioner [ ] Respondent	[ ] Both [ ] Petitioner [ ] Respondent
		[ ] Both [ ] Petitioner [ ] Respondent	[ ] Both [ ] Petitioner [ ] Respondent
		[ ] Both [ ] Petitioner [ ] Respondent	[ ] Both [ ] Petitioner [ ] Respondent
		[ ] Both [ ] Petitioner [ ] Respondent	[ ] Both [ ] Petitioner [ ] Respondent

This section MUST be completed in any case in which custody or visitation may be an issue.

The present address of my minor children is: [ ] Petitioner's address; [ ] Respondent's address; [ ] Other: _____

During the last five years my minor child(ren) has/have resided at the following additional addresses:

_____

I [ ] have [ ] have not participated as a party, witness, or in any other capacity in any litigation concerning the custody of my children in Georgia or in any other state.
I [ ] have [ ] do not have information of any custody proceeding concerning my child(ren) pending in a court of Georgia or any other state.
I [ ] know [ ] do not know of any person, not a party to this action, who has physical custody of my child(ren) or claims to have custody or visitation rights with respect to my child(ren).
If you answered affirmatively ("I have/know") to any of the above questions you must list and describe all such cases, including the name of each court(s), and the most recent judgment or order: _____

_____

6. The Respondent has committed the following acts of Family Violence against the Petitioner or the minor children: **(Please refer to the legal definitions on the instruction sheet. A family violence petition MUST set out facts to support at least one of these offenses. If none of these offenses has occurred, you should consider another more appropriate legal remedy.)**

[ ] Simple Battery   [ ] Battery   [ ] Simple Assault   [ ] Aggravated Assault   [ ] Criminal Trespass

[ ] Criminal Damage to Property   [ ] Unlawful Restraint   [ ] Stalking   [ ] Aggravated Stalking

[ ] Other Felonies

7.   The specific facts concerning the above listed acts of Family Violence are as follows (Attach additional sheets an exhibits as necessary):

_____

_____

_____

_____

_____

_____

_____

_____

_____

_____

_____

_____

_____

_____

_____

_____

_____

8.   Other documents supporting the allegations of Family Violence committed by the Respondent are attached hereto a Exhibit A, consisting of _____ pages. (Police reports, medical or hospital records, photographs, etc.)

9.   The Petitioner alleges that Family Violence has occurred in the past and is reasonably likely to occur in the future f the following reasons:

[ ]   The Respondent has made threats of future violence/stalking.

[ ]   There is an established pattern of behavior by the Respondent involving acts of family violence as set fort above.

[ ]   The Respondent has a pattern of continued substance abuse which has caused family violence in the pas

[ ]   The Petitioner requests that the Court evaluate certain factors and the history of family violence occurrence which affect the risk of future violence, which is hereto attached as Exhibit A, entitled "Factors & History (Family Violence, and is incorporated by reference herein.

[ ]   Other: _____

_____

_____

10.   The Respondent should be restrained from committing further acts of family violence.

Wherefore, the Petitioner requests the following relief be awarded the Petitioner (check all that apply):

[ ]   Exclusive and immediate possession of the residence located at:_____

[ ]   Immediate custody of the minor child(ren). The Respondent [ ] should [ ] should not be awarded reasonable visitation rights under such supervision as the Court deems just and proper.

[ ]   Exclusive and immediate possession of the following vehicle(s):_____

[ ]   Alimony for the support of Petitioner.

[ ]   Child support for the support of the minor child(ren).

[ ]   Payment of certain debts.

[ ]   Award of reasonable attorney fees.

[ ]   **That the Court issue a Family Violence Ex Parte Protective Order protecting all the persons I have listed on the attached form entitled "Petitioner's Identifying Information."**

Furthermore, the Petitioner requests that:

(a)   A Family Violence *Ex Parte* Protective Order issue *ex parte* immediately restraining and enjoining the Respondent from committing acts of violence against Petitioner and the child(ren);

(b)   The Court issue a *Rule Nisi* order requiring the Respondent to appear and show cause why the relief demanded by the Petitioner under the Family Violence Act should not be granted;

(c)   The sheriff, any deputy sheriff or any other state, county, or municipal law enforcement officer shall implement any order of this Court; and

(d)   For such other and further relief as this Court deems just and proper.

I have read the above Petition and hereby swear or affirm that the allegations made herein are based upon my personal knowledge and are true and correct.

_____
Petitioner Signature

_____
Printed Name

Sworn to and subscribed before me this _____ day

of _____, 20_____ .

_____
Clerk of Court/Notary Public/Judicial Officer

Exhibit A
History & Factors of Family Violence

(Petitioner should initial **ALL** that apply. Respondent is the defendant.)

History

_____ Choking of petitioner.

_____ Respondent has destroyed, or threatened to destroy, the personal property of the petitioner.

_____ Increasing frequency and severity of violence against petitioner.

_____ Respondent has threatened to use weapon or threatened to kill partner.

_____ History of prior calls to law enforcement and/or prior filings for protective orders.

_____ History of defying protective orders or law enforcement.

_____ History of substance abuse. Respondent assaults petitioner when drunk or high.

_____ Stalking of petitioner by respondent.

_____ Excessive jealousy and excessive control of petitioner. Currently threatens petitioner because he/she believes that petitioner is cheating with another.

_____ Respondent has expressed fantasies about homicide or suicide.

_____ Respondent has killed or injured pets or threatened to do so.

_____ Respondent has threatened or attempted suicide.

_____ Respondent has told petitioner words to the effect, "If I can't have you no one can."

_____ Respondent threatens to injure or flee with petitioner's children. Or, has done so in the past.

_____ Respondent has mental health impairment, such as depression or schizophrenia or paranoia.

_____ Respondent has threatened to take petitioner hostage or has a history of hostage taking, with or without law enforcement intervention.

_____ (Optional) Respondent has forced petitioner to have sex against will of petitioner.

FACTORS

_____ Parties have recently separated.

_____ Gun present in home or readily accessible to respondent.

_____ Petitioner believes that the respondent may try to use deadly force against petitioner.

_____ (Optional) Petitioner has begun a new relationship with a new partner.

INSTRUCTIONS FOR FILING
PETITION FOR RELIEF UNDER FAMILY VIOLENCE ACT

Under O.C.G.A. '19-13-3 the clerk of the court may provide forms for petitions and pleadings to victims of family violence and to any other person designated by the Superior Court to advise victims on filling out and filing such petitions and pleadings.

These instructions have been prepared on behalf of the Superior Court to assist you in making your own determination whether you should file an action under the Family Violence Act in the Superior Court. They are only general instructions and exceptions may be applicable to your case. **If you have any additional questions which are beyond the limited scope of these instructions you should consult an attorney, or the local representative with the Partnership Against Domestic Violence (770-963-9799), The Family Violence Project, a division of Atlanta Legal Aid, (678)376-9844) or conduct your own legal research. The Family Violence Act is set forth in O.C.G.A. '' 19-13-1, et.seq..**

THE CLERK AND DEPUTY CLERKS OF THE SUPERIOR COURT ARE PROHIBITED BY STATUTE FROM GIVING YOU LEGAL ADVICE. DO NOT ASK THE CLERKS FOR LEGAL ADVICE. THEY CANNOT GIVE YOU LEGAL ADVICE.

These instructions explain the numbered paragraphs on the Petition For Relief Under the Family Violence Act.

Section 1.

You must be over the age of 18 years to file this action. If you are under the age of 18 years you may have an adult approved by the Court file on your behalf.

Section 2.

The Defendant is the "Respondent." For a Protective Order to be now be listed on the statewide Protective Order Registry, you must be able to provide at least one of the following items of information. These items are: Respondent's social security number, date of birth or driver' license number & state. Please use your best efforts to get this important information. You also need to complete the form entitled "Respondent's identifying Information." It is important that you provide as much detailed information as possible so that Respondent can be quickly served with the Protective Order.

Section 3.

You must file your action in the proper county. There are two basic rules for jurisdiction under the Family Violence Act.

(1) Under the Georgia Constitution, this action **MUST** be filed in the county where the Respondent resides. "*To reside*" means generally to live at a location with the intent of remaining there indefinitely. A place of residence is not changed until a new location is established with the intent to remain indefinitely at the new location. If the Respondent lives in the State of Georgia, you must file your case in the county in which the Respondent resides. If the Respondent does not live in this county, but lives in another Georgia county, you must file this action in the Georgia county where the Respondent resides.

(2) If the Respondent lives **outside** the State of Georgia you may file your case in (a) the county where you live, or (b) the county in which the act of family violence occurred **if** the Respondent:
- (i) has committed an act of family violence inside the State of Georgia, or
- (ii) has committed a tortious injury inside the State of Georgia caused by an act of family violence committed outside the State of Georgia, and the Respondent has other "minimum Contacts" with the State of Georgia (see O.C.G.A. 9-10-91).

 Do not file this action in this County Superior Court unless jurisdiction is proper in this court under the above rules. If you have any questions about whether or not the Respondent is a resident of this County you should consult an attorney to help you make this determination. You **must** file your action in the correct county. The law does not permit any exceptions on this issue.

Section 4.

Only persons who have certain relationships can file for relief under the Family Violence Act. Do not file this Petition unless you have one of the specific relationships listed under this section.

Section 5.

If there are minor children residing in the household who will be effected by this action you should list their names, ages and to whom they are related; i.e. Petitioner, Respondent, other family members, or step children, etc.
The supplemental section sets forth the required elements of O.C.G.A. 19-9-69. This information is required if custody of a minor child or visitation with a minor child is involved in this action.

Section 6.

Only certain criminal acts provide a legal basis for relief under the family violence act. Do not file this action under the family act unless at least one of the required acts has occurred. The acts are defined generally as follows:

X   Simple battery: See O.C.G.A. ' 16-5-23 -- to cause physical harm; make contact of an insulting or provoking nature.

X   Battery: See O.C.G.A. ' 16-5-23.1 -- to cause substantial physical harm; to cause visible bodily harm.

X   Simple Assault: See O.C.G.A. ' 16-5-20 -- an attempt to commit a violent injury; to commit an act which places another in reasonable apprehension of immediately receiving a violent injury.

X   Aggravated assault: See O.C.G.A. ' 16-5-21 -- an assault with :(1) an intent to murder, to rape or rob; (2) a deadly weapon; or(3) with any object when used offensively against a person is likely to or actually does result in bodily injury.

X   Criminal trespass: See O.C.G.A. ' 16-7-21 -- to knowingly and without authority enter upon the land of another person, vehicle, etc.: (1) for an unlawful purpose; or (2) after receiving, prior to such entry, notice from the owner, rightful occupant that such entry is forbidden; (3) to remain on the above described after receiving notice from the owner, rightful occupant, authorized agent to depart. (This code section may not apply in some instances between spouses who each have rights of ownership, etc., in their mutual property.)

X   Criminal damage to property: See O.C.G.A. ' 16-7-22 -- to knowingly and without authority interfere with any property in a manner so as to endanger human life; intentionally damage any property of another person with consent and the damages exceeds $500.00. recklessly or intentionally by means of fire or explosive damage the property of another person.

X   Unlawful restraint: See O.C.G.A. ' 16-5-41 -- an act in violation of the personal liberty of another which arrests, confines or detains a person without legal authority.

X   Stalking: See O.C.G.A. ' 16-5-90 -- to follow, place under surveillance, or contact another person at or about a place or places without the consent of the other person for the purpose of harassing and intimidating the other person -- "place or places" shall include any public or private property occupied by the victim other than the residence of the Respondent -- cannot be the property of the Respondent -- "harassing and intimidating" shall mean a knowing course of conduct directed at a specific person which causes emotional distress by placing such person in reasonable fear to himself/herself or a member of his/her immediate family.

X   Aggravated Stalking -- See O.C.G.A. ' 16-5-91 when such person violation of a temporary restraining order, preliminary injunction, or permanent injunction or condition of pretrial release, condition of probation, or condition of parole in effect prohibiting the behavior described herein follows, places under surveillance, or contacts another person at or about a place or places without the consent of the other person for the purpose of harassing and intimidating the other person.

X   A felony -- the commission of a crime punishable by more than one year incarceration and is the type of felony which would support the allegation that family violence has occurred in the past and is reasonably likely to occur in the future.

Section 7.

Write out the specific facts setting forth EACH OF THE LEGAL ELEMENTS of the above listed offense(s) which you believe support your allegation that one or more of these required criminal acts of family violence have occurred.

Section 8.

You may attach copies of any documentary evidence which you believe would support your allegation that any of the required criminal acts of family violence have occurred.

Section 9.

Family violence actions involve a two-part test. First, the judge must first find probable cause that one of the required criminal acts of family violence has occurred; and, second, there is probable cause that family violence is reasonably likely to occur in the future. An isolated or singular instance of family violence may, or may not, be enough to prove an action of family violence under this code section. Be sure to complete the list of history and factor of family violence which is attached as Exhibit A.

Section 10.

Check only the sections which you are requesting that the Court consider for your case. You must also complete the document entitled "Petitioner's Identifying Information." This lists all the persons for whom you are requesting that a protective order issue.

COURT COSTS

There are NO costs associated with the filing of a Family Violence action.
Read very carefully the information provided before filing your action. If you have any questions you should consult an attorney, contact the local representative at one of the Domestic Violence referrals in Form _____ or research the law yourself before proceeding.

This page intentionally blank.

ORI Number_____

THE SUPERIOR COURT FOR THE COUNTY OF_____

STATE OF GEORGIA

_____,)
          Petitioner,   )   Civil Action File
    v.   )
)
_____,)   No._____
          Respondent.   )

DISMISSAL OF TEMPORARY PROTECTIVE ORDER

IT IS HEREBY ORDERED, ADJUDGED, and DECREED that the (Petition)(Counter-Petition)(Both Petition and Counter-Petition) [strike through appropriate] for Temporary Protective Order filed on the _____ day of _____, 20_____ is hereby dismissed without prejudice:

[ ] on (Petitioner's)(Respondent's)(Both Petitioner's and Respondent's) motion to dismiss.
[ ] on (Petitioner's)(Respondent's)(Both Petitioner's and Respondent's) failure to appear and proceed.
[ ] on (Petitioner's)(Respondent's)(Both Petitioner's and Respondent's) failure to prove by a preponderance of the evidence the allegations contained in the (Petition)(Counter-Petition)(Both Petition and Counter-Petition) for Temporary Protective Order.
[ ] due to lack of service on (Petitioner)(Respondent)(Both Petitioner and Respondent).
[ ] OTHER: _____

This _____ day of _____, 20_____.

_____
JUDGE, SUPERIOR COURT
_____ County

_____
Print or stamp Judge's name

❑ Transmitted to Georgia Protective Order Registry   Date _____ Clerk _____

This page intentionally blank.

ORI NUMBER:_____

IN THE SUPERIOR COURT OF _____ COUNTY
STATE OF GEORGIA

_____   )   Civil Action File No:
              Petitioner   )
)
              vs.   )   _____
)
)
)
_____   )
              Respondent   )

FAMILY VIOLENCE *EX PARTE* PROTECTIVE ORDER

The petition having come on for an *ex parte* hearing, pursuant to O.C.G.A. 19-13-1 *et.seq.* that a Protective Order be issued; petitioner alleged that Respondent has committed acts of Family Violence and that Petitioner is in reasonable fear of the Petitioner's safety (and the safety of Petitioner's child(ren), and the Court having read and considered the petition and having heard the sworn testimony of the Plaintiff, the Court finds probable cause exists that family violence has occurred in the past and may occur in the future. **IT IS HEREBY ORDERED AND ADJUDGED THAT:**

1.   These proceedings be filed in the office of the Clerk of this Court.

2.   This Order applies in every county throughout the state of Georgia and it shall be the duty of every court and every law enforcement official to enforce and carry out the provisions of this order pursuant to O.C.G.A. 19-13-4(d). Law Enforcement officers may use their arrest powers pursuant to O.C.G.A. 19-13-6 & 17-4-20 to enforce the terms of this order.

3.   A copy of this order be given to law enforcement and the Respondent be served with a copy of this Order the Petition for Temporary Protective Order instanter.

4.   **The Petitioner and Respondent named herein shall appear before the Superior Court of _____ County, on the _____day of _____ 20_____, at _____o'clock ____.m. at _____, Georgia, Courtroom _____, to show cause why the demands of the Petitioner should or should not be granted. (Absent a consent agreement, the Court ordinarily will not enter a mutual protective order on issues connected with O.C.G.A. 19-13-4(a)(1), (a)(2), (a)(5), (a)(9) or (a)(11), or any combination thereof, unless the Respondent has filed a verified petition as a counter-petition pursuant to O.C.G.A. 19-13-3 no later than three days, not including Saturdays, Sundays, and legal holidays, prior to the hearing and the provisions of O.C.G.A. 19-13-3 have been satisfied.)**

5.   **Respondent is hereby restrained and enjoined from doing, or attempting to do, or threatening to do, any act of injury, maltreating, molesting, following, harassing, harming, abusing or stalking the Petitioner and the Petitioner's minor child(ren), if any. Respondent is not to interfere with Petitioner's travel, transportation or communication. The Respondent shall not follow, place under surveillance, or contact the Plaintiff at any place for the purpose of harassing and intimidating the Plaintiff. Any violation of this order may be considered a violation of O.C.G.A. 16-5-90 and may subject the Respondent to prosecution for Aggravated Stalking, in violation of O.C.G.A. ' 16-5-91, a felony; and Federal Law, Title 18 U.C.S., Chapter 110-A/Domestic Violence, Sections 2261-2266.**

6.   Respondent is enjoined and restrained from doing or threatening to do any act of injury, maltreating, molesting, harassing, harming or abusing the Petitioner's family or household.

Civil Action File No: _____

7.   This Court has determined that it had jurisdiction over the parties and the subject matter under the laws of this state of Georgia and the Court ordered that the Respondent be given reasonable notice and opportunity to be heard sufficient to protect the Respondent's due process rights. This order shall be presumed to be valid and pursuant to 18 U.S.C.A. 2265(a) shall be accorded FULL FAITH AND CREDIT by any other state, tribe or local jurisdiction as if an Order of the enforcing state, tribe or jurisdiction. The Petitioner has validly filed this Family Violence *Ex Parte* Protective Order; therefore, this Order is legally enforceable by any appropriate law enforcement official or court of any State pursuant to 18 U.S.C.A. 2265.

ONLY THE FOLLOWING PROVISIONS APPLY THAT ARE INITIALED BY THE JUDGE

_____ **8.**   **That until further order by this Court, Petitioner is awarded sole and exclusive use and possession of the (family) residence located at:**

_____

_____ 9.   Respondent is ordered to leave the above listed (family) residence immediately. The members of the _____ County Sheriff's office or any other duly authorized law enforcement officer are ordered to:

[ ]   Assist the Petitioner in returning to this residence;

[ ]   Remove and evict the Respondent from this residence, together with Respondent's clothing, personal effects, prescription medication, and tools of his or her trade or profession;

[ ]   Require Respondent to surrender to law enforcement any and all keys, garage door openers and other security devices to the (family) residence and to insure that these items are delivered to Petitioner.

[ ]   Effectuate the custody placement of the minor children as set forth herein;

[ ]   Assist the Petitioner in removing from the residence the Petitioner's clothing and personal effects, together with those of Petitioner's children, if any.

_____ 10.   Respondent is ordered to provide suitable alternate housing for the Petitioner and/or Petitioner's children by this date: _____.

_____ 11.   Petitioner's address is ordered to be kept confidential.

_____ **12.**   **Respondent is ordered to stay away from: (1) Petitioner's residence, workplace & school and any subsequent residence, workplace, school of Petitioner; (2) the residence, workplace & school, and any subsequent residence, workplace, school of the minor children whose custody is awarded to Petitioner;**

Said residence is listed as: [ ] the address as listed in # 8, herein above;

_____

Petitioner's current workplace is: _____

The current school(s) is/are: _____

_____ **13.**   **Until further order of this Court, Respondent is restrained and enjoined from approaching within _____ yards of Petitioner and/or the minor children of the Petitioner.**

_____ **14.**   **Respondent is ordered to not have any contact, direct or indirect or through another person with Petitioner by telephone, pager, fax, e-mail or any other means of communication excepting as specified in this Order; and excepting any communication with any attorney representing Petitioner.**

_____ 15. Petitioner is awarded temporary custody of the minor child(ren), namely:

_____	DOB _____	Sex _____
_____	DOB _____	Sex _____
_____	DOB _____	Sex _____
_____	DOB _____	Sex _____
_____	DOB _____	Sex _____

Unless otherwise permitted by order of this court, the Respondent shall not have any contact with these minor children until further hearing and order of this Court. Respondent is ordered not to interfere with the physical custody of the children.

_____ Check here ONLY if Respondent is awarded temporary custody of the minor child(ren), namely:

_____	DOB _____	Sex _____
_____	DOB _____	Sex _____
_____	DOB _____	Sex _____
_____	DOB _____	Sex _____
_____	DOB _____	Sex _____

_____ 16. [ ] Reserved until hearing after notice to both parties; or [ ] The Respondent is ordered to pay temporary child support for the minor children to Petitioner in the amount of $ _____ every _____, beginning, _____. All payments shall be made:

       _____ By an income deduction order; _____ To the child support receiver;
       _____ by mail directly to Petitioner;
       _____ by _____.

_____ 17. [ ] Reserved until hearing after notice to both parties; [ ] The Respondent is ordered to pay temporary support to the Petitioner in the amount of

$ _____ every _____, beginning, _____.
All payments shall be made:

       _____ By an income deduction order; _____ To the child support receiver;
       _____ by mail directly to Petitioner;
       _____ by _____.

_____ 18. Respondent, **only when accompanied by a law enforcement officer**, shall be able to remove his/her clothing, personal effects, prescription medication, and tools of his or her trade or profession as follows:

_____

_____

       [ ]   As coordinated and scheduled with the _____County Sheriff's Dept. Family Violence Unit, phone _____.

_____ 19. Both parties are hereby enjoined and restrained from transferring, selling, pledging as collateral for a loan, contracting to sell, concealing, or otherwise disposing of or removing from the jurisdiction of this Court, any of the property belonging to the parties, the children of the parties, pets of the parties, except in the ordinary course of business or for the necessities of life.

_____ 20. [ ] Respondent [ ] Petitioner [ ] Both Respondent & Petitioner is/are ordered not to disconnect or have disconnected the home utilities, including but not limited to electricity, gas, water, telephone; change or have changed, or cancel, or have canceled, auto, health, or life insurance for Respondent, Petitioner, Petitioner's children, Respondent's children, or interfere with his/her/their mail.

Civil Action File No: _____

_____ 21. Petitioner is awarded sole, exclusive temporary possession of the below listed vehicle. The Respondent shall not exercise any control over such vehicle. All keys, proof of insurance and registration to this vehicle shall be surrendered to law enforcement and law enforcement shall immediately turn said items over to Petitioner. No changes shall be made to any existing insurance coverage on the vehicle. Vehicle(s) is/are:

Make: _____ Model: _____; Year _____; Color_____

[ ]   As coordinated and scheduled with the _____ County Sheriff's Dept. Family Violence Unit, phone _____

_____ 22. Petitioner shall be allowed to remove the following property from the family residence for Petitioner and/or Petitioner's children's use: his/her/their clothing, personal effects, prescription medication, and tools of his/ her trade or profession and the following items:

_____

_____

[ ]   As coordinated and scheduled with the _____County Sheriff's Dept. Family Violence Unit, phone _____.

_____ 23. Respondent shall be required to return the following property for Petitioner and/or Petitioner's children's use: _____

_____

on or before the following date: _____.

[ ]   As coordinated and scheduled with the _____County Sheriff's Dept. Family Violence Unit, phone _____.

IT IS FURTHER ORDERED:

_____ 24. Other _____

_____ 25. Each party shall complete, notarize and file with this Court a true and correct **Domestic Relations Financial Data Sheet before** the hearing date set forth above.

_____ 26. **REFERRAL TO VICTIM SERVICES & SAFETY PLANNING GUIDANCE**

[   ] Petitioner [   ] Respondent shall **immediately** seek victim services and safety planning guidance from the Partnership Against Domestic Violence – phone _____. Information on safety planning has been given to said party. In the event there is a ending misdemeanor case connected with this action, this party shall contact the Solicitor's office, phone _____ victim-witness services. In the event there is a pending felony case connected with this action, this party shall contact the District Attorney's office, phone _____, victim-witness services.

_____ 27. Respondent shall immediately attend evaluation, treatment and counseling through: _____ _____Court Services – phone _____-- for (alcohol)(drug)(violence) counseling or through another equivalent professional treatment program.

SO ORDERED, this _____day of _____, 20_____ at _____ ___.M.

_____
Judge, _____Superior Court

[ ] by designation

Print Name:_____

Civil Action File No: _____

Violation of this Order May Be Punishable By Arrest

Notice to Respondent
1. Violation of this Order may result in immediate arrest and criminal prosecution that may result in jail time and/or fines and/or may subject you to prosecution and penalties for contempt of court.
2. This Order shall remain in effect unless specifically superseded by a subsequent signed and filed Order, by operation of law, or by Order of Dismissal, whichever occurs first. Only this Court can void, modify, or dismiss this Order. Either party may ask, in writing, or during any hearing, that this Court change or dismiss this Order.
3. A person commits the offense of Aggravated Stalking when such person, in violation of a temporary or permanent protective Order prohibiting this behavior follows, places under surveillance, or contacts Petitioner on public or private property for the purpose of harassing and intimidating the other person. This activity can subject the Respondent to arrest and prosecution for the felony Aggravated Stalking, which carries penalties of imprisonment for not less than 1 year nor more than 10 years and a fine up to $10,000.00.

Note: This form is promulgated as a Uniform Superior Court Rule under the auspices of O.C.G.A. 19-13-53. To order a specific provision, please initial in the space provided. The court should delete or otherwise make inoperative any provision in the standardized form which is not supported by the evidence in the case or in order to comply with the court's application of the law and facts to an individual case.

[ ] Transmitted to Georgia Protective Order Registry: By: _____, Deputy Clerk	Date Submitted by Deputy Clerk:

This is to certify this is a true and correct copy of the foregoing Family Violence Ex Parte Order, as the same appears of record in _____ Superior Court . Given my hand and seal of this court,

this _____ day of _____, 20_____.

By: _____, Deputy Clerk, Superior Court, _____ County, GA

This page intentionally blank.

Civil Action File No: _____

ORI NUMBER:_____

IN THE SUPERIOR COURT OF _____ COUNTY
STATE OF GEORGIA

_____
Petitioner

v.

_____
Respondent

) Civil Action File No:
)
) _____
)
) **[ ]** The clerk shall mail a copy of this order
) to Respondent at last known mailing
) address, or _____
) _____

THREE YEAR OR PERMANENT
FAMILY VIOLENCE PROTECTIVE ORDER

A hearing was held on this matter on _____, 20 _____, for which the Respondent had notice as required by law, and at which the Respondent appeared and/or had the opportunity to be heard and Petitioner requested that the Protective Order entered in this case be converted to a Permanent Family Violence Protective Order. This Court has determined that it had jurisdiction over the subject matter and the parties. Having heard the evidence presented, reviewed the Motion and entire record concerning this case and for good cause shown, **IT IS HEREBY ORDERED AND ADJUDGED THAT:**

1.   These proceedings be filed in the office of the Clerk of this Court.

2.   This Order applies to every county throughout the state of Georgia and it shall be the duty of every court and every law enforcement official to enforce and carry out the provisions of this order pursuant to O.C.G.A. 19-13-4(d). Law Enforcement officers may use their arrest powers pursuant to O.C.G.A. 1-13-6 & 17-4-20 to enforce the terms of this order.

3.   This Order and the Order issued _____, 20 _____, shall be permanent pursuant to O.C.G.A. 19-13-4(C) and have NO expiration date.

OR

3.1.   This Order shall be in effect for three (3) years and shall expire on _____, 20 _____.

The Clerk of the Superior Court shall submit a copy of this order to the Protective Order Registry in the manner required by law. The clerk shall issue a copy of this Order to the Sheriff of _____ County, Georgia and to the _____ County Police Department, who shall each retain a copy for so long as this Order remains in effect.

4.   **Respondent has violated the Family Violence Act, O.C.G.A.19-13-1 et.seq., by committing family**
[pco01]   **violence has placed the Petitioner in reasonable fear for Petitioner's safety, and represents a credible threat to the physical safety of Petitioner and/or Petitioner's child/ren. Respondent is hereby restrained and enjoined from doing, or attempting to do, or threatening to do, any act of injury, maltreating, molesting, following, harassing, harming, abusing or stalking the Petitioner and the Petitioner's minor child(ren), if any. Respondent is not to interfere with Petitioner's travel, transportation or communication. The Respondent shall not follow, place under surveillance, or contact the Petitioner at any place for the purpose of harassing and intimidating the Petitioner. Any violation of this order may be considered a violation of O.C.G.A. § 16-5-90 and may subject the Respondent to prosecution for Aggravated Stalking, in violation of O.C.G.A. § 16-5-91, a felony; and Federal Law, Title 18 UCS, Chapter 110-A/Domestic Violence, Sections 2261-2266.**

Civil Action File No: _____

5. **Respondent is enjoined and restrained from doing or attempting to do, or threatening to do, any**
[pco02] **act of injury, maltreating, molesting, harassing, harming or abusing the Petitioner's family or household.**

6. This Court has determined that it had jurisdiction over the parties and the subject matter under the laws of this state of Georgia and the Court ordered that the Respondent received reasonable notice and had the opportunity to be heard before this order was issued sufficient to protect the Respondent's due process rights. This order shall be presumed to be valid and pursuant to 18 U.S.C. 2265(a) shall be accorded **FULL FAITH AND CREDIT** by any other state, tribe or local jurisdiction as if an Order of the enforcing state, tribe or jurisdiction. The Petitioner has validly filed this Family Violence Ex Parte Protective Order; therefore, this Order shall be enforced as if an Order of the enforcing state, tribe or local jurisdiction and by any appropriate law enforcement official or court of any State pursuant to 18 U.S.C.A. § 2265.

ONLY THE FOLLOWING PROVISIONS APPLY THAT ARE INITIALED BY THE JUDGE

_____ 7. **Respondent is ordered to stay away from Petitioner's residence, workplace & school and**
[pco04] **any subsequent residence, workplace, school and the residence of Petitioner's, or of the minor children for whom custody is awarded to Petitioner;**
Said residence is:

_____

Petitioner's current workplace is: _____

The current school(s) is/are: _____

_____ 8. **Respondent is restrained and enjoined from approaching within _____ yards of**
[pco01,04] **Petitioner and/or Petitioner's minor children.**

_____ 9. **Respondent is ordered to not have any contact, direct or indirect or through another**
[pco05] **person with Petitioner by telephone, pager, fax, e-mail, or any other means of communication except as specified in this Order; and excepting any attorney representing Petitioner.**

_____ 10. Petitioner is awarded temporary custody of the minor child/ren, namely:
[pco09]

_____ DOB _____ Sex _____

_____ DOB _____ Sex _____

_____ DOB _____ Sex _____

_____ DOB _____ Sex _____

_____ DOB _____ Sex _____

Respondent is ordered not to interfere with the physical custody of the minor child/ren.

_____ [pco06] **Initial here ONLY if Respondent is awarded temporary custody of the minor child/ren, namely:**

_____ DOB _____ Sex _____

_____ DOB _____ Sex _____

_____ DOB _____ Sex _____

_____ DOB _____ Sex _____

Civil Action File No: _____

_____ 11. **[ ]** **CHILD SUPPORT**

[ ] Petitioner; [ ] Respondent; shall pay to [ ] Petitioner; [ ] Respondent; for the support and

maintenance of the above minor children the sum of $_____, commencing

_____, payable:

[ ] weekly, on [ ] Sun [ ] Mon [ ] Tue [ ] Wed [ ] Thu [ ] Fri [ ] Sat [ ] Sun

[ ] bi-weekly, on [ ] Sun [ ] Mon [ ] Tue [ ] Wed [ ] Thu [ ] Fri [ ] Sat [ ] Sun

[ ] semi-monthly, on the _____ and the _____ of each month

[ ] monthly, on the _____ of each month.

All payments shall be made:

_____ By an income deduction order; _____ To the child support receiver;

_____ by mail directly to Petitioner;

_____ by _____.

In determining child support the Court finds as follows:

The gross income of the father is:_____ monthly or $_____ yearly;

The gross income of the mother is:_____ monthly or $_____ yearly;
The applicable percentages of obligor's gross income to be considered by the trier of fact to determine child support are:

1 child, 17-23%; 2 children, 23-28%; 3 children 25-32%; 4 children, 29-35%; 5 children, 31-37%

In this case child support is being determined for _____ child/ren and the applicable percentage of gross income to be considered is_____ to _____ percent. The court has considered the existence of special circumstances as has found:

[ ]   no special circumstance apply;

[ ]   the following special circumstances exist: _____

_____

The Court finds that such payments are in compliance with the *child support guidelines*.

_____ 12. The Respondent is ordered to pay temporary support to the Petitioner the sum of

$_____, commencing _____, payable:

[ ] weekly, on [ ] Sun [ ] Mon [ ] Tue [ ] Wed [ ] Thu [ ] Fri [ ] Sat [ ] Sun

[ ] bi-weekly, on [ ] Sun [ ] Mon [ ] Tue [ ] Wed [ ] Thu [ ] Fri [ ] Sat [ ] Sun

[ ] semi-monthly, on the _____ and the _____ of each month

[ ] monthly, on the _____ of each month.

Civil Action File No: _____

All payments shall be made:

_____ By an income deduction order;

_____ To the child support receiver;

_____ by mail directly to Petitioner;

_____ by _____.

[ ]   PAYMENTS THROUGH SUPPORT DIVISION

The recipient of child support and/or alimony has specifically requested that all such payments be made through the Support Division for the term of this Order and the recipient has freely and voluntarily agreed to pay the applicable fees for collection during the term of this Order from the proceeds received from the payor. Therefore, the payor of all such payments required hereunder is ordered to make all such payments at the times specified by cash, cashier's check, or money order, personally or by mailing the same to:

Mailing Address:

_____

_____

_____

The parties shall immediately complete all documents necessary for payments to be made through the Support Division. Internal Operating Procedure Case Management, is incorporated herein by reference and made a part of this Order.

Payments shall continue until further order of a Court of competent jurisdiction, or until this Order expires by operation of law pursuant to O.C.G.A. § 19-13-4(c), six months from the date of issuance of this Order, unless otherwise extended by O.C.G.A. § 19-13-4(c).

[ ]   HEALTH INSURANCE

[ ] Petitioner [ ] Respondent shall provide and maintain medical/hospitalization insurance coverage

[ ]   comparable to the present coverage maintained by that party

[ ]   as follows: _____

to cover and pay at minimum the same equivalent portion of the medical, drug, clinic, hospital, and outpatient charges incurred for the benefit of [ ] each child [ ] Petitioner [ ] Respondent. The party maintaining said medical insurance shall from time to time hereafter, upon request, furnish to the other party duly signed insurance claim forms or an insurance card which shall be submitted to the requesting party within ten (10) days of the date of said request.

If the other party has paid a portion of such bill that is actually covered by insurance, then the party receiving the insurance proceeds shall remit the received insurance proceeds to the other party immediately upon receipt thereof.

Medical expenses incurred for the minor child(ren) of the parties which are not covered or paid by

insurance shall be paid as follows: [ ] by Petitioner _____%, [ ] by Respondent

_____%.

Civil Action File No: _____

Medical expenses incurred for the parties which are not covered or paid by insurance shall be paid as

follows: [ ] each party pays own, [ ] by Petitioner, [ ] by Respondent, [ ] as follows:

_____.

Each party shall pay their share of uninsured medical costs within thirty (30) days of the date of mailing of any such bills to that party by regular, first class mail.

_____ 13.   **VISITATION   [ ]** No Visitation

[ ]   No visitation until _____

[ ]   All visitations shall be supervised by a third party as follows:

_____

_____

[ ] Petitioner [ ] Respondent shall have the right to visit each child as follows:

[ ]   Alternate weekends from _____ ___.m. on _____ until _____

___.m. on _____, commencing _____.

[ ]   Weekdays, on _____, from _____ ___.m. until

_____ ___.m.

[ ]   Thanksgiving from _____ ___.m. on _____ until _____ ___.m.

on _____

[ ]   Christmas from _____ ___.m. on _____ until _____ ___.m. on

_____

[ ]   The children shall be with the mother on Mother's Day from 9:00 a.m. until 6:00 p.m.

[ ]   The children shall be with the father on Father's Day from 9:00 a.m. until 6:00 p.m.

[ ]   For a period of _____ weeks during the children's summer vacation. Said weeks may be agreed upon by the parties, in writing, prior to May 1. In the event the parties cannot agree, said weeks of summer visitation shall commence_____ at

_____ ___.m. and shall end _____ at _____ ___.m.

[ ]   The custodial parent shall have an uninterrupted period of _____ weeks during the children's summer vacation. Said weeks may be agreed upon by the parties, in writing, prior to May 1. In the event the parties cannot agree, said weeks of summer visitation shall

commence _____ at _____ ___.m. and shall end

_____ at _____ ___.m.

Civil Action File No: _____

[ ]   The following holidays from 9:00 a.m. until 6:00 p.m.:

[ ]	New Years Day	[ ]	MLK Birthday	[ ]	Presidents' Day
[ ]	Easter Sunday	[ ]	Memorial Day	[ ]	July 4th
[ ]	Labor Day	[ ]	_____	[ ]	_____

Other: _____

[ ]   VISITATION REQUIREMENTS

In the event the non-custodial parent intends to exercise visitation rights, he/she shall give at least forty eight (48) hours telephone or written notice to the custodial parent. For all visitation set forth herein, the non-custodial parent shall have the duty to pick up and return each child from and to the following location: (Strict compliance with this visitation provision shall not be a violation of the restraining provisions of this Order.

[ ]   the residence of the custodial parent

[ ]   _____

Unless prior arrangements have been made and agreed to by both parties. With respect to all visitation, the non-custodial parent shall give notice in the event he/she must cancel any visitation previously

_____ 14.   Both parties are hereby enjoined and restrained from transferring, selling, pledging as collateral for a loan, contracting to sell, concealing, or otherwise disposing of or removing from the jurisdiction of this Court, any of the property belonging to the parties, the children of the parties, pets of the parties, except in the ordinary course of business.

_____ 15.   [ ] Respondent [ ] Petitioner [ ] Both Respondent & Petitioner is/are ordered not to disconnect or have disconnected the home utilities, including but not limited to electricity, gas, water, telephone, change or have changed, or cancel, or have canceled, auto, health, or life insurance for Respondent, Petitioner, Petitioner's children, Respondent's children, or interfere with his/her/their mail.

_____ 16.   Attorney Fees: [ ] Petitioner [ ] Respondent shall pay attorney fees to the [ ] Petitioner's

[ ] Respondent's attorney in the amount of $_____, at the rate of $_____

per _____, commencing _____. In the event any

payment is ten (10) days overdue, the entire remaining balance shall become due instanter.

[ ] Each party shall pay their own attorney fees.

_____ 17.   **Petitioner/protected party is either a spouse, former spouse, parent of a common child, Petitioner's child, child of Respondent, cohabitates or has cohabitated with Respondent and qualifies for 18 U.S.C. 922 (g). RESTRICTIONS ON POSSESSION OF FIREARMS Pursuant to 18 U.S.C.A. 922(g)(8) and/or 922(g)(9), the Respondent is prohibited from shipping, transporting, possessing, or receiving any firearm or ammunition which has been shipped or transported in interstate or foreign commerce. Respondent shall be entitled to the immediate return of said items upon the expiration of this order, provided there is no other legal adjudication prohibiting such possession. Respondent is hereby ordered:**

[ ] to immediately surrender all firearms and ammunition in his/her possession to the _____ County Sheriff's Office.

Civil Action File No: _____

[ ] to provide to the Court proof that such items have been delivered to a third party and shall remain in the possession of that party until further order of this Court or the expiration of this Judgment, whichever first occurs.

It is further ordered as initialed below:

_____ 18.　　IT IS FURTHER ORDERED

[pco08]

_____

_____

_____

_____

_____

_____

IT IS HEREBY ORDERED THAT each of the parties shall abide by the foregoing terms and provisions of this order. Any party who contends that the other party is in contempt of Court may bring the matter back before the Court by filing a Motion for Contempt, under the same case number, with proper service upon the other party. Such motions must be filed prior to the expiration of this Order. Furthermore, an offending party may be subject to criminal prosecution as well. (See below notice.)

So ordered this _____ day of _____, 20_____ at _____ _____.M.

_____

Judge, _____ Superior Court [ ] by designation

Print Name:_____

Civil Action File No: _____

CONSENT

The parties have consented to the provisions of the above order and agree to comply with the terms and provisions thereof:

_____	_____
Petitioner	Respondent
_____	_____
Attorney for Petitioner	Attorney for Respondent
Bar No: _____	Bar No: _____

Violation of this Order May Be Punishable By Arrest

Notice to Respondent

1. Violation of this Order may result in immediate arrest and criminal prosecution that may result in jail time and/fines and/or may subject you to prosecution and penalties for contempt of court.

2. This Order shall remain in effect unless specifically superseded by a subsequent signed and filed Order, by operation of law, or by Order of Dismissal, whichever occurs first. Only this Court can void, modify, dismiss this Order. Either party may ask, in writing, or during any hearing, that this Court to change or dismiss this Order.

3. If after a hearing, of which the Respondent received notice and opportunity to participate, a protective order is issued which retrains Respondent from harassing, stalking, threatening an intimate partner, Respondent is prohibited from possessing, receiving, or transporting a firearm or ammunition which has been shipped or transported in interstate or foreign commerce for the duration of the order, 18 U.S.C. 922(g).

3. A person commits the offense of Aggravated Stalking when such person, in violation of a temporary or permanent protective Order prohibiting this behavior follows, places under surveillance, or contacts Petitioner on public or private property for the purpose of harassing and intimidating the other person. This activity can subject the Respondent to arrest and prosecution for the felony Aggravated Stalking, which carries penalties of imprisonment for not less than 1 year nor more than 10 years and a fine up to $10,000.00

Note: This form is promulgated as a Uniform Superior Court Rule under the auspices of O.C.G.A. 19-13-53. To order a specific provision, please initial in the space provided. The court should delete or otherwise make inoperative any provision in the standardized form which is not supported by the evidence in the case or in order to comply with the court's application of the law and facts to an individual case.

[ ] Transmitted to Georgia Protective Order Registry By: _____, Deputy Clerk	Date Submitted by Deputy Clerk:

to certify this is a true and correct copy of the foregoing Family Violence Twelve Month Protective Order, as the same appears of record in _____ Superior Court. Given my hand and seal of this court.

This _____ day of _____, 20_____.

By: _____, Deputy Clerk Superior Court, _____ County, GA.

IN THE SUPERIOR COURT OF _____ COUNTY

STATE OF GEORGIA

_____, Plaintiff v. _____, Defendant	)))))))))	CIVIL ACTION FILE NO. ____-CV-_____

DOMESTIC STANDING ORDER

Pursuant to O.C.G.A. §19-1-1(b) and the implementing order of the Court filed on the _____day of _____, 20____ (minute_____, page _____), this standing order binds the parties in the above styled action, their agents, servants, employees and all other persons acting in concert with such parties.

Each party is hereby enjoined and restrained (prohibited) from doing any of the following:

a)   causing or permitting the minor child(ren) of the parties to be removed from the jurisdiction of this court without written permission form the other party;

b)   doing, attempting to do or threatening to do any act injuring, maltreating vilifying molesting, or harassing the other party or the child(ren) of the parties or following, placing under surveillance, or contacting the other party or child(ren) of the parties without their consent for the purpose of harassing and intimidating the other party or child(ren) of the parties;

c)   selling, encumbering, trading, contracting to sell, or otherwise disposing or removing from the jurisdiction of the court any of the property belonging to one or both of the parties, except in the ordinary course of business.

The Court further orders all parties to complete and file a financial affidavit, as required by Uniform Superior Court Rule 24.2, within 30 days from receipt of this order, and within 90 days from receipt of this order, properly complete and file a domestic pre-trial order form, unless the case is uncontested.

Additionally, parties with minor children shall, within 60 days from receipt of this order, attend and submit proof of attendance at the "Seminar for Divorcing Parents", as required by standing order of this circuit.

SO ORDERED, this ___day of _____, 20____.

_____   _____
Chief Judge, Superior Court   Judge, Superior Court

_____
Judge, Superior Court

Index

B

bar association, 19, 41, 43, 48, 73

Basic Child Support Obligations, 66, 67, 68-69

bills, 10, 45, 47, 51, 52, 143, 144

blood test, 1, 148

bonds, 51, 55

C

case heading, 74

case law, 20, 26, 27

case style, 57, 74

ceremonial marriage, 1, 2, 3

Certificate of Service, 79, 80, 101, 109, 115

Child abuse, 63, 116

child custody, 4, 9, 10, 14, 16, 17, 18, 21, 22, 23, 25, 30, 34, 37, 47, 52, 61, 62, 63, 64, 71, 86, 88, 89, 90, 93, 94, 96, 99, 104, 106, 113, 116, 117, 122, 125, 139, 142, 143, 145, 147, 149

    joint custody, 62, 90, 93

    sole custody, 93, 142

child support, 7, 10, 17, 18, 20, 21, 22, 23, 25, 31, 47, 52, 64, 65, 66, 67, 68, 71, 86, 89, 90, 97, 98, 109, 111, 117, 119, 120, 122, 123, 125, 128, 129, 139, 145, 148

Child Support Guidelines Worksheet, 65, 90, 109

Child Support Recovery Office, 128, 129

Child Support Worksheet, 65, 68

common-law marriage, 2, 3

consent divorce. *See uncontested divorce*

contested divorce, 20, 21, 23, 24, 25, 29, 38, 49, 53, 59, 61, 70, 71, 75, 80, 85, 86, 100, 103, 104, 105, 106, 107, 109, 111, 113, 115, 116, 117, 119, 127, 135

contingency fee, 37

counseling, 10, 11, 13, 14, 30, 31, 34, 64, 139, 140, 141

county clerk, 75

court clerk, 18, 22, 23, 24, 26, 33, 75, 78, 79, 80, 86, 103, 104, 110, 111, 115, 126, 128, 129, 138, 143

D

dating, 3, 9, 10, 12

death, 8, 9, 17, 57, 69

debt, 4, 9, 14, 21, 51, 52, 53, 54, 60, 61, 71, 86, 91, 106, 112, 147

Debt Inventory, 60, 112

defendant, 65, 74, 75, 77, 78, 79, 80, 87, 88, 90, 91, 93, 100, 106, 109, 110

Department of Human Resources Report, 120

depository. *See Child Support Recovery Office*

I

impotency, 5
incest, 7
income, 10, 17, 31, 46, 49, 50,
    51, 53, 64, 65, 66, 67, 68, 69,
    81, 90, 92, 97, 98, 106, 107,
    108, 109, 110, 111, 112, 117,
    118, 120, 126, 128, 129, 130,
    138, 144, 145
    adjusted, 65, 67
    annual, 65, 97
    gross, 64, 67, 68, 69, 108, 120
    monthly, 65, 108, 109
Income Deduction Order, 98,
    128, 129, 130
income shares model, 64
inheritance, 52, 54, 114
insurance, 7, 51, 52, 54, 56, 57,
    58, 66, 68, 91, 108, 147
Internal Revenue Service (IRS),
    70, 144, 145
Internet, 12, 34, 41, 57
interrogatories, 112
investment papers, 51

J

jewelry, 57
jury, 16, 24, 25, 31, 67

L

legal research, 20, 26, 27
legal separation. See separate
    maintenance

LegalZoom, 40
liability, 21, 31, 34, 37, 59, 60,
    70, 106
loan, 57, 60, 61, 91, 111

M

manners, 38, 81
marriage certificate, 2
marriage contract, 1, 3, 4
marriage license, 1, 2, 3, 74
mediation, 18, 30, 31, 33, 34
    arbitration, 33, 34, 48
    church, 6, 34
    collaborative mediation, 33,
        34
    court-ordered mediation, 33
    guardian ad litem, 33, 34
    independent mediation, 32-33
medical expenses, 52, 67
Medicare, 68
mental cruelty, 4
mental disability, 7
mental illness, 5, 7, 30, 69
military, 25, 26, 58, 71, 137,
    146, 147
morality, 5, 63, 93, 97, 116
mortgage, 51, 55, 60, 68, 91,
    114, 115, 143

N

name changes, 137, 148
negotiation, 30, 85, 89, 113, 121,
    122, 123, 146
no-fault divorce, 4, 5

W